SASS

MF! Momentary Futures in Black Studies

L. H. STALLINGS, EDITOR

Venturing into futurity and speculation, this series focuses on Black thought experiences, challenges the parameters of current theories, advances new ideas about knowledge production, and escapes finite approaches to the field of Black studies.

A complete list of books published in MF! Momentary Futures in Black Studies is available at https://uncpress.org/series/mf-momentary-futures-in-black-studies/.

J FINLEY

SASS

BLACK
WOMEN'S
HUMOR
AND
HUMANITY

The University of North Carolina Press   CHAPEL HILL

© 2024 Jessyka Finley
All rights reserved
Manufactured in the United States of America

Designed by Lindsay Starr
Set in Charis by codeMantra

Cover art: Lorna Simpson, *Famous Statue*, 2013. Found photograph and collage on paper, 29½ × 21⅝ in. (74.9 × 54.9 cm); framed: 31 × 24 × 1⅝ in. (78.6 × 61.1 × 4.1 cm).
© Lorna Simpson. Courtesy of the artist and Hauser & Wirth; photograph by James Wang.

Library of Congress Cataloging-in-Publication Data
Names: Finley, J, author.
Title: Sass : Black women's humor and humanity / J Finley.
Other titles: Black women's humor and humanity |
MF! Momentary futures in Black studies.
Description: Chapel Hill : The University of North Carolina Press, 2024. |
Series: MF! Momentary futures in Black studies | Includes
bibliographical references and index.
Identifiers: LCCN 2024005604 | ISBN 9781469680026
(paperback ; alk. paper) | ISBN 9781469680019 (cloth ; alk. paper) |
ISBN 9781469680033 (ebook) | ISBN 9781469682150 (pdf)
Subjects: LCSH: African American women comedians. |
African American women—Social life and customs. |
African American wit and humor. | Comedy—Political aspects.
Classification: LCC E185.86 .F524 2024 | DDC 305.48/896073—dc23/eng/20240304
LC record available at https://lccn.loc.gov/2024005604

Portions of chapters 1, 2, 4, and 5 appeared earlier, in somewhat different form, in, respectively, Jessyka Finley, "Black Women's Satire as (Black) Postmodern Performance," *Studies in American Humor* 2 (4) (2016): 236–65, https://doi.org/10.5325/studamerhumor.2.2.0236; Jessyka Finley, "Raunch and Redress: Interrogating Pleasure in Black Women's Stand-up Comedy," *Journal of Popular Culture* 49 (4) (August 2016): 780–98 (© 2016 Wiley Periodicals, Inc.); Jessyka Finley, "From Awkward to Dope: Black Women Comics in the Alternative Comedy Scene," in *The Joke Is on Us: Political Comedy in (Late) Neoliberal Times*, edited by Julie A. Webber (Lanham, MD: Lexington, 2019); and Jessyka Finley, "Irreverence Rules: The Politics of Authenticity and the Carnivalesque Aesthetic in Black South African Women's Stand-Up Comedy," *Journal of Aesthetics and Art Criticism* 78 (4) (September 2020): 437–50 (used by permission of Oxford University Press).

For my children, Desmond and Inge

CONTENTS

ix   ACKNOWLEDGMENTS

1   INTRODUCTION
Cut-Eye and Suck-Teeth: Theorizing Black Women's Sass as a Discourse Genre

37   CHAPTER 1
Never to Be Conquered: Sass, Subjection, and Black Women Self-Possessed

67   CHAPTER 2
Hard-Core Laughter: Sass and the Politics of Raunch

91   CHAPTER 3
Butch Lives Matter: Sass, Masculinity, and Failure

125   CHAPTER 4
From Awkward to Dope: Sass, Interiority, and Black Women's Alternative Comedy

157   CHAPTER 5
Irreverence Rules: Sass and Diaspora Culture

181   CODA
You Don't Quit, Bitch, Unless *You* Wanna Quit

185   NOTES
201   BIBLIOGRAPHY
211   INDEX

ILLUSTRATIONS

- 3   Jada Pinkett Smith at the 94th Academy Awards
- 10   Cardi B's November 2020 Instagram post
- 22   Michelle Obama at the 2013 Inauguration Day luncheon
- 53   Jackie "Moms" Mabley in men's clothing
- 55   Jackie "Moms" Mabley performing in character
- 93   The author performing stand-up
- 103   Gladys Bentley

ACKNOWLEDGMENTS

This book has humbled me, and I'm grateful for the compassion, guidance, and expertise of the many people who have helped me bring what was a dream to reality. Thank you, Mama, for bringing me into the world and passing on to me the love of books and the gift of curiosity. To my family, who has always encouraged and supported me (and chin-checked me when necessary), thank you for everything. A special shout-out goes to Aunt Arlene, Aunt Dee, Uncle Blue, Aunt Bibby, and all my cousins. I miss my grandma Mary Murphy and the stories she told over and over. Thanks, Grandma, for all your love and the history you passed on. The first person I ever remember laughing with was my brother, Jeremy Finley. I miss him every day, and my sense of humor is colored by growing up with his silly ass. He's not here, but he's here. So is his son Dariyan, who made me the auntie I am today. And Noah, my little boo, I see you and I love you. Special thanks go to my Cook family, Joyce, Bruce, and Lizzie, for believing in me and supporting me through this long process.

This project would be nothing without the comics who generously shared their insight, knowledge, and history with me, and I am profoundly grateful to the comics and Black comedy stewards who have contributed to this work. Specifically, I would like to thank Karinda Dobbins, Hope Flood, Kamane Malvo Marshall, Khristee Rich, Aisha Tyler, the late Paul Mooney, Luenell, Laura Hayes, Vanessa Chambers, Niroma Johnson, Jennifer Weeks, the late Jane Galvin-Lewis, Thea Vidale, Naomi Ekperigin, Calise Hawkins, and Gina Yashere. I would also like to thank Ayoka Chenzira and Debra Robinson for kindly providing copies of their films. Michael Williams shared a wealth of knowledge about Black comedy, and I appreciate his kindness and support.

There were many times when I did not believe in this project, and my editor, Dawn Durante, never faltered in her encouragement and support. I am so blessed to have found an editor who believed in this book, who understood and cared about what I have been trying to say, and who graciously ushered me through this process like the boss she is. Thanks, Dawn, Carol Seigler, and the editorial staff at the University of North Carolina Press for your support and guidance through this process, along with the anonymous reviewers whose generous and candid feedback has enhanced the quality of this book. I also want to thank L. H. Stallings for being an inimitable model for beautiful, no-nonsense writing and for the extensive advice and suggestions for revisions that have made this a better book.

Call the building whatever you want at UC Berkeley, but the sixth floor is the sixth floor when it comes to the Department of African American and African Diaspora Studies, and that place made me; it's the place where the words and ideas in this book were born. Thank you to all the professors, staff, and mentors on the sixth floor who have inspired me, pushed me, believed in me, and literally paid my bills—especially Lindsey Villareal, Brandi Wilkins Catanese, Leigh Raiford, the late Vévé Clark, Robert L. Allen, and Charles Henry. I'm grateful for the place that will always feel like home. Catherine Cole is a force and a wonderful advocate—thank you for the entry into ethnography, which continues to shape the work I do. A shout-out goes too to the homies and colleagues I spent so much time learning and growing with on the sixth floor—Jasmine Johnson, Michael McGee, Gabrielle Williams, Malika Crutchfield, the late Carmen Mitchell, Ronald Williams II, Lia Bascomb, Ameer Hassan Loggins, Ianna Hawkins Owen, Katherine Benjamin, Shaun Osei-Owusu, Zach Manditch-Prottas, and Chris Petrella.

I remember the first time I encountered Ula Taylor's work as an undergraduate student, working on an essay about Black womanhood and the politics of respectability. Ever since I read her book, her words have inspired me, and I could not believe my good fortune in 2006 when I learned I would have the chance to be her student in grad school. The first time I worked closely with Ula was in the fall of 2009 when we took on an independent study together on Black women's humor. She was no expert on the topic, she informed me, but she was undaunted and enthusiastic. We chose and read the texts together, each week discovering exciting lines of inquiry and archives untapped. It was during this independent study that I began to understand how archives work, and slowly, the process of conducting research and crafting interesting and critical intellectual questions was demystified. It was difficult work that Ula guided me through, challenging me week after week not only to answer questions about Black women's humor but also to craft them, redraft them, and constantly sharpen my analytical lens. Ula is one of one, someone who has shown me through example what it means to be original, to be creative, and to embrace my scholarly voice. She has also been there in my very lowest moments with warmth, grace, and her precious time. Thanks for everything, Ula; I hope this work makes you proud.

This work was generously funded by the Andrew Mellon Foundation while I was a postdoctoral fellow at Middlebury College, support for which I am deeply appreciative. My colleagues and friends at Middlebury have been instrumental in my growth as a scholar and teacher, and I am especially grateful for American studies people Holly Allen, Susan Burch, Deb Evans, Ellery Foutch, Rachael Joo, Will Nash, and Michael Newbury. I appreciate each of you for making space for me in the program to come into my own, and your comments on my work through the years have made such a positive impact. So much love and thanks go to Rachael Joo, who has been one of my main advocates, a writing partner, and a great friend! Special and heartfelt gratitude goes to Laurie Essig in Gender, Sexuality, and Feminist Studies too—I appreciate your early comments on my work and ongoing encouragement. I also want to thank the homies at Middlebury, Carly Thomsen, Jenn Ortegren, Jason Vrooman, Alvin Henry, and Matt Lawrence, who have made me laugh, made me food, and made me grateful for the seven years I spent in the Green Mountain State.

Moving across the country during the pandemic was a struggle. A special shout-out and love go to Prageeta Sharma, Amanda Lagji, Diana Linden, Peter Ross, Emily and Alex Linden-Ross, whose friendship in that transition has made my life more joyful and fun. And thanks go to Ted Hekman for helping me with the images for the book.

Over the past decade I have had the privilege and great fortune of working with some incredible undergraduate students whose careful attention to detail as research assistants has not only lightened my load but also fundamentally contributed to the arguments I present in this book. Thank you, Addie Mahdavi, Amanda Oluwatosin Eric, and Saténa Charles-Luciani, for your curiosity, consistency, and dedication. I appreciate each of you very much and the work you've helped me accomplish—I'll take all the credit though, for all mistakes, misreading, or errors otherwise.

It has been an honor and pleasure to work with my colleagues at the American Humor Studies Association. I want to thank Beck Krefting specifically for organizing the First Book Workshop, where I got so many valuable resources and strategic information about book publishing—game changer!

My students have been instrumental in sharpening the way I think about humor and comedy, and my classes have been the incubator for a lot of the thoughts I commit to the page. I want to thank my students at Middlebury and Pomona in the classes Black Comic Cultures, Black Queer (After)Lives, and Black Womanhood in Popular Culture for keeping me on my toes, helping me keep my ideas fresh, and not letting me off the hook—working with you all has been a privilege and pleasure, and you all have helped me make this a sharper book.

To my A-1 day ones, my friends who have been here before I was J, when I was just Jessyka—Rosemary Sims, Ashley Jackson, Andrea Aikin—thank you all for holding me up, holding me down, crying with me, laughing so hard we cried together, thank you. We've been through so much together, and I am incredibly grateful to be sliding through life with y'all. ;) To my friends whom I met in the transition from Jessyka to J—Jon Sribnick, M'issa Fleming, Lexie Bouwsma, Aran Jones, Jeena Zografos, and Pepe Lopez—thank you for always letting me be myself.

In this game (of life . . .), everybody needs a good therapist. Lindsay Jernigan, my therapist, walked with me through the good, the bad, and the ugly with such grace and kindness that I learned how to show myself those qualities, too. This book is a testament to it, because in the darkest moments when I could not see where I was going, she showed me that I can be my own light.

Toni Cook is my hand-holder, my laugh maker, my joke writing partner, my joke making partner, my tear catcher, my line reader, my baby mama, my love. "Thank you" doesn't capture the gratitude I feel for you and all you do for me. You've been here right from the start, taking on all kinds of roles, whatever's necessary at the time. I appreciate and love you with all I have, and I hope you're proud of me. My babies, Dez and Inge, thank you for making me a mama. All this is for you.

SASS

INTRODUCTION

CUT-EYE AND SUCK-TEETH: THEORIZING BLACK WOMEN'S SASS AS A DISCOURSE GENRE

> Sassy conduct is itself a strategy for resisting social devaluation.
>
> —JOYCE WEST STEVENS, *Smart and Sassy*

The smile slowly faded from Jada Pinkett Smith's face at the 94th Academy Awards on March 27, 2022. She was seated in the front row next to her husband, Will Smith, who had been nominated for Best Actor for his role in the film *King Richard*. She clasped her hands tightly in her lap and sent a sharp cut-eye toward the Oscars' host, comedian Chris Rock, who had just told a joke at her expense. "Jada, I love ya [*pointing down to her*]. *GI Jane 2*, can't wait to see it, aight?!" Pinkett Smith was wearing a close-cropped natural, nearly bald that night owing to her alopecia. She had publicly spoken about her struggle with the autoimmune disorder and its physical and emotional effects. A few days before she sat at the Academy Awards ceremony and became the target of Chris Rock's joke, she had uploaded a video to TikTok explaining to her following that she had come to terms with her shorn hair after years of ambivalence and Hollywood expectations of Black feminine propriety.

I always had to do my hair in ways that didn't feel natural to *me*, because I was trying to play the game. So, if I'm doing a [magazine] cover, everybody's [like], "No, we want your hair straight, flowy." I'm like, "All right, cool. . . . But that's not what my hair likes to do. [*Laughs to self.*] So, I had to get the courage to just go, "Nah, I'm not doing that." Which is why I feel the freedom *today*. I don't give two craps what people feel about this bald head of mine. 'Cause guess what [*pointing to herself with both thumbs*]? I love it.[1]

The crowd at the Academy Awards was laughing with Chris Rock, including her husband, Will Smith, and actress Lupita Nyong'o, who were shown on camera directly after the insulting joke. Pinkett Smith tightened her posture and rolled her eyes, registering at the very least her displeasure at publicly becoming the butt of a joke, especially in what could be read as an ad hominem attack on her seeming failure to meet Hollywood standards of femininity, based on Rock's reference to the film *GI Jane*. As Marlon M. Bailey and Matt Richardson have noted, "Gender performance has tremendous material consequences, as it is meticulously scrutinized and assiduously policed, and those who do not follow the logic of heterogender are often subject to violence and death."[2] Pinkett Smith was relegated by Rock to the category of *unwoman*, a distinction particular to Black women since the period of enslavement, facing constant defeminization in popular culture, in "scientific" analyses, in political discourse, and in everyday life to the effect of shaming their sexual practices, devaluing and exploiting their bodies, silencing their critiques of power, and rendering them objects of comedic ridicule.

When Chris Rock publicly derided Jada Pinkett Smith, her reaction—to cut her eyes and create distance between herself and the object of her sass—reverberated across time and space. It reached back to enslaved women, to sharecropping women, to Black women like Shirley Chisholm, Kamala Harris, and now Ketanji Brown Jackson who share the distinction of being "firsts." All along, Black women have endured dehumanization through gritted teeth, empowered by the ingenuity of spirit and the exigency of their circumstances to deflect insult and injury. Sass has been a powerful agent of deflection and humanization in a world that sees and often treats Black women as perennial punching bags and scapegoats, bearing the brunt of white supremacist, patriarchal power.[3]

Will Smith stood up, walked onto the stage, and ceremoniously slapped the shit out of Chris Rock before returning to his seat in the stunned audience. "Keep my wife's name out your fucking mouth," Smith roared twice before

Jada Pinkett Smith reacts to a joke at her expense at the 94th Academy Awards, March 27, 2022. Screenshot by author from *The Daily Mail*, clip courtesy A.M.P.A.S. © 2022, www.dailymail.co.uk/tvshowbiz/article-10658717/Oscars-2022-Smith-Chris-Rock-Jada-Pinkett-Smith-row-moment-moment.html.

Rock—shook and nearly speechless—moved on to present the next award. This became the story. Debates swirled. Did Rock deserve it? Did Smith go too far? Did this incident further sully Black people's already battered public image? Was Smith protecting Black women appropriately? Can comedians go too far? Is comedy dead? These are all valid questions, but they are for someone else to answer. What struck me is the way Jada Pinkett Smith's response to the joke was usurped and elided by her husband's bid to publicly claim and assert his fragile, patriarchal masculinity. Pinkett Smith had said she felt *free* a few days before the Oscars. What that freedom meant was that she no longer had to hold on to other people's ideas about who she should be, what she should look like, and how she should act. Indeed, she had moved beyond mere acceptance of her difference in terms of how she presented her femininity; she had transcended feelings of ambivalence and moved to the side of loving herself—the ultimate individual enactment of Black feminist politics that could set the very foundation for collective action. "I don't give two craps what people feel about this bald head of mine. 'Cause guess what? I love it."

That hands-clasped cut-eye at Chris Rock registered Pinkett Smith's moral assessment of Rock and her will (no pun intended) to be resolute in the face of it all, to do as First Lady Michelle Obama once advised, "When they go low, we go high." Her silent deployment of sass was an enactment of her humanity, the latest high-profile moment in which we see a Black woman powerfully speaking back to authority in a way that would register to people who would

INTRODUCTION   3

be attuned to look for it. The subtlety of Pinkett Smith's sass was buried in the avalanche of her husband's hubris. Not only was power wielded against Pinkett Smith by Rock, who made her appearance the target of his humor, but power was also seated next to her as her husband-cum-savior, who with one cinematic blow snatched whatever potential for power Pinkett Smith's enactment of sass might have yielded.

That cut-eye she directed at Rock could have smarted more than the smack Rock received. Had Will Smith left well enough alone, had Pinkett Smith's critique of power in her sharp glance not been subsumed by the brute force of patriarchy, something more compelling and subtle could have taken root: we might have been forced to confront the inner lives of Black women on their own terms, to grapple with the notion that Black women's sass is serious and does real work if we let it; it calls attention to the contours of power and the conditions in which Black women make use of it. It is also funny.

The moment of Jada Pinkett Smith's sass could have been a viral meme, a citational response, cut and repurposed to answer authority and assert humanity in the age of the Internet. It could have been, absent Smith's brutish intervention, a moment where we might understand the complex meaning of freedom for Black women. As Pinkett Smith explained in her TikTok video, the *feeling* of being unapologetically self-possessed in the face of a history and forces seeking to discipline and mock the manifold ways of being a Black woman—that is freedom. The main issue with this moment at the 2022 Academy Awards is that Black women's sass has been erased from public discourse, and with that erasure comes the consequence of obscuring this foundationally significant genre of discourse that has been a means by which Black women have offered glimpses into their inner lives and asserted their humanity. This follows a similar course of Black women's sass being misunderstood and delegitimized, which effectively means that Black women's humor, of which sass is the central binding feature, could fall victim to a similar fate.

Calling this book *Sass* is an intentional, meaningful gesture that marks the pain Black women have endured owing to centuries of mistreatment, misunderstanding, and dehumanization. At the same time, it calls up the ingenuity of and pleasure taken in the responses we have created to feel free despite that history. I hope readers will come to see that there is something powerful and subversive about taking a trope assumed to be essentialist and offering an alternative reading to show that it is *not* what mainstream culture presumes it to be. While sass is the overarching lens through which Black women's humor is examined here, there is no intent to treat sass as a descriptor that must apply to *all* Black women humorists. Furthermore, *not* all Black women humorists deploy sass in their comedy, nor is Black women's humor a category in which all Black women who are humorists fit. Sass as a framework, though, offers a through line that makes manifest the historical conditions and the ongoing afterlife of slavery that have wrought it as Black women's most salient discursive feature, expressed variously across genre, generation, and geography. Understanding the work that sass does in speaking back to power helps us make sense of how it has become the most recognizable feature of Black women's humor.

"The struggle for recognition," argues Melissa Harris-Perry, "is the nexus of human identity and national identity, where much of the most important work of politics occurs. African American women fully embody this struggle."[4] The struggle for recognition and human rights is at the center of what it means to be a Black woman, for better or for worse. Wrenching humor from that struggle, making politics funny by confronting and counteracting (dis)order, disciplinary power, and racial and sexual tropes through the stories we tell and the sass we use, are enduring demands that the terms on which we must be understood are our own. In recognizing the efficacy of sass, we chart a new path toward a more complicated understanding of liberation and how Black women move toward it.

Black women's interiority is at the center of sass. It is here where inner longings to be seen and heard as the complex human beings we are, especially in the face of violent repression and domination to which we have historically been subjected, are many times outwardly expressed. Of course, people are naturally inclined to speak back to authority, but Black women have developed an entire performative genre around that inclination, which has given birth to the particularity of Black women's humor. Across generations, time, and space, Black women have engaged creative strategies to adapt to their conditions and stay human under the crushing conditions of white supremacist, patriarchal domination. It is along the steep cliffs and within the deep valleys of these circumstances that Black women's humor has developed and thrived, and we cannot lose sight of sass as anything less than a distinctly American art form and unconventional mode of self-expression and politicking.

First and foremost, this is a book about Black women's humor, but it is also a book that showcases the mutually constitutive nature of Black women's humor and humanity, and the moment is urgent given the ongoing debates about misogynoir, gendered violence, and racial politics embedded in contemporary comedic traditions. Jada Pinkett Smith's treatment by Chris Rock, Dave Chappelle's enduring onstage disrespect of trans people, and the blackballing of legendary comedian Mo'Nique within the broader entertainment industry and in the stand-up scene in particular because of her speaking out against gendered pay inequity demonstrate this urgency. When we think of Black women's humor, the sites that typically come to mind are the stand-up stage and sketch comedy skits; Black women's poetry and literature are shot through with biting humor as well. Yet, Black women's humor is everywhere if we are looking for it. Whether onstage, in the audience, or in the quotidian state that most of us experience—existing—even when met with existential threats, sass is the core of our humor, and it has established our North Star. It guides us to find and express the understanding deep down inside ourselves that we are worthy to be free, just as we are. Institutions like churches, schools, comedy clubs, and even award shows function as sites that regulate the production of race, gender, and sexuality, and humor has always loomed large in that discursive production.

Rather than present a complete history, *Sass* offers a genealogical sketch of Black women's humor, drawing the contours of its comedic elements and aesthetic practices and placing them in the broader sociopolitical context of Black popular culture. Each chapter engages a thematic examination—most with ethnographic analysis—of a specific aspect of the aesthetics and political efficacy of Black women's humor, situating it within the context of the discourse of sass elucidated in this introduction. This book foregrounds how Black women's humor responds to and intervenes in disciplinary structures that seek to regulate, subjugate, or annihilate Black women, whether in the public sphere of popular culture or in the quotidian spaces of everyday life, which is why I began with the Academy Awards moment that blurred the boundaries of entertainment culture and "real" life. Black women's comedic practices emerge within the material conditions of living in a white supremacist, patriarchal, capitalist order, and humor is an everyday mode of human communication that anticipates the political and imaginative projects Black women undertake in the collective sphere of public culture. I open this discussion by analyzing another legendary pop cultural moment where we see how Black women's humor travels between bodies and spaces (both ideological and material) and illuminates the aesthetics and politics of contemporary Black women's comedic practices.

The Pleasure and Politics of Black Women's Humor

Suddenly the beat dropped from loudspeakers over the cacophony of the crowd. The most recognizable, most downloaded, and most controversial anthem of 2020, Cardi B and Megan Thee Stallion's "WAP" (Wet Ass Pussy), blared to the delight of those assembled at Black Lives Matter Plaza, right across the street from the White House, behind the "unscalable" barricades erected in the run-up to the 2020 presidential election. The crowd was of a singular mind and spirit, bouncing to the beat, scream-singing each syllable in unison. "Whores in this house, there's some whores in this house! / Yeah you fucking with some wet ass pussy!" The topsy-turvy world inaugurated by the Trump era had suddenly gone topsy-turvy again, and one could feel the catharsis as the beat thumped and the crowd gleefully sang along. Pussy started Donald Trump's reign, and "WAP" was a pointed, perfect bookend to his presidency. Instead of the pink pussy hats marching on Washington that cold day in January 2017, now it was Black and brown pussies—wet ones, too—that called forth the masses to reclaim their bodies, their rights, and their pleasure in this moment.

On November 7, 2020, during the celebration outside the White House after Trump's defeat, the jubilant chant "Bring a bucket and a mop for this wet ass pussy" flipped the entire script on pussy grabbing, as if to say, "Whose pussy is this, President Trump?" If Trump's so-called locker-room talk captured on the leaked *Access Hollywood* recording had been for men, by men—for power, by power—"WAP"'s celebratory incantation was a political revelation right at the seat of power: the kind of sexual pleasure invoked by the song was for (Black) women, by (Black) women, and the inversion of power as this song was chanted by thousands on national television was poignant and hilarious! The explicit speaking of truth to power in the song itself, and as a prop for the moment, indicates the reach of Black women's humor and their sass. The comedic moment sprang from the marshaling of Megan Thee Stallion and Cardi B's raunchy anthem as a Black feminist credo, an unconventional and brazen inversion, at least representationally speaking—of Black female sexuality as a marker of mainstream political empowerment. As Katelyn Hale Wood puts it, Black feminist comedy "is both visceral and epistemological," and Black feminist humor "hold[s] space for the pleasures, communities, and spiritual experiences that thrive in the face of, and in spite of, legacies of racialized grief."[5] Speaking back to authority becomes necessary, and its mode of expression shifts with the winds. Yet sass remains constant—Black women are constantly finding ways to claim their humanity and their rights, no matter how "unscalable" the barrier, and making people laugh with their acts of transgression.

Was this triumphant moment an ephemeral illusion of the descent of legitimate power, a "temporary liberation from the prevailing truth and from the established order," as Mikhail Bakhtin described carnival time?[6] I would venture to say there is something more than a carnivalesque moment of comedic switcheroo, catharsis, and return to the status quo. That "WAP" became the anthem for this particularly historic political moment sheds some light on the transformative power of Black women's humor—especially their extravagant, sexually explicit humor—which has been castigated as simple, vulgar, and largely relegated to the realm of lowbrow entertainment, targeted to a narrow audience with limited political consciousness and power. Of all the songs available to those celebrating outside the White House, why was "WAP" such an appropriate repudiation of Donald Trump? Why was this song, infused with Black women's humor, so perfect for this political moment?

Rather than reflect some "innocent amusements and harmless pleasures," in Saidiya Hartman's words,[7] the performance of the song outside the White House in 2020 enables us to grapple with the seriousness of Black women's humor and with the way it serves feminist ends to put out in the open and redress the scenes of discursive and structural marginalization. In *Cracking Up: Black Feminist Comedy in the Twentieth and Twenty-First Century United States*, Wood locates the inherently subversive power of Black feminist humor—how it breaks down racism, sexism, homophobia, and all sorts of other forms of violence and erasure to which Black women have historically been subjected—and opens new pathways for the transformation of our social world via the knowledge and political consciousness that Black feminism engenders. Wood names this expressive force "cracking up," for the way Black feminist humorists break down normative sociocultural constructs to build a sociality that is newer and better, a space that is capacious enough to hold the variety of Black women's experiences unburdened by the usual structures of power to which they are routinely subjected. *Cracking Up* "archives artists who understand that the stage can be a place of transformation, progression, and freedom," Wood argues, and "their Black feminist performance is in service of continued illumination rather than contained, ephemeral happenings."[8] This work builds on Wood's analytic of Black feminist humor as a mode of political illumination as Black women's humor travels through and across bodies and spaces—traversing stages, airwaves, genres, and the streets. As the crowd in 2020 sang along to "WAP," they marked an important transition, and not simply one from Trump to Biden in that ephemeral moment in front of the White House. Rather, there was a subtler, more interesting and compelling ontological and political shift that the song and the embodied verve of its collective performance instantiated as it moved from the ether through the crowd assembled at Black Lives Matter Plaza.

The raunchiness itself undergirding Cardi B and Megan Thee Stallion's anthem is an expression of Black women's sass that "offers an important expression of frustration, a source of resilience, and the experience that in one's own mind one is free, even if it is not ... socially or politically transformative."[9] The song lyrics, and their celebratory performance outside the White House, demonstrate how contemporary evocations of Black women's sass—here, articulated in the extravagant excess of the lyrics' raunchiness—are a politically salient element of their humor. For Meg and Cardi, the regular discourse around sex, desire, and pleasure do not dictate their expression, and the song's first line inaugurates a transformative moment. The White House crowd triumphantly chanted, "I say, certified freak, seven days a week / wet ass pussy make that pullout game weak!" The mood is set, and the "freak" is coming for what she wants. Freaks, James Baldwin once said, "are called freaks and are treated—in the main, abominably—because they are human beings who cause to echo, deep within us, our most profound terrors and desires."[10] The articulation of desire and sexual arousal are often the site of humor in "WAP" because of the very explicit ways the artists express them. They brazenly call up "the possibilities of the human being in whom the awakening of desire fuels imagination and in whom imagination fuels desire."[11] The song "WAP" and its initial performance by Meg and Cardi foregrounds the embodied experience of the erotic and the ecstatic energy it summons. As Jennifer C. Nash succinctly puts it, ecstasy refers "both to the possibilities of female pleasures within a phallic economy and to the possibilities of black female pleasures within a white-dominated representational economy."[12] The embodied state of ecstasy expressed by the "certified freaks" reverberated through the assemblage at Black Lives Matter Plaza and to viewers who experienced the moment captured by mainstream news media. The explicitness of the incantation introduced and the crowd exerted a kind of sexual force that undercut expectations of the normative public/private binary.

Mireille Miller-Young has argued that Black women performers, especially in pornographic productions, participate in "illicit erotic economies" to "mobilize deviant, outlaw racialized sexuality as vehicles of consumption and labor as well as of contestation and consent."[13] As a strategy for sociopolitical subversion, Black women like Cardi B and Megan Thee Stallion, whose cultural production exquisitely straddles the humorous and pornographic, engage with practices of illicit eroticism as they "put hypersexuality to use ... manipulat[ing] ... racialized sexuality ... in order to assert the value of their erotic capital."[14]

Cardi B's video post on Instagram showing the crowd chanting the lyrics from "WAP," November 7, 2020. Screenshot by author, clip courtesy of Instagram (Meta).

Those chanting the lyrics outside the White House repositioned themselves and, perhaps by proxy, Black women more generally speaking as the freaks of a Trumpian, right-wing nightmare. "Put this pussy right in your face, swipe your nose like a credit card," they shouted, reveling in this topsy-turvydom. Cardi B clearly understood the magnitude of the moment, posting a shot of the scene on Instagram with the caption, "BITCH WE ON CNN OUTSIDE OF THE WHITEHOUSE LITTY LIKE MY TITTIES!!!" Black women's humor can be playful, crass, and politically transformative, all in one fell swoop. This is its superpower—not that it is inherently transformative but that it offers "a chance for change."[15] Cynthia Willett and Julie Willett ask us in *Uproarious: How Feminists and Other Subversive Comics Speak Truth* to think about how people who are marginalized, and many times are invisible as legitimate subjects, might use humor to challenge structures of power that give rise to marginality—structures like race, gender, and sexuality—and Meg and Cardi's "WAP" does just that.

Willett and Willett offer an alternative reading of the efficacy of feminist humor outside of the other major theories of humor, what they imagine as humor-as-catharsis-sharing that speaks truth. The "WAP" celebration of the end of the Trump administration provides some insight into how we might imagine the way Black women's humor functions—how it can do the work of redressing, on the public stage, the kinds of marginalization to which they have historically been subjected. Indeed, as the crowd recited the raunchy, humorous lyrics—with each expression of desire, "I wanna gag, I wanna choke. I want you to touch that little dangly thing that swing in the back of my throat"; with each explicit utterance of sexual arousal, "Macaroni in a pot, that's some wet ass pussy"; and each claim on pleasure, "Make it cream, make me scream," the artists and chanters alike redistributed the pain of marginality and the trauma of sexual shame to audaciously reclaim sexual pleasure and power in the public sphere. We will see throughout this book the way Black women deploy explicitness through humor as an aesthetic mode that promotes self-care, moments of embodied ecstasy, and the subversion of gendered and racialized expectations and social orders. Black women's humor many times turns to pleasure and the erotic to imagine what freedom *feels* like. The subversive practices of humor that emerge in Black women's language and discourse enables frank discussions about Black women's bodies that eschew fear, shame, and abjection, and the explicitness of "WAP" is an expression of embodied sass—it foregrounds desires and pleasures, to be sure—but the raunch-cum-humor of the lyrics and the crowd's citation of them also indicate "their rage and their longing."[16]

In *Wayward Lives, Beautiful Experiments: Intimate Histories of Social Upheaval,* Saidiya Hartman discusses how young Black women in the early twentieth century used their voices productively while they were incarcerated at Lowell Cottage at Bedford Hills Women's Reformatory in upstate New York to register their dissent, their refusal to be quietly dehumanized and brutalized. "Songs and shouts were the instruments of struggle," Hartman says of the Black women's singular, cacophonous chorus. "Terms like 'noise strike' and 'vocal outbreak' described the soundscape of rebellion and refusal," a limited means of redressing their conditions, to be sure, but these chants of revolt "made manifest the latent rebellion simmering beneath the surface of things."[17] The gathering outside the White House in 2020 most certainly was not *only* Black women engaged in a defiant "vocal outbreak," but what was happening there was certainly *Black noise* that was amplifying and politicizing Black women's aesthetics, humor, and desire for social and cultural transformation. "The collective, *orchestrated fury* of Black women can move the whole world," Brittney Cooper notes.[18] Building on that idea of a collective politic hewn of many voices, we might see the "WAP" moment as an expression of Black women's rage as Black feminist world-making.

When Black women publicly, brazenly, and explicitly express their sexual desires and practices, they push back on normative discourses of respectability that demand a "good" Black woman be a "lady in the streets and freak in the sheets." As Cardi B and Megan Thee Stallion lay bare, one can be a "certified freak, seven days a week," and still demand to be seen, heard, and respected as a human being and a political subject. The proof is in the pudding. Regardless of what critics may say about the artistry and reception of "WAP," Cardi B and Megan Thee Stallion have politically benefited themselves, and so have Black women more broadly, from the platform upon which "WAP" propelled them. Cardi B was invited by the last two Democratic presidential candidates in 2020, Bernie Sanders and Joe Biden, to the mainstream political conversation to discuss issues affecting people publicly and privately to whom they were campaigning. Megan Thee Stallion, in a powerfully moving and timely performance on *Saturday Night Live*, rebuked Daniel Cameron, Kentucky's attorney general, for his handling of the case against the police officers who barged in Breonna Taylor's apartment with a no-knock warrant and murdered her. Meg was particularly attuned to that specific case but also to the way it symbolized the failure of American institutions and individuals to protect Black women from violence and early death. Indeed, after the success of "WAP" and her own experience with domestic violence, she has become an outspoken advocate for Black women suffering violence and abuse.

The idea that Black women are mired in "controlling images" has gained so much currency in Black feminist discourse that it has become almost obligatory to theorize representations and practices of Black women in popular culture through that discursive lens. Patricia Hill Collins makes the case that "the mass media has generated class-specific images of Black women that help justify and shape the new racism of desegregated, colorblind America."[19] Collins suggests that representations of the "Black bitch," who is "loud, pushy, confrontational, aggressive," is "designed to defeminize and demonize Black women."[20] Melissa Harris-Perry locates the trope of "the angry Black woman" as a controlling image, a representation that "holds Black women responsible for power they do not possess, power that is, in fact, being utilized in very real ways by members of social groups who can claim emotional innocence as they hide behind, and persecute, the 'Black Bitches' of our cultural imaginations."[21] The "angry Black woman" and the "Black bitch" are indeed permutations of the "sassy Black woman" who has become an essentialized stereotype, but they lack the ability to lodge the kind of critique of power that is the hallmark of Black women's sass as an agentive, contextualized, subversive cultural practice. This project offers a Black feminist reading of Black women's humor in the spirit of the Black radical tradition, a reading that centers Black women's sass as an expression that interrogates how a history of violence and disempowerment undergirds Black women's expressions of humor and humanity but moves toward joy, pleasure, and even ecstasy.

No Problem with Sass: Representations of the "Sassy Black Woman"

Sass is *not* a concept around which there is consensus among contemporary Black women comics, and in deed, they understand its efficacy differently. Some comedians like Naomi Ekperigin see sass as a confining stereotype.

> JF: Let's talk about Black women comedians. Would you say that you are outside of the mainstream?
>
> NE: Yes, and I don't know why. Um, I think I am because . . . I don't think I can be easily pegged. And that's not to say that I'm so amazing. I can give you both. I'm aware of what you expect to see.
>
> JF: Which is?
>
> NE: *Sassy*. Which is my least favorite word ever. But I love it 'cause sometimes they'll say, "She's funny, she's *sassy!*" And then they'll say my name, and I'll be like, "By sassy he meant *Black*."[22]

It was this frustrated comment Ekperigin made in 2011 that left me with one of the biggest questions this book seeks to answer: How might we codify the particularity of Black women's humor without being essentialist? It is important to remember that depending on the audience, Black women's humor may not always have the intended outcomes of laughter and rebellion. DoVeanna Fulton points out one of the biggest hurdles Black women comics face: in the wide circulation through various media of stereotypically degrading images of Black women, countless opportunities emerge for misinterpretation of cultural and historical knowledge.[23] For any comic, but especially Black women comics, cultivating a community of laughter is the most difficult part of stand-up comedy. Skillfully using personal experience, especially the inversion of marginality from a burden to an asset, can, however, be entertaining, empowering, healing, and, for lack of a better term, sticky. That is, Black women's humor creates a unique cultural product with affective power both familiar and off-putting as Sara Ahmed notes, "in which emotions align some bodies with others, as well as stick different figures together, by the way they move us."[24] Yet, the fact remains that for a variety of reasons—not least the legacy of chattel slavery's cultural and social impact, or neoliberal imperatives that value certain narratives of Black womanhood over others—Black women comics have a difficult time succeeding as professional stand-ups.

I met comedian Karinda Dobbins at a comedy show at the Layover Bar in downtown Oakland, California, in the summer of 2010 and had the chance to watch her perform live in several venues, from comedy clubs to hole-in-the-wall bars to the LGBT community center in San Francisco during Pride Week. Dobbins describes her comic style as "witty, thought-provoking social commentary," and she has opened shows for W. Kamau Bell, Trevor Noah, Gina Yashere, and Dave Chappelle.[25] Dobbins takes on a range of social and political issues that specifically affect her. "I think I have a different voice than a lot of comedians I've heard. I have a very unique perspective. I'm Black. I'm a woman. I'm gay. And I work in corporate America. It's a very unique set of circumstances."[26] Given the particular obstacles Black women comics face in attaining professional success, Dobbins must constantly engage with how the stories she tells onstage butt up against historical ideas about what Black womanhood means and what Black women can and should talk about on the comedy stage: "It's tougher [for Black women comics to succeed] because from our perspective a lot of things aren't funny if you don't know the history of Black women. . . . There's a difference between laughing at it and getting it. And that's one of the hurdles we face. And secondly, it's just really hard to make our experiences funny without making them trivial. There's a fine line between me telling you this is my reality and having you laugh at it and not trivialize it."[27] It *is* possible to theorize the particularity of Black women's humor. Contested as it is, sass is a discourse genre that is foundational to Black women's humor, a conceptualization that changes the very nature of sass as an object of study.

Black feminist scholar Brittney Cooper has discovered her superpower of "eloquent rage," which she chronicles in her eponymous 2018 book. "Eloquent rage" feels like a reimagination of sass, shorn of the negative connotations that have congealed it into the figure of the "sassy Black woman." For Cooper, this figure is a representational trope, like the Madea character in Tyler Perry's films, who "put[s] white folks at ease."[28] Sass, Cooper argues, is a form of expression to which Black women turn "when rage is too risky. . . . When it comes to Black women, sometimes Americans don't recognize that sass is simply a more palatable form of rage. Americans adore sassy Black women. You know, those *caricatures* of finger-waving, eye-rolling Black women at whom everyone loves to laugh."[29] A "sassy Black judge" would be much easier to cast in a film role than "a character who is a charismatic drug dealer with a penchant for parliamentary procedure and aspirations of quitting drug dealing and becoming a legitimate businessman," echoes media scholar Kristen Warner. As Warner sees it, the "'sassy Black judge' is easily digestible because within the description lies recognizable iconography."[30] Indeed, "sassy" is an iconic marker that has come to characterize representations of Black womanhood in popular culture—including film, television, advertisements, and Internet memes.

Tyler Perry's character Madea and Warner's "sassy Black judge" inhabit the legacy of the "baad bitches and sassy supermamas" popularized by Blaxploitation films in characters like Christy Love and Cleopatra Jones, tough women "who show no fear, take on powerful whites and men, and according to the genre's expectation, win."[31] These kinds of characters project a "fantasy of power" as Stephane Dunn puts it, in which the heroines use sass, style, sexuality, and grit to claim personal victory rather than real liberation. The "sassy Black woman" hinges on these fantasy spectacles, which are merely projections of power. My theory of Black women's sass as a genre of discourse complicates the idea that *all* sass is an ossified spectacle meant to entertain and placate white people into believing the lie that Black women are physically strong but politically impotent. Using sass to exact revenge, whether in an extreme or subtle way, can be both personal and about a broader kind of political liberation at the same time—like Cooper remarked on the great Serena Williams, "Her shots are clear and expressive. Her wins are exultant. Her victories belong to all of us, even though she's the one who does all the work."[32] When a Black woman enacts sass, it may seem like a personal enactment, which it inherently is, yet if the victories belong to us all, I am drawn to the idea that sass *can be* about a collective kind of liberation.

There is a note of radicalism embedded in Cooper's notion of eloquent rage in its articulation of an embodied politics of anger, which is a productive source for personal and social transformation, in the Lordeian sense. "Rage is a kind of refusal," Cooper argues, "to be made a fool of, to be silenced, to be shamed, or to stand for anybody's bullshit. It is a refusal of the lie that Black women's anger in the face of routine, everyday injustice is not legitimate."[33] Eloquent rage might look like the "I-refuse-to-be-bothered-ness" of Michelle Obama's casual, everyday, not-for-public ponytail at the inauguration of Donald Trump in January 2017.[34] To be sure, Cooper's eloquent rage foregrounds the affective, interior dimensions of Black women talking back to authority, a crucial element of the enactments of sass. However, she seems to dismiss sass *only* as a strategy of caricatured figures of toothless derision based on gestures and the cultural knowledge commonly attributed to Black women that circulates globally.

In Cooper's reading, sass is what Black women turn to when rage is too risky, because sass is theorized as a *palatable* alternative expressive resource to rage. In the examples Cooper offers, from her own experience as a cultural critic to Michelle Obama and Cooper's own mother, seem to embrace *the work* of sass while rejecting the term itself. "So in this book," Cooper declares, "I am doing what Black women do best. I'm calling America out on her bullshit about racism, sexism, classism, homophobia, and a bunch of other stuff."[35] Cooper is doing the important work of calling out and speaking back to structures of domination, and I believe Cooper is enacting sass, which we can a see in the intentions, aesthetics, and stylistic choices the author makes in the book and in its reception.

Departing from Cooper, though, I do not believe we have a "problem with sass," as her opening chapter's title suggests, or that sass needs a new palatable name. Sass is not the problem. Sass does, however, need a new critical lens and a new understanding of how it functions as a powerful resource in Black women's expressive tool kits. Much of the scholarship on Black women's sass focuses on it as a verbal language practice, overlooking not only its gestural components but also the broader constellation of discursive elements in which it produces humorous affect and, at times, transformative meaning. Drawing on performance theory and contemporary Black feminist thought, I theorize sass as a genre of discourse—embodied practices allowing us to move beyond seeing sass as text to something more dynamic and contingent. Sass is something Black women *do* or *perform* in specific situations to assert a sense of autonomy, a performative tool that in its primal scene operates as an affirmation of one's humanity. Building on the articulation of the righteous anger that is at the heart of Cooper's notion of "eloquent rage," the discourse of sass enunciates Black women's inner lives within conditions of constraint toward an affective politics of pleasure and joy in the pursuit of human connection. Used in humorous contexts, sass can be a subversive tool like irony and satire with which one can defiantly, even if figuratively, assert authority and superiority over those considered to be in a higher position. To put it differently, *Sass* is most concerned about what Black women can *do* with sass, especially with how it functions as an index of Black women's humor and humanity.

Genre theory reframes texts as dynamic interactions. I think it is fair and appropriate to think of representations like stereotypes, for example, as texts in that they are static, not contingent on a particular moment, but seemingly flattened into objecthood. My theory of Black women's sass holds that it is not simply a representational matrix of tired stereotypes. For Black women, sass is agentive. It has come to encompass expressions that are purposefully deployed within specific cultural and social contexts, and it is used as an instrument of appraisal and most importantly as a strategic tool for asserting one's humanity. Sass is also a response—it comprises seemingly innocuous yet distinctive gestures and communicative styles as reactions to pressures to "stay in one's place." Enactments of sass are not always about humor, but if one is literate in its generic conventions and historical functions and understands the social conditions from which it springs in the moment of its expression, it is highly possible that it will be humorous. Creating humor is not *always* the intention of sass, but its uptake does always have the potential to produce laughter in those who recognize the fundamental subversion of power that sass always intends to express.

Anger and Eros: Or, the Politics of Black Women's Sass

Why am I getting so theoretical about Black women's sass? It is not simple, is the simple answer. To treat sass seriously is a political act that does much more than impart an intellectual heft to a practice historically held in such low esteem. I have watched hundreds of live comedy acts since I began this work, and it seems like everyone, as if by requirement, has a "sassy Black woman" joke in their repertoire, even bits that are supposedly trying to be progressive and celebrate Black women. Every July, Montreal plays host to the biggest comedy festival in the world, Just for Laughs, where hundreds of comics from around the world bring all manner of comedy to dozens of stages around the city. In 2016, I headed to one of the late-night shows that caught my eye at the MainLine Club, a show called "Urban Dictionary" hosted by comedian James Davis. Davis has been the host of the Netflix series *Hood Adjacent* since 2017 and opened the show by explaining "hood adjacent comedy" as "knowing the dude that got shot but didn't get invited to his retaliation meeting." The host had some tight jokes exploring a few different words in the online Urban Dictionary: curve, Netflix and chill, glowed-up, and staywoke.

After a few white men performed mediocre sets, the internationally known comedian Iliza Schlesinger came on as the show's special guest. The host made a point of talking about how busy she was and how much work she had been getting lately, and it turns out Schlesinger was probably practicing some of the jokes that would end up on her third Netflix comedy special, *Confirmed Kills* (2016). She came onstage in a black tank top, blue jean Daisy Dukes, and some fashion wedge sneakers. Schlesinger's jokes were in the Amy Schumer style of unabashed sex talk, confident imperfection. She hit on the perils and privileges of being a fit, tan, blonde, witty white woman who is not afraid of her own voice. The set ended with a joke about how Black women's self-esteem is unshakable: "Go up to a Black woman, *I dare you.*" Even approaching a Black woman might be dangerous in Schlesinger's story. "Go up to a Black woman and tell her she looks fat in that shirt. First of all, *I dare you.*"

There were about ten Black people at the small, intimate show. I was the only one sitting directly in her sight line in the middle section. She looked me straight in the eyes as she delivered this joke, or at least it felt like she was staring at me. I tried not to flinch or blink because I knew where the joke was going. I did not want to seem afraid or call attention to myself. I also wanted her to tell me exactly what she thought *I* might say to someone who walked up to *me* and told *me* I looked fat in my clothes. I wanted her to look at me straight when she reduced me and robbed me of my individuality with her grotesque mimicry. She raised her arm and tooted her hip out, rolling her neck slightly. "Whatever. I see you lookin'!" This was the standard "sassy Black woman," a fantasy that discursively produces *all* Black women as such via Schlesinger's recitation. The crowd was with her on it. The laughter was not gut-busting, but it was hearty. It got her a good round of applause.

I laughed a little, but I laugh at a lot of jokes that are not funny. For better or worse, it is contagious. I was also deeply aware of myself as a Black woman in the mostly white audience, and there is always a part of me that fears exposure. Yes, I am a humor scholar, but I am also a Black feminist trying not to be a killjoy. Laughing is a profoundly social, pleasurable experience, and when jokes disempower me for whatever reason, it is difficult to reject that pleasure for myself and sit in inherent judgment of the rest of the community's laughter. So, many times I laugh not only from its contagiousness, but as a Black woman and an ethnographer, I laugh too out of an instinct for self-preservation. This cuts to the heart of a common dismissal of feminists, that we are humorless. Being hailed as humorless never happens in a vacuum but is an epithet lodged in relation to the humor other people are enjoying. When I got home from Schlesinger's show, I thought about how people see Black women and how I had been seen that night. You must fear us because we cannot be hurt? I wondered. We talk back, but we do not say much of substance—is that it? We do not delve into legitimate problems, but we express them away until we have made personal insults against us less meaningful by the way we can deflect them with the roll of the neck, a cut of the eye, and a shimmy of the hips. That must be how they see us. I was enraged.

The "sassy Black woman" is the problem. I see Black women's sass as a hermeneutic for teasing out Black women's liberatory comedic strategies in the ever-tightening grip of a constantly shifting capitalistic, white supremacist, patriarchal vise. Sass is more than cursing someone out in public or having unshakable self-esteem while cursing someone out in public. Sass is a complicated expressive resource for Black women and becomes powerful, first and foremost, to claim one's humanity. One has the right to express that interiority, even in the face of multiple and overlapping systems of oppression. The political significance of Black women's sass cannot be overstated because it is a means of seizing control of one's (inner) life in conditions of overwhelming constraint. Brittney Cooper brings this into stark relief as she notes the worldly value of Black women's use of sass. Black women "have jobs to keep, families to feed, and bills to pay."[36] Black women's sass exists in the tradition of Black performance in which compulsory compliance and acquiescence to domination has at times been mitigated only by covert acts of insurgency. Sass has become a means by which Black women express anger and lodge moral critiques in hostile conditions; it can also manifest a subversive, revelatory, embodied laughter, unimpeachably indicating *life* from below.

Sass is a pleasurable practice that has deep roots as a transformative tool in the Lordeian sense—anger and eros at the same time—to keep Black women psychologically and spiritually (and at times, physically) alive. The aim here is to think about sass as a mechanism through which Black women stake claims to their humanity in specific moments. It bears mentioning, though, that the concept of the human, with all the racial and gendered logics that have rendered it coherent, could be seen as limited and limiting when it comes to Black women, who have struggled to access its rewards and to mobilize it as a meaningful sociopolitical category. Yet, I think it is possible to understand sass as a productive response to the dehumanization it often speaks back to; it is an embodied appeal to *aliveness* that undercuts the brutalizing effects of force and ideology aimed at keeping Black women in their places. In spite of Black women not being seen or treated as human beings, sass insists on their aliveness not just as a feeling but as a *doing* in the intentionality of its expression.

Comprising a repertoire of stylistic tools, sass involves language, style, gesture, and intention. It has functioned historically as a performative technique for communicating a sense of control, empowerment, and moral evaluation, and at times it exposes and transcends normative categories of social identity, like the "sassy Black woman" recited by Iliza Schlesinger. Sass's expression, verbal or otherwise, is preceded by an *internal* appraisal that indicates one has evaluated oneself as having the right to resist and the ability to assert one's humanity to a superior. Its expression is materialized as the speaking back to the object of sass. As Thomas DeFrantz and Anita Gonzalez note, "Black expressive performance springs from the need to communicate beyond the limited events of words alone."[37] Bringing off the gesture or using language to convey that evaluation—to sass someone—is the end point of sass, not where it begins.

Sass provides a framework for thinking historically about Blackness, and Black womanhood in particular; it is a way to think about the processes by which those categories come to cohere in the act of performance and its inextricable link with Black women's experiences of everyday life. Black women's humor and comedy are practices that facilitate this kind of knowledge. The conceptual language of sass as a genre of discourse enables us to move to a space where Black women's humor is understood as fundamental to the Black performance tradition that is part of liberationist struggles toward a new order. We can see it more for what it is: a site for the transgression of disordered social and cultural norms; a claim on pleasure; release and redress in the process of speaking and acting on behalf of the self and the collective. "Much attention has been given to the dominative mode of white enjoyment," Saidiya Hartman argues, "but what about forms of pleasure that stand as figures of transformation or, at the very least, refigure Blackness in terms other than abjection?" Black women's sass is indeed a "self-conscious form of racial pleasure"[38] that generates limited forms of redress "aimed at relieving the pained body through alternative configurations of the self and the redemption of the body as human flesh, not a beast of burden."[39]

The Discourse Genre of Black Women's Sass

Black women's sass is a discourse genre, "a structure of relations of synonymy, paraphrase and substitution—which determines what can and should be said in and through a particular register."[40] In John Frow's work from 1980, discourse genres were limited to "the major and clearly-defined genres and exclud[ed] the nuanced subgenres" such as "highly situational acts like telling off a superior."[41] Black women's sass is fundamentally an act of "telling off a superior," yet I believe we can extend Frow's theory to encompass sass as a discourse genre. Historically, Black women have existed in an uninterrupted state of alterity in the United States that has demanded, in different times and places, a means of ascending to a position of moral superiority; sass is a genre of discourse engaged by Black women subjects that can be codified to encompass what Black women say and how they say it in certain situations to speak back to authority and lay claim to their humanity. Darryl Dance sees sass as a critical linguistic element of Black women's humor, and Joyce West Stevens submits a compelling account of sass as a form of social capital for young and poor Black girls.[42] Yet, a theory of sass as a genre of discourse enables us to think about how Black womanhood (and girlhood) is *done* in practice, through complex processes that create a link between the ways that Black women's humor became legible in the past and the ways it does so in the present.

William F. Hanks provides two views of genres: first, the ahistorical framework in which generic types are grouped by "thematic, stylistic, and compositional elements," which may "differ by the features or configurations by which they are defined, irrespective of the historical conditions under which the types come to exist and of the social values attached to them in a given context."[43] In this view, we can see how an ahistorical "sassy Black woman" has become legible. Hanks's second definition of genre is germane here; a discourse genre "can be defined as the historically specific conventions and ideals according to which authors compose discourse and audiences receive it."[44] Hanks analyzed a set of texts produced in early colonial Mexico by Mayan native officials and elucidated a conceptual framework for understanding how discourse genres work. "In their formal and functional details," Hanks argues, "the texts reflect a process of local innovation, blending Mayan and Spanish discourse forms into novel types. They document the rapid emergence of new genres of language use, new types of action in colonial society.... One is led to treat genres as *historically specific elements of social practice*, whose defining features link them to situated communicative acts."[45] Furthermore, it is this *historicity* of Black women's sass that secures its status as a discourse genre.

Cut-Eye and Suck-Teeth

In 1976, linguists John Rickford and Angela Rickford published a study of gestures known as "cut-eye and suck-teeth," the classic paralinguistic markers associated with "sassiness." Rickford and Rickford surveyed Black and white informants in the United States, the Caribbean, and African nations to examine the extent to which these gestures "might represent African 'survivals,'" finding that it was Black women in each locale who had the most knowledge of the gestures and the most competency at performing them.[46] Cut-eye (or rolling the eyes), they argue, "is a visual gesture which communicates hostility, displeasure, disapproval, or a general rejection of the person at whom it is directed,"[47] and suck-teeth is "an expression of anger, impatience, exasperation, or annoyance ... often used in combination with [cut-eye],"[48] the "gesture of drawing air through the teeth and into the mouth to produce a loud sucking noise."[49] These iconic gestures are part of the symbolic gestural repertoire that Black women have historically used as part of the discourse genre—sass—to produce meaning and communicate a sense of moral superiority in situations where speaking back to power is required.

As already mentioned, bringing off the gesture, or using language to convey one's moral evaluation, is the end point of sass, not where it begins.

Michelle Obama at the 2013 Inauguration Day luncheon. *The Atlantic* GIF, January 21, 2013, https://cdn.theatlantic.com/media/mt/politics/eyeroll.gif.

Sass has functioned historically for Black women, even in times when verbal language was unavailable, as a means for communicating her values, and it works as a clearly defined discourse genre that can be understood as "a constellation of recognizable forms bound together by an internal dynamic . . . a fusion of substantive, stylistic, and situational elements" that function as a range of possible "strategic responses to the demands of the situation."[50] In its primal scene, sass is first and foremost *for* the subject of sass—she who deploys it. One of the most iconic "cut-eyes" happened in January 2013 at President Barack Obama's second Inauguration Day luncheon. First Lady Michelle Obama was captured on camera seated between the president and Republican John Boehner, Speaker of the House of Representatives at that time.

We do not know exactly why Michelle Obama cut her eyes at Boehner—a person who was often at political odds with the president—as he spoke. But we can all understand that the rolling of the eyes is an expression of negative affect. Why was Michelle Obama's gesture an act of "world-historical shade," in the words of one Gawker writer?[51] The impact of the first African American presidential family is deep, as is the racist discourse that has circulated about the Obamas. Former Speaker Boehner symbolized the power structure, at that time, that was checking President Obama at every turn. Although the First Lady could not pass legislation through Congress, she sure could cut her eyes at the man undermining her husband. Analyzed within Rickford and

Rickford's framework, Michelle Obama "convey[ed] that he is not admired or respected."[52] Michelle Obama's sassy behavior was a symbolic means of communicating her values, and it was *not* for us as spectators. Yet, if we share in those values and all the history attached to them based on what we see in the video clip, Michelle Obama's cut-eye and the meaning it produced in that context might have made us laugh and feel like we got to peek behind the curtain of the polite and agreeable front that public appearances typically demand of the First Lady.

Let me offer a provisional codification of Black women's sass (which is synonymous with *sass* throughout the book) as a discourse genre. Sass is a dialogic, intelligible pattern of address, operating primarily via oral expression to an assumed superior in institutional or interpersonal settings. It is characterized by verbal expression and paralinguistic elements; that is, (e.g., a gestural repertoire including posture, intonation, or aesthetic elements) consistent with marking a slight (real or perceived). The expression of sass creates meaning by combining instrumental rhetoric (appraisal, questioning, provoking)[53] with experiential processes (asserting, reinforcing) and follows from the *internal imperative* of the subject to flout normative rules of decorum (the rules, whatever they are, being the object of sass). Black women have a long, ubiquitous history of enacting sass to "tell off a superior," so long and pervasive that it has come to form a capacious discourse genre in which Black women challenge domination in all its intersecting forms. They often revel in the assertion of humanity that sass produces, and the inversion that takes place in the enactment is often to humorous effect.

Put differently, sass is a repertoire of stylistic tools involving *language*, *style*, *gesture*, and *intention*. More than a stylistic convention of performance, or "an attitude," as Marcyliena Morgan puts it,[54] sass is an embodied strategy of separation, a technique igniting Black women to move "out of their place," detaching themselves from people or ideas they find irritating, insulting, confining, or degrading. In this framework, sass cannot function as a permanent affect or essential trait—if one is "always out of one's place," then one is never in one's place! Sass is necessarily ephemeral, tied to a particular temporal moment.

Black Women Politicking: Performance as a Politics of Liberation

Foregrounding the performances, artistry, and voices of Black women humorists, this work is fundamentally interdisciplinary, drawing on Black and feminist theories of humor, sass, performance, politics, and popular cultural interpretations of Black women's expressive culture. I make use of these sources to reveal the ways humor functions as a zone of freedom wherein Black women are at liberty to define themselves through narrative and in performative gestures; take refuge from life's hardships; break down representational stereotypes; feel embodied pleasure; and grapple with and engage the politics of everyday life. Nevertheless, the scholarship on Black women's humor as a specific, stand-alone cultural and political formation is notably lacking, and *Sass* offers a critical intervention in these areas of inquiry. For example, scholars have compellingly theorized performance as a primary vehicle of resistance for racial and gender minorities, especially in the way humor facilitates the development of collective cultural and political consciousness. Black women's humor tends to function in these literatures as a subgenre, theorized primarily as representational tropes divorced from the humorists themselves. Instead of being rooted in what Dwight Conquergood calls the "view from above," the knowing *that* and *about* Black women's humor and humanity, *Sass* privileges the "ground view"—knowing *how* and *who*, that which is anchored in practice.[55]

Indeed, *Sass* departs significantly from this body of knowledge, contributing a utility-based analysis of Black women's humor where performance, pleasure, identity, and political expression is front and center. That is, in thinking about how Black women's humor is codified and located within a cultural, political, and intellectual history, this work reveals not only how Black women's humor is a fundamental constituent of Black (expressive) culture but also how it sheds light—through time and space—on the cultural and political meanings of Americanness in new ways. *Sass* troubles the classic feminist debate between discourse and materiality, focusing on Black women's performance as both representational and embodied. In this historical moment of artistic expression, feminist politics, and social transformation, the Black Lives Matter movement, the Women's March, and the #MeToo movement are key sites for contextualizing the efficacy of Black women's humor. Black women humorists are political actors engendering major cultural shifts, similar to the way that in the 1960s and 1970s Black feminists gave meaning to their personal experiences and transformed American culture. This calls attention to the intersection of self-making and redress that is always animating how I think about the efficacy of Black women's humor, especially how it forces critical examination of the meaning of politics and politicking.

This book argues that Black women's humor is a genre of popular culture with a unique intellectual, cultural, and aesthetic history—specifically marked by the discourse of sass. But I would be remiss to locate this particularity outside of the history of the broader tradition of women's and feminist humor.

By the same token, some of the Black women comics I am working with in my theory of sass often challenge mainstream notions of "ladyhood" by incorporating racialized sexual politics in their comedy. Bearing in mind Peggy Phelan's critique of "the ideology of visibility,"[56] which is the idea that marginalized people can attain political power via more visibility, we will see that identifying and recognizing Black women as cocreators of the Black humor tradition is in fact political. As Toni Morrison reminds us, "Canon building is empire building. Canon defense is national defense. Canon debate, whatever the terrain, nature, and range ... is the clash of cultures. And *all* of the interests are vested."[57] More specifically, my aim is to identify and analyze Black women's humor as a mode of performance facilitating personal, intellectual, and political expression in the public sphere.

Saidiya Hartman's notion of subterranean politics is germane for understanding the intersection of performance practices and the cultural politics of Black women's humor. In *Scenes of Subjection: Terror, Slavery, and Self-Making in Nineteenth-Century America*, Hartman argues that the subversive politics of everyday performances for enslaved people did not necessarily produce "freedom" or a remedy to the condition of slavery but enabled a communal space for the expression of their pain.[58] It is precisely in the space of subterranean politics and in the sociality of comedic events that sass creates that we can locate the political efficacy of Black women's humor. I use the term *politics* in this spirit, yet Black women's comedic expressions are far from simple romantic acts of resistance. These enunciations are provisional, local, and limited practices that are sometimes right on the surface and many times are subterranean, similar to the practices Hartman theorizes.

Sass is a Black feminist project, part of a proscriptive effort that reflects and generates "a wider range of choices and resources" for Black women.[59] Black women's humor and those who practice it are part of a broader intellectual and political tradition that enables us to understand who Black women are and how they create, maintain, and enjoy the spaces they inhabit. In this book, I show how Black women often elicit more than laughter with their humor, but also—and importantly—they often depict for their audiences the potential for *liberation*, a sense of freedom that engenders alternative or new forms of sociality or cultural relations. Scholarly studies of women's and feminist humor have abounded, and Black women humorists have generally been part of those conversations—likely mentions being Jackie "Moms" Mabley, Florynce Kennedy, Whoopi Goldberg, and Wanda Sykes among those categorized as performing feminist humor. Far less attention, however, focuses on how Black women's comedic politics address the specific experiences and concerns around issues of economic, social, and political marginalization. Katelyn Hale Wood's work is an outlier in this respect as her trailblazing book, *Cracking Up*, characterizes Black feminist stand-up comedy as responding to and telling the truth about systems of power and marginalization (racism, homophobia, sexism) in order to subvert or dismantle them. *Sass* builds on Wood's astute and timely elucidation of Black feminist stand-ups who "deploy the art of joke-telling to 'stand up' against oppression and 'stand up' for joyful expression."[60] Focusing on the granularity of Black women's humor, *Sass* examines the subversion of power inherent in Black women's humor and how that subversion has materialized as the discourse of sass, whether onstage, in sketches, or in the everyday lives of Black women. *Sass* offers a different kind of insight into the specificity of Black women's humor as it traverses time and space and brings sometimes disparate bodies into close proximity.

I draw from performance theories to interrogate Black women's humor as a cultural formation and use the term "performance" in the spirit of performance studies scholars, who see it as a structural category of behavior by which we can understand how we as social and political subjects make meaning and affirm social values. According to performance studies scholar E. Patrick Johnson, "Black performance is at the interstices of Black political life and art, providing the lynchpin that sustains and galvanizes arts and acts of resistance."[61] Even when Black women's humor operates under the radar, the performance of Black women's humor facilitates the processes of social and political transformation—it transmits historical material, entertains and educates, opens space for resistance to all forms of oppression, and sets a foundation for personal and collective political consciousness and liberation.

Black women's sass is a mode of cultural performance, and this work explores several iterations of it that Black women humorists undertake: (1) performance as epistemology and acts of self-making; (2) performance as pleasure; and (3) performance as political praxis. Further, I analyze how Black women use humor to break down negative stereotypes but also to embody and articulate alternative renditions. Humor enables Black women to narrate their experiences and publicly make themselves, and it also creates a path for audiences to better understand and accept their own subjectivities and the histories out of which they are constituted. Joyce West Stevens's definition of *self-efficacy* encapsulates the crucial role of sass in Black women's humor, both on the stage and in everyday life. To possess self-efficacy, as Stevens theorizes it, one has "the ability to exercise mastery and competence in one's social environment or to feel that one has control over one's environment because of proficient abilities. Self-efficacy is the developmental marker that can be accomplished by a variety of means. Self-efficacy can be achieved in the competition of athletic games learned in the school setting, in the autonomy and independence of decision making learned by taking part in family and community processes, and in the mutuality and caring of friendships developed in the peer group and neighborhood."[62]

This book is informed by and expands on Rebecca Krefting's notion of *charged humor*, a brand of humor performed by minoritarian subjects who connect with their audience by calling attention to personal experiences or intimate knowledge of what it means to be marginalized in order to disrupt the structures of power that enable that marginality.[63] Indeed, the humorists in this study often use jokes to grapple with feelings of being an outsider or an outcast from various communities, and they are generating other means of making community given their experiences of exclusion. But more importantly, Black women's humorous performances also function as a means through which new forms of Black feminist praxis and understandings of liberation can emerge. Moreover, the political charge of Black women's humor is undertheorized in scholarship on satirical and racial humor. The discourse of sass originated in the conditions of chattel slavery—abject disempowerment and dehumanization—conditions that frame the inherently political nature of the performative repertoire itself. For Black women to talk back has always been a political act, and when we situate sass as the center on which the particularity of Black women's humor coheres, it becomes easier to reevaluate the way we think about the mutual imbrication of politics and performance and how Black women's humor can function in service of it.

Danielle Fuentes Morgan's book *Laughing to Keep from Dying* explores Black satire's ethic of justice, arguing that satirical performance moves the audience to see the world differently and act accordingly. The Black satiric mode, Morgan argues, is a platform for self-making, a process through which contemporary African American satirists might make known what she calls *kaleidoscopic Blackness*, "the various ways Blackness might be experienced, performed, and lived as self-directed expression," the recognition of which "is an ethical move that leads to social justice in its revelation of the multiple ways of performing Blackness and being Black, where social justice is the freedom to be, freedom to articulate and perform one's own autonomous identity."[64] For Morgan, Black satirical readings reveal the post-racial as *the* mythology around which contemporary Black satirists explore the paradox of race and racism in the twenty-first century, highlighting contemporary performances of Black humor as political praxis oriented toward justice. Morgan mainly focuses on readings of Black satire in which the subjects use humor to "keep from dying," a radical kind of laughter that seeks personal autonomy as a form of justice, which highlights my analysis of how the performance of sass in Black women's humor functions as a mechanism of *liberation* through which Black women assert their humanity and wrest a modicum of empowerment from conditions in which we were "never meant to survive."[65]

Critical (Auto)ethnography

Over the course of more than a decade, I conducted fieldwork in a variety of comedy venues around the United States, South Africa, and Canada. I have amassed a significant and unique archive of Black women's comedy, which is foregrounded in *Sass* to provide both a broad image and a granular examination of Black women's comic culture. Since 2010, I have conducted extensive, semi-structured oral history interviews with nearly thirty professionals in the comedy industry, including nationally and internationally known comics Paul Mooney, Luenell, Aisha Tyler, Hope Flood, Miss Laura Hayes, Thea Vidale, Jane Galvin-Lewis, Naomi Ekperigin, and Gina Yashere, among many other lesser-known comics. Interviews addressed family history, comedic influences, joke writing, onstage experiences, audience perception and reception, and the embodied sensations of performing comedy. Furthermore, participant observation of the moment of performance is central in setting the terms for debates around comedy as a medium through which Black women articulate and redress cultural, social, and political marginalization. The bulk of the oral history interviews were completed between 2010 and 2015, and I have used interview data where permission to publish it could be obtained in 2023. None of the interviewees declined to have portions of their interviews included in the book after I reached out to get permission, but several comics were unreachable or unresponsive to requests for permission to use their original interview material. Where permission could not be obtained, I used interview data that appears in the public domain, which provided information similar to what the original interviews offered.

The majority of live performances I watched took place in the United States, but I attended more than a dozen live comedy performances over the course of two weeks at the Just for Laughs comedy festival in Montreal in 2015 and 2016 and another four performances at a large commercial venue in that city, Club Soda. I watched nearly ten stand-up performances and two comedy shows at large casinos in Durban and Johannesburg, South Africa, in 2015, I caught four live performances of celebrity stand-ups at larger commercial performance venues in the United States seating thousands of patrons: the Paramount Theatre in Oakland, California; Mountainview Winery in Saratoga Springs, California; Treasure Island Casino in Las Vegas; and the Arie Crown Theater in Chicago. All interviews but one were conducted in person and audio recorded. I offered to use pseudonyms, but each interviewee declined. Many excerpts and quotes from live comedy shows I attended are from my personal archive of audio recordings, fieldnotes, and transcriptions.

I learned how to write jokes and perform stand-up comedy as part of this research. My fieldwork included a five-week night course in 2009 that met on Wednesday evenings for three hours at the San Francisco Comedy College, which bills itself as the "most attended stand-up program in the United States."[66] It was there that I learned the technical aspects of joke writing and routine development. One aspect of comedy writing that I learned at SFCC was to jot down anything that might become a joke or bit, and since taking the course I have written hundreds of jokes, scattered over notecards, scraps of paper, Microsoft Word documents, and phone memoranda. Since 2010, I have performed about thirty distinct stand-up sets, from five to twenty-five minutes in length, at open mic nights at bars, as an opening act for a national headlining stand-up act, as an invited performer at the Vermont Comedy Club, in a showcase at a mainstream Black comedy club in Los Angeles in front of veteran professional comics, as an opening act for an improv show at the famed Second City theater in Chicago, and as a feature act at two academic conferences.

From my interviews, I have come to understand the personal and financial struggles that often define the lives of professional stand-ups, and learning to write jokes and continuously reaching for the courage to perform stand-up set me as somewhat of an insider in the broader stand-up scene. Performance ethnography is an ethical research methodology I engaged to mitigate the sense of myself as a disconnected researcher unproblematically trying out an art form and profession that mean so much to my interlocuters. Being a researcher who was trying to become a part of the community that I was studying challenged me to write the best and tightest jokes, to practice and revise them, and to never take the craft lightly. The uncomfortable experience of simultaneously inhabiting two seemingly contradictory worlds (scholar and comic) is par for the ethnographic course. One might perceive the seriousness of intellectual inquiry and the entertaining function of stand-up as conflicting modes of theorization. But as autoethnography, stand-up comedy becomes a method and product of academic analysis. D. Soyini Madison reminds us, "The performer must be committed—doing what must be done or going where one must go—to experience the felt-sensing dynamic of that world: its tone-color—the sights, sounds, smells, tastes, textures, rhythms—the visceral ethos of that world."[67] For me, that meant first spending many nights in dark, dank clubs with individuals working to get their "big break" and then interpreting the difficulties for Black women of achieving such a goal.

I folded many moments of my life (my youth, grappling with my sexuality and gender presentation, my weight, personal relationships, and the like) into my jokes and routines. My humor, like that of the Black women comics I interviewed and observed, was rooted in my own experiences. My attempt to become a stand-up was in earnest, while I was fully aware of the privileges I had in terms of being financially secure with no children (at the time I began performing) to provide for. Unlike many women who labor on the road as comics who must perform where they *can* get work, I had the luxury of choosing where I would perform; most of the time, it was at venues in progressive urban areas where audiences had the cultural and social knowledge that made my humor legible to them. I did not have to make the sacrifices that many Black women make to create a viable career.

A Note on Blackness

Sass highlights the link between race, gender, sexuality, experience, and performance. "It is not skin color which makes a Negro American," Ralph Ellison remarked, "but cultural heritage as shaped by the American experience, the social and political predicament."[68] When I use the term *Black* or *African American*, I follow E. Patrick Johnson's assertion that racial Blackness is performatively produced and is "historically, socially, and politically contingent upon terms of its production."[69] As Johnson notes, "Blackness does not only reside in the theatrical fantasies of the white imaginary that is projected onto black bodies, nor is it always consciously acted out; rather it is also the inexpressible yet undeniable racial experience of black people—the ways in which the 'living of blackness' becomes a material way of knowing."[70] This is not to say that Blackness is not also rooted in corporeality, because as Jayna Brown reminds us, the Black body is a site of race and racism, and "race and racist regimes are made out of flesh—muscle and ligament, blood and bone."[71] However, Toni Morrison draws up a beautifully contingent and supple definition of Blackness as it intersects with womanhood, which she harnessed to create the character Sula in the eponymous novel. Morrison's idea is especially appropriate in elucidating the way the Black women humorists of this work were selected. "I always thought of Sula as quintessentially black, metaphysically black . . . which is not melanin and certainly not unquestioning fidelity to the tribe. She is New World black and New World woman extracting choice from choicelessness, responding inventively to found things. Improvisational. Daring, disruptive, imaginative, modern, out-of-the-house, outlawed, unpolicing, uncontained and uncontainable."[72]

Many of the humorists and comedians who appear in this work were chosen because of my previous knowledge of their work, but I discovered many people whom I had not known of in the process of conducting ethnographic and archival research. This book does not pretend to provide an exhaustive list of Black women comedians and humorists, nor does it insist that Blackness and womanhood are unilaterally applicable to all the women under investigation. But to be sure, there are many connections we can draw between the history of racial slavery, colonialism, and imperialism and Black women's comedic practices across the African diaspora and on the continent. Gabeba Baderoon makes the case that slavery had a fundamental effect on the ways race and gender are understood and lived out in South Africa to the same extent that the institutional apparatus and cultural practices of apartheid shaped Black life. Chattel slavery across the African diaspora and on the continent "created continual intimate proximity," Baderoon argues, and "forms of discipline such as surveillance, whipping and sexual violence were deployed in an attempt to violently assert boundaries amid such nearness."[73] Slavery rendered Black people in the modern South African state—Black women specifically—disposable, yielding the kinds of social and political conditions that require Black women to make certain kinds of claims on their humanity in the face of unyielding domination.

Avoiding too facile a comparison between Black women comics in the diaspora and on the continent, I do, however, want to foreground a dialogic connection between Black women who have used creative tactics and practices to get out of place, take up space, and "extract choice from choicelessness," as Morrison put it. "Central to this space," Pumla Gqola maintains, "is the creation of new language, new vision and new realities as we world our environs anew."[74] There is a sense of affinity between Black diasporic women, despite "lives [that] have been diverse and differentiated on the basis of a range of factors such as culture and custom, class and citizenship status, socioeconomic level, political and economic context, and historical period."[75] Sass as a genre of discourse is distinctly African American, yet the will of Black women all over the world who have been subject to white supremacist, patriarchal domination to speak back to power is diffuse. Indeed, each of the Black women comics featured in chapter 5, which addresses Black South African women's comedic practices, has performed at the iconic stand-up showcase Blacks Only, and "Black" is as salient a political and cultural identity in South Africa as it is in the United States, on the continent, and across the diaspora. Furthermore, the art of contemporary stand-up is an American genre, and the comics under investigation in South Africa have all expressed that they have been deeply influenced by the art, aesthetics, and politics of Black American humorists.

Another Diasporic Black woman comedian included in this study is British Nigerian comedian Gina Yashere, who lives in the United States but grew up in East London and performs comedy all over the world. "I'm a storyteller," she explained in a promotional interview for her 2023 stand-up tour. "So, I'm basically telling stories from my life. From living in London, growing up in England in the seventies and eighties."[76] Yashere actively seeks out Black comedic spaces, which is where she got her start in the UK and the United States. She performed in the urban scene in London, made up mostly of Caribbean and African acts and audiences, and she was the first non-US-born Black person to be featured on HBO's *Def Comedy Jam*. Yashere clearly has a certain intimacy and affinity with Black people across the diaspora, even though she pitches her comedy to a wide variety of audiences. Yashere has a global audience and enjoys a successful career as a stand-up, a television actress, and a writer for the American CBS sitcom *Bob Hearts Abishola*, and her comedy and the stories she tells illuminate the capaciousness and reach of Black women's humor as it becomes a sought-after form of cultural capital, traversing continents, genres, and bodies.

The will to speak back to authority and assert humanity within ongoing conditions of racial and sexual alterity draws together the Black women of this study. They may not name it "sass," but the practice of asserting one's humanity and speaking back to power or authority in particular situations in which one feels slighted has become a critical element of Black women's humor across the diaspora and on the continent, and I have selected for inclusion in this study Black women whose work demonstrates the particularity and limited continuity of Black women's humor, even across gulfs as wide (spatially, culturally, ideologically, historically) as the Middle Passage. To use Hartman's poignant words, "The collective movement points toward what awaits us, what has yet to come into view, what they anticipate—the time and place better than here; a glimpse of the earth not owned by anyone.... Inside the circle it is clear that every song is really the same song, but crooned in infinite variety, every story altered and unchanging: *How can I live? I want to be free. Hold on.*"⁷⁷ The Black women in this book sing the same song, "crooned in infinite variety." It is a song that reaches toward freedom, and with sass we hang on. Sass *moves* people, jolts and awakens from comfort zones, affecting social relations and igniting embodied sensation, be it terror, pleasure, relief, or release. Infused in Black women's humor, sass can make you laugh, and it can help you *live*.

Overview of *Sass*

Chapter 1 outlines the roots of Black women's sass, emphasizing the role of chattel slavery and patriarchal power in its development. I demonstrate the ways that Black women used sass as a tool to struggle against and protest conditions of subordination, enabling them to make manifest their consciousness and a sense of their humanity. Overall, this chapter charts how Black women's sass has transformed over time and become the most discernible and efficacious element of their humor. To understand how sass has become a foundational comedic technique, it is necessary to examine how social structures and relations of power shape the performative choices to which Black women have had access in conditions of profound constraint and within the context of deeply held beliefs about Black womanhood. I suggest not only that Black women's sass enables an inversion of power that allows Black women to envision and enact a limited form of liberation, but also that this inversion calls up alternative relations for audiences who must confront what that liberation from subordination might look like, too.

Chapter 2 examines Black women's raunchy humor, taking as its subject the laughter evoked from explicit sexual jokes and how, for Black women, they can excite different kinds of pleasure, from the psychological to the erotic. This analysis reconsiders how humor works on and through the body when Black women stage explicit, illicit sexual encounters to titillate and touch their audiences. I foreground the ways Black women's raunchy humor functions in the framework of sass to redress, on the public stage, the marginalization of sexual subjectivity and the will, by many scholars and critics alike, to primarily frame Black women's sexuality and erotic desires as sites of violence, subject to erasure and silence.

Indeed, Black women's raunch and the stories they tell signal the liberationist potential of Black women's humor, its raunchiness and excess not only a challenge to the white supremacist, patriarchal order but also a call to celebrate and appreciate Black bodies and the erotic pleasures housed within them. Black women's raunchy humor is more than a low-brow form of entertainment, and the poetics dimension, or what I call corporeal orature, challenges conventional readings of raunchy humor as unserious and low-hanging fruit in the economy of humor and stand-up comedy. Along with readings of LaWanda Page's comedic oeuvre, my ethnographic observations of contemporary Black women's stand-up illuminate sexually explicit routines as instruments of amusement, erotic pleasure, and feminist politics.

Chapter 3 considers how sass functions for Black women comics to produce meaning in transformative ways—specifically, how Black masculine women deal with their butchness onstage. Anchored in autoethnography and fieldwork, this chapter helps us examine the comedy and experiences of Black masculine-presenting women, and in so doing we gain a deeper understanding about the ways sass functions in Black women's humor, especially how it enables comics and spectators alike to expand their ideas of what Black womanhood means and how Black butch women enacting sass involve nuanced and fundamentally political ways of claiming their humanity.

Addressing what I call butch body politics, the performativity of gender, and the overarching trope of failure, I argue that we must treat Black lesbian gender styles seriously to think about the seriousness of Black masculine gender presentation. It functions for Black women comics to produce meaning in transformative ways—specifically, dealing with the physicality of butchness onstage, claiming humanity, and understanding the politics of sass that have always been in play in Black women's comedy.

Chapter 4 examines comics who have come of age in the twenty-first century and are on the cutting edge, employing surrealism and offbeat quirk to address some of the same comedic material. This chapter looks at the aesthetics and sensibilities taken up by Black women performing in the alternative comedy scene. Black alternative acts include Naomi Ekperigin, Nicole Byer, Marina Franklin, and Sasheer Zamata, and I argue there is no easy distinction between Black women's "urban" and "alternative" comedy.

The aesthetic and stylistic elements of Black women's alt-comedy illuminate important insights regarding how Black women are engaging in Black feminist performance practices—especially sass—through which they show Black comics' desire to be regarded as complex, thinking human beings. Black women have become relatively ubiquitous in the US comedy scene in the twenty-first century, holding promise and the risk of exploitation . Centering their comedic narratives and the stories they tell about themselves in interviews, I argue that some current instantiations of Black women's humor insidiously share certain features—the embrace of individuality and a penchant for almost continuous innovation—with the neoliberal cultural and economic order that defines twenty-first-century life. I closely read sketch, podcast, and stand-up comedy to argue that insecurity, political consciousness, and neoliberal imperatives frame Black women's humor in the twenty-first century.

Finally, in chapter 5 I examine the stand-up comedy of Black women in South Africa and how they deploy the language and discourse of sass in their comedy. Employing participant observation and secondary sources related to the comedy and lives of comics like Celeste Ntuli, Tumi Morake, and Khanyisa Bunu, I suggest the carnivalesque as a useful way to think about how Black women comics in South Africa use humor and sass to call into question social and political power dynamics and potentially subvert or reorient dominant norms associated with Black womanhood. These comics show comedy as a powerful means by which to challenge and dislodge old ideologies and social orders, especially the gendered racial order of apartheid. When these comics deploy aesthetics of the carnivalesque that are imbued with the discourse of sass, they openly celebrate their experiences, their bodies, and their capacity to speak and be heard.

I argue that stand-up is a genre of diaspora culture meant to contend with issues of anti-Black racism, patriarchy, and economic and social marginalization. Ultimately, this chapter examines how humor and comedy manifest transnational intimacies and affinities via the circulation of Black women's comic culture, intimacies that are critical to understanding sass and to troubling theories of the African diaspora wherein Africa is always the locus of dispersal. As marginal comics within a sprawling global industry, the comics examined in this chapter use stand-up to call out certain cultural values that consign Black people, and more specifically Black women, to the margins by mocking and ridiculing them. These practices of social and cultural critique are performed in a stance where irreverence rules; as Khanyisa Bunu described her style, "few, if any," subjects are taboo.[78] When irreverence rules, humor enables the four women highlighted in this chapter to share their experiences with audiences in ways that subvert discourses of Black womanhood and express political ideas in new and exciting ways that engender a broader Black feminist diaspora culture, where the Black woman self is a site of celebration, in all its various incarnations.

Sass is a story about Black women who have used creative tactics and aesthetic practices to "get out of place," for one reason or another, within conditions so limited and constrained that the very act of speaking back might end in death. Indeed, Black women's humor is a fundamental element of a culture of Black people on the continent and in the diaspora defying material conditions to carve out spaces to be heard. What is essential to this process of world-making is the way the women of this study have created courageous ways of speaking and acting as we press on toward new visions of liberation.

CHAPTER 1

NEVER TO BE CONQUERED

SASS, SUBJECTION, AND BLACK WOMEN
SELF-POSSESSED

> The war of my life had begun and though one of God's most powerless creatures, I resolved never to be conquered.
>
> —HARRIET JACOBS, *Incidents in the Life of a Slave Girl*

American treasure Fannie Lou Hamer put her body and livelihood on the line in her mid-forties as an activist from the Mississippi Delta, working in the Black freedom struggle during the 1960s and 1970s. Hamer is most remembered for her efforts to secure the vote for Black Mississippians during the 1960s. Despite the ongoing threats of violence and terror from the state and racist vigilantes, Hamer was a field organizer for the Student Nonviolent Coordinating Committee to agitate for the Black vote in Mississippi. She became the face of the Mississippi Freedom Democratic Party, an integrated alternative to the mainstream Democratic Party, which arose to oppose or be seated along with the all-white delegation sent to the Democratic National Convention to represent Mississippi in Atlantic City in 1964. Hamer had first tried to register to vote in August 1962 but was denied, along with seventeen other people she had traveled with, and was subsequently fired from her job as a timekeeper on the plantation where she had worked for decades. In 1964, Hamer famously delivered a speech before the Credentials Committee at the DNC in Atlantic City that was so poignant and powerful that President Lyndon B. Johnson—who could perceive a threat to white supremacy in her words—insisted the coverage be interrupted for a pointless news conference in order to silence her story. Nevertheless, major networks at the time played the almost nine-minute testimony in its entirety that night, and the story had profound implications, reverberating across time and space.

In her testimony, Hamer dramatically recalled a savage event that would change her life and shape her resolve to secure full citizenship rights for Black people in the United States, even under the intractable threat of terror and danger. She recounted a night in the summer of 1963, when after attending a voter registration workshop her bus was stopped by state police and she was arrested at a rest stop. Hamer was already well known as an advocate for the Black franchise, and she was targeted that night and subjected, along with several other people with whom she was traveling, to a devastating beating from which she would never fully physically recover. Hamer told the harrowing, explicit details of her experience on live television for the world to hear. Like that of her forebears in the slave narratives, Hamer's testimony was affectively and politically moving in one fell swoop, barraging listeners with imagery and sensations of the brutality she had experienced in the service of moving people to action.

> They left my cell and it wasn't too long before they came back. He said, "You are from Ruleville all right," and he used a curse word. And he said, "We are going to make you wish you was dead." I was carried out of that cell into another cell where they had two Negro prisoners. The State Highway Patrolman ordered the first Negro to take the blackjack. The first Negro prisoner ordered me, by orders from the State Highway Patrolman, for me to lay down on a bunk bed on my face. I laid on my face and the first Negro began to beat. I was beat by the first Negro until he was exhausted. I was holding my hands behind me at that time on my left side, because I suffered from polio when I was six years old. After the first Negro had beat until he was exhausted, the State Highway Patrolman ordered the second Negro to take the blackjack. The second Negro began to beat and I began to work my feet, and the State Highway Patrolman ordered the first Negro who had beat me to sit on my feet—to keep me from working my feet. I began to scream and one white man got up and began to beat me in my head and tell me to hush.[1]

Hamer's unrestrained attention to detail and sense of urgency in the moment are striking. Her testimony is probably most well-remembered for the way white supremacist violence is foregrounded and the way she endured it. The particulars incite a call to action among those forced to see and hear the truth about what it means to be a Black American a full century after the Civil War had officially ended chattel slavery.

At the end of Hamer's narrative to the Credentials Committee, she makes the American paradox plain:

> All of this is on account of we want to register, to become first-class citizens. And if the Freedom Democratic Party is not seated now, I question America. Is this America, the land of the free and the home of the brave, where we have to sleep with our telephones off the hooks because our lives be threatened daily, because we want to live as decent human beings, in America?

Exposing the American paradox is persuasive and highlights Hamer's political acumen. Yet, there is another portion of her testimony that is crucially important for the way it demonstrates the nature of Black women's *sass* as an enactment of her humanity, toward liberation—the foundation upon which political action can be carried out. The interaction Hamer describes "illuminate[s] the entanglement of slavery and freedom and offer[s] a glimpse of the futures that will unfold."[2] Before her beating commenced, Hamer endured an excruciating wait: "After I was placed in the cell I began to hear sounds of licks and screams, I could hear the sounds of licks and horrible screams." Being forced to listen to others brutalized instilled fear and terror. Yet, what Hamer heard in addition to the sounds of blows and cries was a chilling interaction between the police and Annell Ponder, a Southern Christian Leadership Conference activist who had also been arrested that day. This interaction was surely familiar to Hamer, reminiscent of the antebellum master-slave dialectic that still characterized southern life in the mid-twentieth century.

> And I could hear somebody say, "Can you say, 'yes, sir,' nigger? Can you say 'yes, sir'?" And they would say other horrible names.

The woman's response—a response that inverted that very same dialectic—no doubt had an overwhelming effect on Hamer, enraging and frightening her but also strengthening her resolve to endure, even in the face of torturous brutality.

She would say, "Yes, I can say 'yes, sir.'" "So, well, say it." She said, "I don't know you well enough." They beat her, I don't know how long. And after a while she began to pray, and asked God to have mercy on those people.

Hamer heard a powerful inversion, a sense of topsy-turvy that may have struck in her terror or laughter, perhaps some combination. When the officer demanded to hear "yes, sir" from Ponder, Hamer heard sass in her response, "I don't know you well enough." For the transgression of talking back—for daring to undermine the authority of white supremacy—this woman suffered a relentless beating. All the while, Ponder maintained consciousness of herself as a human being empowered with the agency, even in her absolutely prone position, to speak back to those who would assume they had authority over her. Ponder's sass to the officer, who saw himself as her master, was an active assertion of her sense of humanity *to herself* and to the object of her sass—those beating her—and to Hamer, too. It demonstrated that some other forms of relations were possible outside of the Black-white interactions that characterized mid-twentieth-century southern life. When Hamer narrated the story at the Democratic National Convention, Ponder's sass was not merely a seasoning to the story but the apex, the central feature that revealed Black women's resolve to be free.

Ponder's response to power was clearly important to Hamer, who included it not only in her narrative of the event at the DNC but also for a widely heard radio interview with Radio Pacifica in 1965 when she was discussing the Mississippi Freedom Democratic Party's political platform. The sass Hamer related in the narrative served a critically important role in her own story because it demonstrated to those listening how inspiring and influential it was to others when Black women owned themselves in such a deep, fundamental way—so much so, they were willing to performatively exact it at the risk of dismemberment and death in the cause of freedom. Liberation was an empowered, agentive state of consciousness that sometimes preceded a physical state of freedom for those enslaved, or for women like Ponder and Hamer who were subjected to the institutions and conditions precipitated by the afterlife of slavery.

Sass may be humorous, but this is not *always* the case. It is, however, always about agency in the sense that Cathy J. Cohen has described it, to "choose differently from what is prescribed."[3] In Ponder's sass, the naked function of it as a strategy for liberation can be located. "Real wonder," Toni Morrison mused on the ingenuity and resilience of Black people, "lay in the amazing shapes and substances God's grace took: gospel in times of persecution; the exquisite wins of people forbidden to compete; the upright righteousness of those who let no boot hold them down—people who made Job's patience look like restlessness. Elegance when all around was shabby."[4] This discursive ingenuity and resilience of spirit is reflected in Black women's enactments of sass. One source says that when Ponder received a visitor after her beating in Mississippi, her face was so swollen and battered that she could hardly speak. But she managed to eke out a single whisper, "Freedom."[5] Ponder surely did not mean for her sassy act to be amusing, yet it forces us to think about Black women's humor outside of its usual frames—the way it can unmask and subvert relations of power in moments when Black women must lay claim to themselves as human beings by baring their interiority, a momentary shattering of expectations that potentially evokes laughter. This is a chapter about the dialectic of Black women's humor and humanity.

Fannie Lou Hamer's account of Annell Ponder refusing to kneel to the patriarchal, white supremacist order that threatened to literally crush her reminds us of the historical context of Black women's sass—how it originated in master-slave power relations and how those relations were also fundamentally gendered. Black women found themselves at the absolute social and political bottom, and it is from that abject historical position that they have dared to talk back. The story Hamer tells reminds us of the violent repercussions to which Black women might be subjected when expressing agency and interiority through sass and of how sass originated as an unlikely political tool and a mechanism of self-fashioning in spaces where violence might happen—it is a performative means through which to discover and reveal one's consciousness and humanity. Ponder's act in 1963 also spotlights how Black women's sass has been distorted, exploited, misunderstood, and misrepresented—robbed of the extraordinary power the expression of sass indicates—transmogrified into the classic stereotype of the "sassy Black woman."

Contemporary popular readings of the "sassy Black woman" as stereotype overlook the historical context of Black women's sass as a genre of discourse, including the kinds of power imbalances, violence, violation, and coercion that Hamer and Ponder experienced in the Mississippi jailhouse and that enslaved women endured in everyday life. It is this historical context that has produced the necessity for this genre of discourse to exist, and to engage with Black women's sass ahistorically mistakes it as text or stylistic choice or meaningless aesthetic sensibility. The abstraction of Black women's sass in the contemporary moment is a misreading of *behavior* as an intrinsic *trait*. Enactments of sass require that we probe specific contexts where Black women speak back to power and the ways they deal with the problems they face in their everyday lives, especially the problems of racism, patriarchy, violence, and subjection to narrow scripts of Black womanhood as they navigate their worlds.

In this framework, discourse genres serve more than a taxonomic function. They are pragmatic, born of necessity. As Rinaldo Walcott put it, "For people who have lived their lives in the sphere of oppression and domination, processes of allegory are often developed not only to throw off the smell of danger, but to subvert while maintaining dialogue,"[6] and sass functions precisely as one of those processes. Black women's sass is a genre of discourse with its roots in US slavery, what Erving Goffman termed a "total institution . . . a place of residence and work where a large number of like-situated individuals cut off from the wider society for an appreciable period of time, together lead an enclosed, formally administered round of life."[7] The total institution of slavery rendered Black women's bodies always already sexually available and vulnerable to violence. This violence, which as Saidiya Hartman notes was "necessary and routine," "defined the afterlife of slavery and documented the reach of the plantation into the ghetto"[8] and racially segregated sites that developed in the (dis)order of racial slavery like the so-called homelands and townships of South Africa.

The styles, gestures, and subversion associated with Black women's sass have always emerged from and been shaped in the historical, cultural, and political contexts of their social conditions. Indeed, the narrow circumscription of acceptable behavior within the institution of slavery formed the crucible out of which sass emerged. I want to turn to a discussion of Black women's language practices and power so that we might better understand the genealogical roots/routes of sass as a genre of discourse going back to the institution of chattel slavery. Anchored in readings from the period of enslavement, fin de siècle vaudeville performances of *Uncle Tom's Cabin* by Black actresses, and contemporary comedic material that takes the treatment of Black women within the institution of chattel slavery as its subject, we will see sass as a tactic igniting Black women to move "out of their place," detaching themselves from people or ideas they find insulting, confining, degrading, or dehumanizing—often manifesting laughter in its wake. Sass is a trope for what Hartman calls a "revolution in a minor key,"[9] the way Black women pull from the ordinary resources they have on hand, which may be ineloquent but are coherent strikes at the heart of power that demonstrate in the wildest and most confining circumstances Black women's determination to live free.

While it may seem dark to find humor in the horrors of enslavement and the relations of power it inaugurated, Black women's irreverence within those conditions can be funny. The lowly object speaks back, emerging as the subject—revealing for her audience (even if that audience is herself) the truth about the thing: Black people are human beings. "The flag is drenched with *our* blood. . . . So many of our ancestors," Hamer explained in a 1968 interview, "was killed because we have *never* accepted slavery. We had to live under it, but we never wanted it."[10] The act of speaking back in that context of crushing disempowerment—the expression of sass—renders that fact undeniable, and the inversion, the refusal to accept dehumanization, is a classic trickster moment that can be humorous. We will see how sass has become the definitive element, across time and space, around which Black women's humor coheres.

Black Women's Language and Literacy

In Black women's historical struggle to speak and be heard, language practices have served strategic functions, as Elaine Richardson explains, through which Black women "communicate these literacies through storytelling, conscious manipulation of silence and speech, code/style shifting, and signifying, among other verbal and nonverbal practices."[11] Black women's language practices are central to understanding humor as a serious creative resource for Black women in interpersonal relations and in public culture. Some of the most central elements of Black women's language practices give insight into humor as an emancipatory strategy where Black women not only have tried to neutralize ideas and actions that threatened to silence and constrain them but also have enabled the creation of intimate community and a sense of pleasure at the same time. VéVé Clark has analyzed the overlooked literary tradition of Caribbean women novelists that arose in the mid-twentieth century beside the prominent new letters movements, largely recognized by the literary production of male writers that enabled new ways to think about the African diaspora. In her study "Developing Diaspora Literacy and *Marasa* Consciousness," Clark examines how comprehension of cultural differences in the literatures of Caribbean women writers relies upon a command of what she terms "diaspora literacy," defined by "the reader's ability to comprehend the literatures of Africa, Afro-America, and the Caribbean from an informed, indigenous perspective. . . . This type of literacy is more than a purely intellectual exercise. It is a skill for both narrator and reader which demands a knowledge of historical, social, cultural, and political development generated by lived and textual experience."[12] Extending Clark's analysis of literacy beyond literary texts to consider Black women's performance, Black women's humor operates similarly as a mode of literacy. Black women are particularly attuned to the elements, functions, and aesthetics of humor from their own perspective; to a collective, if ambivalent, history of the circumscription of movement and our ability to speak freely; and to the ongoing efforts to get and be free.

Scholars tend to agree about the particularity of Black women's speech and its capacity to facilitate social identity formation and cultural cohesion. Yolanda Majors's 2004 ethnography of Black women's language explores how Black women employ specific stylistics of language and storytelling in the context of a hair salon to build a shared discourse of "shoptalk," which she frames as a distinct African American speech community. Shoptalk, according to Majors, is an interactional style of Black women's language practices and "literate skills such as narration, signifying, and reading," which "are tools that disrupt and erode borders of culture, gender, race/ethnicity and social class."[13] For the Black women in the midwestern salon, literacy in Black women's language practices facilitates a shared community, and further, the "reading of culture, class, and social relations in oral narrative texts is not only a skill that occurs within this context, but a tool of skilled, practical/life problem solving."[14] Sass's production of meaning in language and gesture is as important as the social reading required for its uptake. To be literate in Black women's sass means one has developed "ways of knowing and acting and the . . . skills, vernacular expressive arts and crafts[,] that help [Black] females to advance and protect themselves and their loved ones in society."[15] Sass is a cultural practice that builds on the production of what Brittney Cooper calls "embodied rhetoric," or the ways Black women have historically "made the body speak,"[16] and the reception of the inherent critique that sass lodges is crucially important.

"Never to Be Conquered"

Black feminist literary scholar Joanne M. Braxton argues that sass in Black women's autobiography, particularly the ex-slave narrative, was a verbal tool Black women used for self-defense against systems of racial and sexual domination. When it comes to the enslaved woman, "her tools of liberation include sass and invective as well as biblical invocation; language is her first line of defense."[17] The 1861 volume *Incidents in the Life of a Slave Girl: Written by Herself* is one of the most celebrated and cited slave narratives, in which Harriet Jacobs (or Linda Brent, which she used as a pseudonym) outlines, among other aspects of chattel slavery, the racialized sexual violence she experienced as an enslaved person. Jacobs used her harrowing experience of escape to move middle-class white women into the struggle to abolish slavery by laying bare the horrid realities of what it meant for a woman to be subject to the brutal institution.

Early in Jacobs's life, at just fourteen years old, she transgressed the social and political conventions of the day by simply regarding herself as a person, even though she was enslaved. "The war of my life had begun," Jacobs wrote, "and though one of God's most powerless creatures, I resolved never to be conquered."[18] This ontological seed of agency toward liberation in Jacobs's inner life, her basic claim on humanity, is the primal scene of sass as an emancipatory tool for Black women and its essential feature: first and foremost it is a recognition of and claim to one's subjectivity *for the self*. After Jacobs's master, Dr. Flint, beat her for answering him in the affirmative when he asked whether she loved another man besides him, Jacobs retorted, "You have struck me for answering honestly. How I despise you"[19]—not only a spoken manifestation conveying her emotional reaction to and moral judgment of her master but also an audacious claim on her *right* to express her feelings, evidenced in the expression itself within the relations of power typified in the master-slave dialectic. Braxton locates Jacob's sass as an important verbal tool of resistance to Dr. Flint's sexual assaults, a means of "gaining psychological space and strength," and when Dr. Flint strikes Jacobs, she "hits back not with fists, but with sass."[20]

Jacobs's sass is a site of Black performance, an instrument of resistance. Her act of speaking back is one of the performative rituals that have historically facilitated reflection and transformation, a means to stay alive and keep a sense of humanity in the most dehumanizing conditions.[21] The words and gestures that frame the discourse of sass establish Jacobs's coherence as a Black woman in a perpetual position of subjection who, as an enslaved person, slipped "out of place" in declaring her intention "never to be conquered." Braxton puts a finer point on it, naming the outraged mother of the enslaved as "the sassiest woman on the face of the earth. . . . She sacrifices and improvises for the survival of flesh and spirit, and as mother of the race, she is muse to Black poets, male and female alike. . . . Implied in all her *actions* and fueling her heroic ones is outrage at the abuse of her people and her person."[22] Like Harriet Jacobs, Annell Ponder in the mid-1960s struck back at the site of power with an expression of sass, through which she fundamentally refused to be dehumanized, even while being savagely brutalized. Though neither instance was meant to evoke humor, one can see how this kind of inversion of power in which Black women refuse ontological domination (if ephemerally) may elicit a bit of amusement in those witnessing the audacity of the event and its absurdity from various angles.

Sass is an element of what Johnnie M. Stover calls "mother tongue," which in the tradition of African American language practices refers to "a combination of words, rhythms, sounds, and silences that woman has encoded with veiled meaning. And it is more. It is also a look, a set of the lips, a positioning of the hand, hip, and head."[23] Charlotte C. Teague analyzed Zora Neale Hurston's use of sass both to a sense of Black cultural identity and as a vehicle to express her individuality—both of which were articulated in her literary works, fiction and nonfiction. Like Harriet Jacobs, Teague makes the case that for Hurston, "sassing is a way to convey a serious point about a conflict without risking defeat, punishment, or blatant offense," a "refus[al] to give up or release her destiny to others fully."[24] In her autobiography *Dust Tracks on a Road*, Hurston illuminates her propensity to employ sass to internally lay claim to her right to her destiny in the world and her right to grasp it. She reflected on her childhood, "My mother . . . conceded that I was *impudent* and *given to talking back*, but she didn't want to 'squinch my spirit' too much for fear that I would grow up to be a mealy-mouthed rag-doll by the time I got grown. Papa always flew hot when Mama said that. He predicted dire things for me. . . . Somebody was going to blow me down for my *sassy tongue*."[25] Hurston's "spirit" was the impetus for the kinds of sassy expressions she became known for in her cultural production. Often infused with Black cultural sensibilities, then, Black women's sass is a mode of Black performance as Thomas DeFrantz and Anita Gonzalez envision it, "the enlivened, vibrating components of a palpable Black familiar— [which] demonstrate the microeconomics of gesture that cohere in Black performance."[26] Hurston's sassy tongue is akin to Harriet Jacobs's assertion that she was "never to be conquered," which is like Annell Ponder's refusal to be dehumanized into submission in the 1960s.

Expressions of sass indicate a claim on humanity. "Conquered" is the word Jacobs used, not "brutalized," not "raped," not "humiliated." To be "conquered," as Jacobs and the other Black women of this chapter indicate, functions on the ontological plane, and the resolution to be unconquered and unconquerable is to lay claim to a deep sense of *full* subjectivity that is the core of one's liberation within a society structured on domination. For Jacobs, to be unconquerable signified interiority and self-possession, an internal sense of agency to which only she had access. Indeed, this resolution to never be conquered is where Black women's sass begins, and its expression in word, gesture, and intent is the endpoint that unmasks the fantasy of Black inhumanity that was the brick and mortar of the institution of slavery. In other words, white supremacy is predicated on the notion that Black people are subhuman, but Black women's enactments of sass show this to be false. Sass says, "How can you claim I am not a human being when I can stand (figuratively) unbothered, blowing this smoke right in your face to indicate my purposeful existence?" What began in the "total institution" of chattel slavery as a mechanism for Black women to claim humanity became a genre of discourse to reveal the farce of white supremacy. When this discourse genre entered the cultural marketplace, the blowing of smoke—the expression of sass—became the site of laughter that signified the conditions of its development and the particularity of Black women's humor.

Black Women's Humor in the Cultural Marketplace

Black women's humor functions simultaneously as a legacy and facet of African American culture more generally and as something truly its own. It forces consideration of the roots of the expressive practices of which Black women on the variety stage at the fin de siècle availed themselves and of the ways slavery and domination—and Black women's creative ingenuity within those conditions—framed those practices. Hartman has described the subterranean practices of the enslaved as deeply constrained "when the force of repression is virtually without limit, when terror resides within the limits of the socially tolerable."[27] It was in these crushing conditions that Black women's sass originated as a tool to assert one's humanity, yet it has become a hallmark of their humor, a signification of the inversion of power relations in which the genre of discourse was developed. It signals Black women's will to redress that history in the limited sense Hartman proffers, "action aimed at relieving the pained body through alternative configurations of the self and the redemption of the body as human flesh, not a beast of burden."[28] The tragicomic imbrication of pain and pleasure has come to define how Black women's sass gets expressed. In *Babylon Girls: Black Women Performers and the Shaping of the Modern*, Jayna Brown examines the performative labor of Black actresses portraying the character Topsy (as opposed to white minstrel performers in blackface) at the turn of the twentieth century. Her study reveals a pivotal moment when the distinctiveness of Black women's humor, with sass as its underlying feature, can be discerned in popular culture. The vaudeville stage was the first place where Black women made significant inroads as professional entertainers and was a site where they expressed themselves authentically to the extent possible, whether their humor was meant to be consumed by white or by Black audiences.

Black women's vernacular performances, especially those that took place on urban variety stages at the turn of the twentieth century, "mark[ed] a crucial moment in the development of modern identities and pleasures," Brown argues. "They were key sites at which Black female urban presence was articulated and expressed, and they were important nodal points in the circulation of expressive forms."[29] Brown beautifully captures how Black women's humor during this period was saturated with the kind of sass I have outlined—with its primal scene firmly seeded in slavery. "The very act of making money through the beauty, grace, and comedy of their bodies' talents reframed what could be produced by physical effort, by sweat, and disciplined tenacity," Brown contends, and moreover, Black women's labor in stage productions of Harriet Beecher Stowe's *Uncle Tom's Cabin* seems to have propelled Black women's humor into public culture.[30] For better or worse, this period was significant in laying the foundation for how we think about the development and consumption of Black women's humor as a distinctly American artistic form.

One of the most profound insights we gain from Brown's analysis of Black women's expressive culture at the turn of the twentieth century is our understanding of how Black women performers—from singers and dancers to actresses and musicians—used humor as a subversive tactic to undermine authority on the variety stage. By the 1840s, blackface minstrelsy had become America's favorite pastime. White actors used burnt cork to blacken their faces and exaggerated stereotypical features associated with Blackness; large red lips and bugged-out eyes were the hallmark features that played up this (mis)representation of Blackness, cementing the image of Black people as strange, funny, folksy, and ignorant. The image of the shucking-and-jiving, laughing Black person that began circulating in the nineteenth century became a mainstay of American popular culture.

Many Black minstrelsy troupes became popular, and even though their performances of degrading stereotypes were often as bad as those of white minstrels, Black comics had become part of the fabric of American popular culture. Performing on the minstrel stages and emerging vaudeville circuits gave hundreds if not thousands of African Americans new opportunities for traveling and economic mobility that had been denied them during slavery, making comedy and musical performance a viable career option for Black people in the late nineteenth century. The international obsession with stage productions of *Uncle Tom's Cabin*, Brown argues, opened the door for Black women to enter blackface minstrelsy, introducing Black women's humor into the public sphere.[31]

After the turn of the twentieth century, the character Topsy was portrayed by Black women instead of white women in blackface, and as Brown persuasively argues, "Black women's performances of Topsy carried different meanings than white women's versions."[32] In "The Story of Topsy" in *Uncle Tom's Cabin*, Topsy is introduced on an auction block, purchased by a white man, Augustine St. Clare, for his cousin, the character Miss Ophelia. Topsy is "ignorant and care-free . . . joyful and mischievous," a frightening sight to Miss Ophelia at first glance. "The Blackest little pickaninny girl [St. Clare] had ever seen," Topsy "was eight or nine years old, and, besides being very Black, had round shining eyes, glittering as glass beads, and wooly hair braided into little tails, which stuck out in every direction. She was dressed in a filthy, ragged garment and was quite the most woebegone little darkey ever seen."[33] Topsy is a naughty child, harshly punished for her ongoing refusal to behave. According to Brown, Topsy is a figure of low farce, "associated with gruesome violence, which she survives and which she is seemingly inured to."[34] Topsy's imperviousness to pain is rendered in the scarification of her back from repeated whippings (because she refused to be disciplined), and Brown goes on to cite Topsy's darkly comic (if unintentional on Stowe's part) mockery of a beating she endured from Miss Ophelia: "Law, Miss Feely whip! Wouldn't kill a skeeter, her whippin's. Oughter see how old mas'r made the flesh fly; old mas'r know'd how!" The performance of naked insolence *by Black actresses*, in the face of the unmitigated power to brutalize Topsy, suggests that Black actresses, "with a sly grin,"[35] were pulling on the one expressive resource they had at their disposal—sass.

The scene becomes farcically humorous to the extent that Topsy "taunts her owners to inflict punishment from which she then refuses to suffer. . . . The figure cannot be slapped down, but keeps rising up, keeps refusing to obey, keeps offering pun and quip."[36] To interpret this scene performed by a Black woman as an enactment of sass recalls the kind of inversion humor common to enslaved Black people, a way of "getting over" that facilitated a sense of control via laughter. Inversion was a way for enslaved Black people to feel superior to their white masters by figuratively and unthreateningly elevating themselves above them.[37] In the trickster tales, for example, Blacks were often portrayed as the weaker animals, like the tortoise, that in the end triumph over the stronger animals, like the rabbit or lion, which represented white people. Black farce in this case sheds light on the fissures in hegemonic claims, "revealing the ways hierarchies breed their own instabilities."[38] If one was literate in the discourse of Black women's sass, it could be inferred that Topsy's performance of it onstage via Black actresses allowed her to harmlessly ridicule the rationality of white supremacy as unmitigated violence and disregard for Black humanity by means of exaggeration, revealing both flawed logic and foolishness. As Brown put it so well, "She has not escaped from suffering, rather she has escaped *through* it; it is her absolute woundedness that has made her body malleable enough to wind through the pain. Everything, and nothing, can now touch her, as she exists in a space beyond suffering. Topsy's imperviousness to pain, her callousness, shows her body to have become resistant to violent claims of ownership."[39] The Black actress as Topsy inhabited a position wholly abject, yet she could assert her humanity not just in the act of getting back up and taking more blows but also in imploring her abuser, "Is that all you've got?" Indeed, these staged iterations of Topsy recall Annell Ponder's sassy enactment in 1963.

Yet, Topsy's act of inversion was a "fantasy spectacle," as Stephane Dunn puts it—an enjoyable illusion depending on the position from which it was consumed.[40] Importantly, Topsy's spectacle incited laughter from those attuned to it, indexing a dangerous if clandestine political consciousness of the self as having the *potential* to get back up one day and get free. Brown calls staged unruliness of this sort "black expressive resilience," another way of thinking through the way Black women in the early twentieth century made use of the discourse of sass. Topsy's expressive resilience, via the Black women who animated her, inadvertently laid the foundation for Black women's humor to become legible in popular culture by way of the subversive (often in-group), well-exaggerated sass they enacted, even though many problematic stereotypes came in its wake as markets distilled and redistributed images of Black womanhood from stock characters like Topsy. Brown's notion of black expressive resilience highlights how Black women have called upon "disruptive creativity" in ways that "resonated in the performance strategies of Black women singers, musicians, and especially dancers into the twentieth century."[41] Actually, Black women's sass was a fundamental mechanism of expressive resilience that came to the fore as an undeniable resource—the ability to make folks laugh and think at the same time—in this period when Black women's humor formally entered the cultural marketplace.

What began as an expressive tool to move out of place and hold on to a sense of humanity within tragic, brutal conditions transformed into the lifeblood of Black women's humor. Critiques of Black laughter are often rooted in the ideology of respectability—or, in the perennial argument that Black comedy is thoughtless, reinforces negative stereotypes, or diverts energy away from structural critiques of domination. Yet Black humor functions on multiple productive levels that go far beyond mere escapism. This humor is potentially dangerous. As Cynthia Willett and Julie Willett persuasively hold, "Laughter's uproar exposes hypocrisy, unjustified privilege, and lies. It can be the scourge of the sociopath and the narcissist."[42] When you make people laugh, you have made them think, and in the case of Black women's sass as the agent of humor, you have made them imagine alternative arrangements in which Black women might be empowered, in which they might be free. Fantasy, it seems, is the seed of consciousness, whose fruit is liberation.

The new kinds of freedom that emancipation afforded Black women, especially over their bodily autonomy and ability to choose the kinds of relationships into which they would enter, shaped and transformed the way Black women made use of sass and the nature of authority to which they spoke back in the public sphere.[43] Control over Black women was almost absolute in the "total institution" of slavery, yet they found creative ways to keep their human dignity—and sass was one of those creative strategies. Slavery's wake did not shift conditions all that much for many Black women for generations, yet their sense of humor—the way they imagined and reached for alternative arrangements to subjection—enabled the ideal to emerge of the tough, resilient Black woman who is not afraid to speak her mind about any subject, no matter how taboo. The legacy of Black women's sass in the blues era is evident in the saying often seen as a feminist slogan on bumper stickers today, signifying on Ida Cox's 1924 classic lyrics "Wild women don't worry, wild women don't have the blues." This is both a fantasy of liberation and a rendition of a fundamental truth when Black women conceive it and express it—they are free. That is the gag. If you get it, you get it. Black women's sass—their propensity to speak back audaciously and creatively to authority, real or perceived—has become the hallmark of what makes Black women's humor distinctive and extraordinary.

Ultimately, the expression of sass is an intentional, aesthetically discernible genre of discourse inaugurating the subject as a Black woman self-possessed. Of course, the immediate proximity to chattel slavery fell away as Black women gained a foothold in the entertainment industry during the first half of the twentieth century. And thus, Black women's sass kept its fundamental purpose—subverting hegemonic and material power for the purpose of asserting one's humanity—yet the saturation of stereotypes associated with hypersexuality, bitchiness, and placating white folks became radically intertwined with how Black women's humor got represented across the pop culture imaginary. There is a general acceptance of Black women's sass as a site of humor, but in many cases the uptake of Black women speaking back to authority is rarely understood or treated as a serious critique of power, rendered inconsequential when wrapped in the cloak of a culture that refuses to hear it.

"I Thought the Red Light Was for Us!"

Jackie "Moms" Mabley was one of the first Black women to perform the monologue style of stand-up comedy in the 1940s, with a career in vaudeville and stand-up spanning from the mid-1930s to the mid-1970s.[44] She was a mainstay of popular Black venues like the Apollo Theater in Harlem, the Regal Theater in Chicago, and the Uptown Theater in Philadelphia, and her down-home southern humor made her hugely successful in smaller venues throughout the nation that catered to Black audiences. Before 1961, the year she made appearances and a recording of her performance at Hugh Hefner's Playboy Club in Chicago, Mabley was not widely known as a mainstream entertainer. Toward the end of her career, in the late 1960s and early 1970s, her comedy was increasingly political, frequently attacking southern racism and the attitudes and institutions that supported it. Mabley, whom we must locate in the still-unfolding history of Black women constrained in the master-slave dialectic, had a popular bit about performing in the segregated South: "Now they want me to go to New Orleans. It'll be Old Orleans 'fore I get down there. The Greyhound ain't goin' to take me down there and the bloodhounds run me back. I'll tell you that."[45] Her humor became more politically incisive as she stepped outside the "wise keeper of the culture" role she played early on in her career.

Mabley was known to those around her as a lesbian who dressed in masculine clothing in her everyday life.[46] "Moms" was Mabley's stage persona, but as one of her contemporaries remembered, Mabley was referred to as "Mr. Moms," a moniker that spoke to her butch presentation of self in her everyday life and that acknowledged both the interiority of herself as a transgressively gendered subject and the political and cultural work her comic persona enabled her to accomplish.[47] Katelyn Hale Wood argues that Mabley's grandmotherly performances, which she locates as queer enactments that "challenged heteropatriarchy," were queer to the extent that the onstage "Moms" was saturated with "Black feminist/Black queer aesthetic practices that privilege the body, history, sexuality, and vernacular articulation of racist/sexist/homophobic US culture."[48] Speaking truths "about white supremacy, gender inequity, class dynamics, and sexuality in blunt, confrontational ways," Mabley's Black feminist comedy laid the foundation for contemporary Black women comics who do Black feminist politicking on stand-up stages, Wood argues.[49] I am inclined to agree with Wood's assessment of Mabley as a foremother of Black feminist stand-up and with the idea that the way she adorned her body onstage mediated her sharp, otherwise unpalatable social and political critiques of power.

As a Black woman with very little political standing at the height of her career, it was clearly not Mabley's masculine drag performance that authorized her to lodge powerful sociopolitical critiques. As a southern Black woman

Jackie "Moms" Mabley dressed in men's clothing.
From Iloveoldschoolmusic.com.

who had been performing since the 1930s, Mabley was keenly aware of the power relations related to slavery in which she lived and performed. Mabley astutely recognized that what I am calling "granny drag" was a route through which she could sneakily achieve uptake of her critiques by hiding them within a familiar and innocuous mouthpiece of humor, infused with the discourse of sass that had come to frame Black women's humor in the early twentieth century—that which called attention to and sent up the master-slave dialectic that continued to characterize postbellum life in the United States. "Mabley's Black queer iteration of a grandmother character," Wood argues, "made space for a singular, mature, funny Black woman to express a brashness and bossiness not culturally 'allowed' for Black women of her time." Mabley's performances as "Moms" mocked and resisted heteronormative femininity and sexuality. "A grandmother or mammy caricature might be selfless and sexless, but Moms was self-possessed and insistent on physical and sexual pleasure."[50] Her brashness, bossiness, and self-possession onstage showcased the extent to which Mabley understood that her performance would work against certain social expectations that disciplined and controlled people's public (and private) behavior. I would like to recalibrate Mabley's brash self-possession as a trope for sass, embodied in her adornment and the politics of her sartorial choices onstage and in the kinds of sociopolitical interventions those choices enabled her to make.

Old women, especially old Black women dressed up like somebody's granny, are generally not socially sanctioned to talk about their sexual desires, not only on account of their old age per se but also because of the way time marks aged bodies as (un)desirable. Mabley's iconic series of jokes about wanting young men is relevant here, and I think there is much to be said of the force of Mabley's embodied politics, how her "corporeal-centered performances displayed the Black woman's body as a site and source of pleasure, anger, sexual desire, and political resistance."[51] For example, on her 1970 album *Moms Mabley Live at Sing Sing*, Mabley began one of these classic bits: "That old man like to run me crazy, children. I don't want nothin' old but some old money. And I'm gonna use it to put an ad in the paper for some young man!"[52] Mabley does indeed use this cycle of jokes to comically undercut and demonstrate the frailty of the male body, as Wood deftly argues. Yet, there is a deeper subversion going on when Mabley foregrounds sex with young men in her jokes. Could it be that the young man of these jokes functions as a subversive, a proxy for the actual women she desired in real life? Afterall, Mr. Moms was an out, butch lesbian off the stage, and it was this sexual desire that necessitated the suppression of her gender performance, because it functioned as a visual cue of that desire. Mabley was *not*, of course, her comic persona, as Wood points out, but "Moms" did Mabley's bidding. Could it also be that not being worried about being old and still expressing erotic desire was a subversive stand-in for not being worried about being a bulldagger—a failed Black feminine subject—and still being desirable? Could it be that the ultimate gag of Mabley's granny drag opened space for

It's Your Thing, Moms Mabley, aka Jackie Mabley, 1970.
Image courtesy of the Everett Collection,
https://everettcollection.com/#/home.

giving Black grandmas and bulldaggers erotic subjectivity—putting Black women's desires, whatever they look like and whomever they are projected toward—front and center? Mabley's granny drag was queer performance that subversively spoke back to authority, an enactment of embodied sass, first oriented toward herself. Granny drag was an enactment of sass where Mabley's Black feminist politics made *her* free first. In its cloaked subversion, her audiences could imagine this freedom, too. Mabley's subversive self-possession was enlivened in her onstage adornment and was an essential component of her queer sass.

Clad in a colorful flowery dress and a floppy bucket hat and often without her dentures, Mabley addressed her audiences with a deep southern drawl, speaking what was formerly unspeakable about the Black experience of race and racism, all under the guise of the harmless granny. Her costume cast her as what anthropologist Lawrence Mintz would call the "negative exemplar," embodied in the various kinds of fools and clowns that audiences can unproblematically laugh at. As the toothless granny, Mabley gained what Mintz terms "comic license" onstage to say things and act in ways that deviated from the norms of what Black women were ordinarily authorized to say in public.[53] This drag performance was important for Mabley as a Black person and as a masculine woman—and if she dared to speak out publicly against white racist violence during the Jim Crow era, she had better seem benign. In another one of her classic bits about southern racism, Mabley exposed how racist attitudes and laws violently circumscribed Black life and prevented mobility, both in the mundane realities of everyday existence and implicitly, in terms of political participation. "One of the big cops come running over to me: 'Hey woman don't you know you went through a red light?' I said, ''Cause I seen all you white folks going on the *green* light I thought the *red* light was for *us*!'"[54]

Mabley's satirical humor breaks down the facade of the doctrine of "separate but equal" in a way that publicly lays bare and renders absurd the social and political arrangements it engendered. It also reveals how Black women use the discourse of sass—the claiming of one's humanity and its outward expression as speaking back to authority—as a comedic technique that not only entertains but also has the potential to plant political seeds of liberation, even if the laugh was ephemeral. Her granny drag permitted this noteworthy performance of sass as queer. As the "comic spokesperson" for Black people, Mabley's grandmotherly persona, which lacked the outspoken bitterness and disgust of other Black satirists like Dick Gregory, relied on a version of drag that allowed her literal toothlessness to obscure the very real teeth of her political critique.⁵⁵ Mabley's queer enactments of sass, while they expressed subversive gender politics, were not entirely tied to her LGBTQ+ identification. In one sense, queer practices are those that trouble hegemonic perceptions of race, gender, and sexuality and the public fantasies that inform them. Queer sass is an anti-normative enactment that challenges and transforms how people think about Black womanhood in general, and especially about the comics themselves—how Black women may *do* Black womanhood differently by not enacting traditional features of sass (for example, its gestural repertoire), which can make their performances even more subversive. For as Wood reminds us, "The interplay between Black feminist comic—whose voice moves through the microphone and then speakers—and her audiences—that shout back with vocal response during the live performance or a playback of the recording—creates sonic and affective modes of community building."⁵⁶ Today, sass has become a familiar trope of contemporary Black women's humor, a trope that illuminates the consciousness, agency, and pleasure of Black women that is first about the self, and the knowledge produced by its enactment moves affectively through the community.

Sass, Subversion, and Satire

"What's your favorite part of the plantation?" Lydia Smith from Allentown, Pennsylvania, asks. Standing in front of a tree with a modern car visible, her name and location displayed underneath her image, Smith asks the question clearly from the contemporary period, in the style of an on-site television newscast. A Black woman whose white kerchief and golden dress signify a time warp back to America's colonial past takes a short breath and faux-contemplatively looks up to the left. "My bed," Lizzie Mae answers, punctuated with a tight-lipped smile that belies her exasperation.⁵⁷ *Ask a Slave* is a web series created by actress and comedy writer Azie Mira Dungey, who portrays the character Lizzie Mae, a housemaid for George and Martha Washington. Lizzie Mae assumes the role of a museum docent charged with educating visitors about life at Mount Vernon from the perspective of an enslaved woman. In this scathingly satirical series that began in 2013, Dungey responds to interminably foolish questions posed by present-day tourists, which Dungey claims in the opening scene of every episode are questions based on her actual experience as a historical re-enactor at Mount Vernon.

Dungey employs various representational technologies that give a sense of vacillation between the historical past of the antebellum South and the purportedly post-racial present. In the first episode, Lizzie Mae explains that her purpose is "to answer all your questions about the Washingtons' home and plantation," but as the questions come, we find out Dungey's true motive in answering visitors' questions. Her aim is to expose not only how racial and gender violence structured early American society but also the ways in which that history is still a feature of contemporary American society. This specter of the past is evidenced in the absurd questions Lizzie Mae pessimistically yet playfully answers.

"Why are you a slave?" asks Jayson Anderson, a young white guy from Pittsburgh wearing a T-shirt. In Lizzie Mae's response, "Because I'm Black," her sass is subtle yet matter-of-fact. She speaks not of "men of their time" or "necessary economic evils." Lizzie Mae gets to the embodied root of chattel slavery, the ritual of dehumanization that was the engine of the brutal institution. Her response "Because I'm Black" simultaneously reveals and lays claim to the humanity of the enslaved with the use of the subject pronoun *I*, a configuration of the human that was meant to be fully quashed in the enslaved. Dungey's character is enacting sass, which is met with an aloof, "Is it through an internship? . . . Are there other internships you could apply for?," an indirect nod toward the ongoing post-slavery condition of Blackness. Another visitor asks, "Where do your kids go to school?" Lizzie Mae simply responds with a derisive chuckle.[58]

Dungey's intertextual citations call up the ideologies that structure how race and gender are understood and acted upon in contemporary American society, appearing in the form of parodied questions and Lizzie Mae's scornful retorts to her clueless interlocutors. These comebacks are infused with the same kind of sass Black enslaved women offered in response to real and presumed authority. Romantic narratives of slavery as a benevolent or harmless institution are reworked, and Lizzie Mae uses her satirical quips to dissect and divest them of their endurance. One episode features abolitionist Tobias Lear, who was also George Washington's personal secretary, and callers phone in to ask both Lizzie Mae and Lear questions. "I agree with Mr. Lear," the first caller claims; "slave masters were just awful, just terrible." Lear responds, "Although the institution of slavery is morally reprehensible, there were, and are, some good slave masters and owners . . . Thomas Jefferson for example." Disgusted, Lizzie Mae leans back in a gesture signaling her sass, "Thomas Jefferson? He has sex with his slaves." In the face of deeply held authoritative beliefs about Thomas Jefferson as an American hero who was "a man of his times," Lizzie Mae keeps it all-the-way real, which is the site of humor. Almost joyfully, Lear responds with an upturned pointed finger, "Ah ha, yes, indeed!"[59] This exchange not only challenges slavery as a benign institution but also underlines the unadulterated racialized sexual brutality to which enslaved Black women were often subject.

As it moves between the late eighteenth and early twenty-first century, *Ask a Slave* engages a deconstructive humor that refuses to see the present moment outside of history, spotlighting the devastating brutality of racist, patriarchal, capitalist violence as a fundamental component of the narrative of the United States—personified in George Washington himself. Dungey's body, swinging between past and present, functions as a transhistorical text upon which the legacy of slavery is theatrically revised. Her satiric humor, imbued with sass, exposes American racism and chattel slavery as a braid woven by a singular ideology.

The web series is shot through with stinging humor that lays bare the selective amnesia that makes possible romantic and twisted founding fathers narratives about patriotism, liberty, and "civic good," narratives that elide the violence and brutality that undergirded the nation-building project. A musical mash-up of the well-known nineteenth-century snare drum introduction of "The Battle Hymn of the Republic," a short colonial flute riff, and a banjo tune opens each episode as a cartoon version of Lizzie Mae sweeps a cloud of dust in the foyer of colonial Mount Vernon, establishing a tongue-in-cheek tone, punctuated by Lizzie Mae's wink and smile. Flouting conventional temporal frames, questions and answers veer across time and space, speaking to the disorientation and sense of cultural fracture that frames contemporary American society, particularly considering the power relations signified and maintained in structures of race, gender, and social class. *Ask a Slave* imparts "a will to unmaking,"[60] as Ihab Hassan puts it, and what Dungey attempts to unmake is the idea that we live in a post-racial society. Indeed, Dungey demonstrates the immanence of race and gender in the lived experiences and ideologies that constrain, contain, corrupt, and subject the most vulnerable in American society to specific forms of violence.

The ways race and gender structured the institution of slavery and continue to shape contemporary American life is the predominant theme of Dungey's humor in *Ask a Slave*. "How did you get to be housemaid for such a distinguished founding father?" A middle-aged white man in a straw sun hat and Hawaiian-style shirt looks straight into the camera and continues, without a hint of irony, "Did you see the advertisement in the newspaper?" It is unclear whether he is asking Lizzie Mae the enslaved character or Dungey the performer how she got the job. A venomous amalgamation of the transhistorical pair answers the man. "Did I read the advertisement in the newspaper? Why yes," Lizzie Mae calmly responds, smiling with her head slightly cocked to the side. "It said: WANTED: One housemaid. No pay. Preferably mulatto, saucy with breeding hips. Must work eighteen hours a day, seven days a week, no holidays. But, you get to wear a pretty dress. And if you're lucky you just might carry some famous white man's bastard child. So, you better believe I read that, and I ran right over and said sign me up!"[61] Lizzie Mae's sass is undeniable, illuminating a fugitive humanity under the yoke of slavery. At the same time that she makes the granularity of slavery visible, she also renders the object of her sass a fool for trying to hide slavery's mercilessness. The reality, as Lizzie Mae's faux advertisement demonstrates, is that violence was meted out on the backs and in the wombs of Black women, a fact made explicit in the "newspaper ad," no longer veiled in subtext. The way her satirical snap boomerangs between the character Lizzie Mae and her twenty-first-century avatar is funny because of its cutting audacity within the conditions of power from which it twice sprang.

Dungey's satire enables her sass to surface, where it had previously been buried, distorted, or relegated to the margins of political speech. The satirical humor of *Ask a Slave* fits with what Glenda Carpio identifies as "a vehicle for catharsis—both a release of racial tensions and for the purging of racist attitudes—but also a medium through which [Dungey] symbolically redress[es] chattel slavery and its aftermath."[62] Dungey's sass exposes and challenges interlocking systems of domination and the possibility of cultural change via new racial and gendered epistemologies generated by her satirical critiques. The sass Dungey enacts in *Ask a Slave* is an instantiation of Black feminist humor, the way paved by humorists like Jackie "Moms" Mabley, whose "legacy solidifies important precedents for Black feminist comics in contemporary US performance, cracking up power structures that attempt to silence Black women and Black queer sexualities."[63] Dungey's litany of never-ending "ignorant" questions she had heard as a docent at the Mount Vernon estate and mockingly cited in the *Ask a Slave* series serves to underscore her view that racist, sexist, and patriarchal ideologies that were at the heart of chattel slavery remain with us today.

For contemporary Black women humorists like Dungey, sass becomes a means by which to unapologetically cut to the quick of ideologies that hold together narratives of post-racialism and egalitarianism. Like other cultural producers, Dungey's sass, deployed by way of satire, is invested in resisting (but not transcending) domination, and part of that process is to call attention to what the reality of racial and sexual domination means for Black people. Or, as one of the most venomous satirists, Paul Mooney, put it in a joke about white America's obliviousness to the pervasive and inescapable reality of racism, "Uh, the elephant [in the room]? Shitting on you?"[64] The afterlife of slavery, or more precisely as Hartman puts it, the afterlife of property, is right out there in the open, "the detritus of lives with which we have yet to attend, a past that has yet to be done, and the ongoing state of emergency in which black life remains in peril."[65] Jokes and humor cannot fully get at the obscene violence of slavery and its afterlives, but as Richard Schechner (and indeed the women investigated here) reminds us, jokes are "indirect, dense actions" in which "obstacles are . . . circumvented. Repressed material is liberated. The listener is bribed by pleasure into helping the joker get at the forbidden object,"[66] which, for Black women, is our humanity. The afterlife of slavery is the elephant in the room that keeps shitting on us, a reality many institutions and individuals refuse to see. Black women wield humor as an illuminating force to reckon with the materiality of that afterlife, first to express their own agency toward liberation and then, many times, toward that of their communities.

Ida Bae Wells

I conclude this chapter with a reflection on Black women's humor and humanity. I turn to Ida B. Wells-Barnett, the dissident journalist of the late nineteenth and early twentieth century whose maverick activism in the service of liberation put a spotlight on anti-Black violence and the ideology of white supremacy in the long aftermath of the Civil War. Wells-Barnett's sass turned the tide of history. Anti-Black violence motivated her journalistic work because she saw white supremacy, in terms of its ideology and of the brutal materiality of it in the form of lynching, as the main barrier to the promise of freedom and equality that postbellum Black citizens so desired. It was Wells-Barnett's mission to expose that ideology and the practices that were its outward symptom, and she took on that task within conditions limited by racial and gendered norms of propriety. In her words and actions on behalf of Black folks trying to get free, Wells-Barnett was constantly getting out of her place. She uncovered and presented the cold, hard facts of anti-Black violence. Journalist and activist T. Thomas Fortune, who was editor of one of the leading Black periodicals of the time, the *New York Age*, wrote of Wells-Barnett,

"She has become famous as one of the few of our women who handles a goose quill with diamond point as handily as any of us men. . . . She has plenty of nerve; she is smart as a steel trap, and she has no sympathy with humbug."[67] Wells-Barnett's most searing and influential work came in the form of the 1892 pamphlet *Southern Horrors: Lynch Law in All Its Phases*, a text that used statistics and careful qualitative documentation to reveal the true nature of the widespread practice of lynching that was brutally visited upon Black women, men, and children at the time.

Lynching was a mechanism of terror, its raison d'être the disciplinary control of Black people after Reconstruction. With *Southern Horrors*, Wells-Barnett struck at the very root of lynching: the fear and anxieties about the illegitimacy of white supremacy and the transformation of economic, political, and cultural relations of power that might precipitate from the revelations therein. "Nobody in this section of the country believes the old thread-bare lie that Negro men rape white women. If Southern white men are not careful, they will overreach themselves and public sentiment will have a reaction; a conclusion will then be reached which will be very damaging to the moral reputation of their women."[68] This is one of *Southern Horror*'s most devastating statements. It is an expression of Black women's sass in form and content—within the enduring conditions of chattel slavery, Wells-Barnett boldly speaks back to authority "by exposing the rawest nerve in the South's patriarchal bosom," as Paula Giddings put it.[69] Not only did she uncover the root cause of lynching as a white supremacist disciplinary spectacle, but she also circulated proof of white women's consensual relationships with Black men. Wells-Barnett believed herself a human being and an American citizen imbued with natural rights, and *Southern Horrors* was a testament to this belief; its publication within the historical and political contexts is an expression of Black women's sass meant to assert humanity in the service of Black liberation. Wells-Barnett's activism on behalf of Black freedom received much backlash; her press in Memphis was torched, and she was under such threat of violence that she was exiled from her hometown of Memphis for decades. Her continued work in the face of injury and even death is a link in the chain of Black women's resolve "never to be conquered." That chain reaches here into the historical present.

In February 2020, just before the novel coronavirus clenched the world in its viselike grip, Pulitzer Prize–winning investigative journalist Nikole Hannah-Jones came to Middlebury College, where I was a professor at the time, to deliver a talk about *The 1619 Project*, which is now a best-selling book and a Hulu miniseries and has even spawned a children's book. In 2020, it was a collection of essays that was a radical reorientation of US history—a revised origin story that put chattel slavery right at the heart of what it means to be American. In 2020, *The 1619 Project* barely had a foothold in popular discourse because it had only been published in August 2019, coinciding with the 400th anniversary of the arrival of the *White Lion*, the ship that would bring the first cargo of enslaved Africans to what would become the United States. "A re-education is necessary," Hannah-Jones explained to us; "we've sanitized what slavery is like because we can't deal with what we've done."[70] Her goal in collecting and framing the essays—which focus on the roles of capitalism, sugar production and consumption, scientific racism, health care, carceral institutions and ideology, the wealth gap, and racial segregation—is to offer a corrective, an uncomfortable narrative in which the ideology and materiality of white supremacy are part and parcel of the "true founding" of the United States, in 1619, not 1776. *The 1619 Project* was published by the *New York Times*, a wide platform upon which it took on a life of its own, but not without the promotion of Hannah-Jones, who successfully advocated for it to be introduced into public and private schools across the United States. Indeed, many school districts adopted *The 1619 Project* as part of their curricula across a range of disciplines and topic areas, a testament to the intellectual weight of the project and to Hannah-Jones's dogged activism to disseminate it.

As its central thesis, *The 1619 Project* holds that race and racism are woven into the fabric of all of the foundational institutions in the United States. This feature, largely unacknowledged, is the ongoing legacy of chattel slavery, the history that as Hannah-Jones put it that evening in Vermont is "foundational to who we are." This premise, that racism is constitutive of what it means to be American, is also the first principle of critical race theory, a political project and body of scholarship dedicated to unearthing and transforming the relationship between racism, institutional structures, and (dis)empowerment. CRT holds that racism is a persistent, permanent feature of American society, yet it is also invested in the elimination of all forms of subordination, two qualities that are mirrored in *The 1619 Project*.

Actually, one could argue that Hannah-Jones's *1619 Project* is the political and intellectual grandchild of Ida B. Wells-Barnett's trailblazing journalism, which had at its core the impetus to correct false narratives that served as the bases of white supremacist violence and that erased Black people from their central role in building up the nation. In 1893, to celebrate the 400th anniversary of the so-called discovery of the "New World," a year after the publication of *Southern Horrors*, Wells-Barnett published another pamphlet, *The Reason*

Why the Colored American Is Not in the World's Columbian Exposition, after Black Americans had failed to be included in the exhibit on American progress at the infamous "White City":

> The exhibit of the progress made by a race in 25 years of freedom as against 250 years of slavery, would have been the greatest tribute to the greatness and progressiveness of American institutions which could have been shown the world. The colored people of this great Republic number eight millions—more than one-tenth the whole population of the United States. They were among the earliest settlers of this continent, landing at Jamestown, Virginia in 1619 in a slave ship, before the Puritans, who landed at Plymouth in 1620. They have contributed a large share to American prosperity and civilization. The labor of one-half of this country has always been, and is still being done by them. The first credit this country had in its commerce with foreign nations was created by productions resulting from their labor. The wealth created by their industry has afforded to the white people of this country the leisure essential to their great progress in education, art, science, industry and invention.[71]

After this preface, Wells-Barnett goes on to lay out in data-supported detail the mechanisms through which Black Americans had been marginalized, brutalized, exploited, and denied full citizenship rights. Like Hannah-Jones, *The Reason Why* locates the year 1619 as a pivotal year in American history and Black people as central to "American prosperity and civilization." One could argue that *The 1619 Project* is part of Wells-Barnett's unapologetic political project of ultimately correcting records in the service of transforming the everyday lives of Black people.

Given Hannah-Jones's success at getting it into so many classrooms since 2020, *The 1619 Project* has become a site of political and cultural contestation. CRT has emerged in common parlance (if many times misunderstood and misinterpreted) and has appeared on local and state election ballots with candidates running on platforms to outlaw the teaching of CRT in schools. *The 1619 Project* has stirred such a deep sense of discomfort and white anxiety that on Election Day 2020 (a fateful day, indeed), then president Donald Trump formed the 1776 Commission by executive order "to better enable a rising generation to understand the history and principles of the founding of the United States in 1776 and to strive to form a more perfect Union." Trump's rationale in forming the 1776 Commission was based on a whitewashed, reactionary idea of American history that harks back to a fantasy of American exceptionalism.

> The recent attacks on our founding have highlighted America's history related to race. These one-sided and divisive accounts too often ignore or fail to properly honor and recollect the great legacy of the American national experience—our country's valiant and successful effort to shake off the curse of slavery and to use the lessons of that struggle to guide our work toward equal rights for all citizens in the present. Viewing America as an irredeemably and systemically racist country cannot account for the extraordinary role of the great heroes of the American movement against slavery and for civil rights.[72]

Trump's 1776 Commission was a direct response to Hannah-Jones, meant to create an institutional structure to offset, if not silence, *The 1619 Project*, and Hannah-Jones's work in the face of this kind of threat from the seat of state power itself reminds us of the relations of power from whence Black women's discourse of sass sprang—in the master-slave dialectic. Those conditions are persistent, as both Wells-Barnett and Hannah-Jones remind us, and remain a feature of the historical present.

It is fitting that on Twitter and Instagram, Hannah-Jones's handle is "Ida Bae Wells," signifying on a person who had the audacity to speak truth to power over and over, even under threats of institutional and bodily violence. Her chosen name signals a "getting out of place" in the ways Wells-Barnett did, in the face of enormous state and extrajudicial power. As she delivered her talk in Mead Chapel at Middlebury College that cold February evening, her cell phone, which sat on the lectern, rang loudly, briefly interrupting her talk. She picked her phone up without looking at it and with perfect timing quipped, "That's probably the feds," bringing raucous laughter from the crowd. The discourse of sass was operating on multiple levels. Most explicitly, her invocation of being surveilled by the federal government because of the political efficacy of *The 1619 Project* suggests that Hannah-Jones understands the way relations of power frame her work as an activist/journalist in similar ways to Wells-Barnett.

Her gag brought those relations of power to the surface and rendered them absurd—and frightening. She dares to own herself and to speak back to authority, even to "the feds." This was a moment of release—release in the collective feeling that fear does not rule the day. Hannah-Jones *was* Ida B. Wells-Barnett in that moment. "She spent her entire life refusing to be silenced," Hannah-Jones said of her shero, "pushing back, and refusing to allow other people to write a script for her life. And that's what I've tried to do as well. I understand that it cost you."[73] Black women's sass can play out as an individual political project toward the liberation of all Black people. Nikole Hannah-Jones's *1619 Project* is the perennial reminder we need that Black women's sass is about humor and humanity.

CHAPTER 2

HARD-CORE LAUGHTER

SASS AND THE POLITICS OF RAUNCH

> You know, I'm a *chick* comic. I'm what they call a *broad*.
> I do shit that broads do. I get drunk. I be in the parking lot fucking.
>
> —LUENELL, *Comedy after Dark*

Comedian Luenell was born in Arkansas and raised in a mostly white suburb, Castro Valley, fifteen miles outside of Oakland, California. As the last-born of eight children, Luenell occupied a position that would force her to struggle for a voice and vie for attention. "I got adopted out of the family. I got seven brother and sisters, and we weren't raised together. I was raised alone. They were raised in the South. The man who raised me was a raging alcoholic, very mean. Verbally abusive, and sometimes physically. And I said on my eighteenth birthday, 'I'm out this bitch.'"[1] After emailing with Luenell for a couple of weeks, I first met her before her show at Pepperbelly's Comedy Club in August 2011. She agreed to sit down for an interview after she finished her hour-long set, for which she was about half an hour late because, as she had told the audience, her driver was pulled over for speeding on the way to the show. She sipped Ketel One vodka and pineapple juice, the same cocktail she ordered and nursed onstage as she performed.

Luenell exudes warmth and has a smile in her deep, gravelly voice. "I'm somebody that people pull for. People who have known me for years have seen the struggles I've been through. . . . I think I'm funny and refreshing, and sexy and crazy. Knowledgeable at the same time. The people know that I really am down for my people. And women. And kids."[2] When I asked her what it feels like to be onstage, Luenell replied that comedy is where she feels free; doing stand-up enables her to speak and be heard. Luenell used to *be* a bad girl. She developed a drug addiction in her twenties, was a prostitute for a very short time, and has been incarcerated for stealing money from her employer. Her bad girl lifestyle fuels her stand-up comedy, where she makes jokes of her life. "You gotta know what you can and cannot drink," one of her standard bits begins. "Personally, I know that I cannot drink gin. I slip and fall on a dick every time I drink that shit. Whoops!"[3] As a bad girl, Luenell gives her audience a more intimate, complex view of the interiority of that life and the emotion and context of some of those choices.

As a comic, Luenell transforms her experiences into a persona, "The Original Bad Girl of Comedy," a title she has been given by others and claimed for herself. Bambi Haggins thinks of comic personae as lenses through which we can understand cultural and societal shifts around how Blackness gets understood and materialized in contemporary popular culture. More specifically, comic personae are roles that comedians construct and perform and are products of the individual choices the artists make based on their aesthetic tastes and stylistic proclivities in conjunction with the kinds of economic and industrial imperatives that exist in that historical moment.[4] Luenell's branding as "The Original Bad Girl of Comedy" has opened numerous professional opportunities for her in Hollywood films and on network and streaming television. Her comic persona has also enabled her to connect with her audiences who are eager to share in her experiences of disclosure, sexual or otherwise.

The Nasty Show

Luenell's first Just for Laughs appearance was in 2015 at "The Nasty Show," sponsored by the website PornHub. The promotional video for Luenell's show describes "The Nasty Show" like this: "The following program is the most shocking comedy ever produced. If you are not offended, we haven't done our job."[5] Club Soda, a multipurpose concert venue and event space, situated on St. Laurent Boulevard in what has historically been the red-light district of Montreal, was hosting the show. I arrived early at the venue and stood in a long line, despite having prepurchased tickets. The stadium seats filled up quickly as a DJ spun hip-hop music to entertain the audience before the show began. By this date, I had already seen Luenell perform a handful of times, from the Bay Area down to Los Angeles, and each time, she radiated the persona of a raunchy aunt or trusted homegirl with whom you might share late-night laughs and probably a few secrets.

At the 2015 Just for Laughs show, unlike any other night I had seen her, she seemed uneasy. Canadian comic Artie Lange was the host of the show, which notably included Luenell, Gilbert Gottfried, Mike Wilmot, and Gina Yashere, among a few others. Luenell came onstage to thunderous applause, greeted the audience, and started dirty. "It's my first time here at the festival," she said, reaching up with her long, manicured fingernails to nervously scratch her head, "breaking my cherry with all of you simultaneously." The crowd laughed and she laughed with them, growing instantly comfortable. This was "The Nasty Show," and as advertised, Luenell's set was raunchy.

A boyfriend had gifted her a pair of thong underwear, Luenell joked, which she pulled ceremoniously from her bosom. She held up the black and red undergarment to the crowd's delight, sizing it up against her body. "I said, 'Baby, I could put it on, but you'll never see the motherfucker again.' . . . I don't know what type of little, tiny, triangular Vietnamese pussy you got to have," she continued, "to fit in this little area of material right here. I'm a grown-ass Black woman from California. If I put this bitch on, it's gon' be pussy lips hanging out on this side [*big swooping gesture to one side*], this side [*swooping gesture to the other side*]. You'll never see this side again, that's over [*pointing to the thong in the back*]." Luenell reveled in the Rabelaisian inversion, her excessive body foregrounded. In this moment Luenell refused to disavow it as a site of repulsion, and the crowd howled in laughter. Raunch is an aesthetic mode that enables the comic and her audience to circumvent the kind of affective response to sexual shame—disgust—that disciplines people into not publicly disclosing the pleasure of sex acts and sexual embodiment.

The biggest laughs came from her raunchiest bits. Like Moms Mabley before her, Luenell frequently discusses the pleasures and perils of dating older men. "My boyfriend Rufus got a hold of a little blue [Viagra] pill that really changed the whole game," she joked. After a night out, the two went back to the assisted living facility and began to get intimate. "'You talking all that shit,' Rufus boasts, 'what you think about this?!'" Luenell mimed with the microphone a scene of Rufus whipping out his chemically induced erection and beating it against herself for a comically long time. The audience's laughter built to applause as the metallic staccato continued. "I said, 'What has gotten into you?!' [*Running away from him.*] He said, 'Yeah, where ya going?! What cha crying for?!' [*Continues rapping his erection at her.*]" The audience was in stitches, and Luenell moved right along to her next couple of bits: "He love to get that dick sucked though. Goddamn. You men fucking love head. Ladies, you may as well take your titties and cut the fuckers off and throw 'em in the garbage. . . . Everybody love to get their dick sucked; that's all they want. . . . If you can suck a dick, you can rule the world! [*Laughter and applause.*]"

Fellatio is a practice that has been considered disgusting and abject, and they who perform it have been similarly described. The oral-genital nexus, for some people, conjures an inherent "nastiness" associated with sexual deviance. Sara Ahmed's notion of the performativity of disgust is instructive here, as she notes disgust's "stickiness," the propensity of emotions to separate bodies in danger of coming into "sensuous proximity."[6] Disgust becomes associated with "the lower regions of the body as it becomes associated with other bodies and other spaces," argues Ahmed, and "as a result, disgust at 'that which is below' functions to maintain the power relations between above and below, through which 'aboveness' and 'belowness' become properties of particular bodies, objects, and spaces."[7] Yet, Luenell's raunchy joke located her as a dick-sucker who in that moment celebrated the erotic pleasure of belowness onstage, delighting in the laughter elicited from her disclosure of the power of performing and being good at oral sex: "You can rule the world!" Luenell's raunch is embodied sass wherein she refuses the disciplinary forces that give shame its power to elicit disgust.

> They don't even give a fuck if you're sleep. You can go out. Girls' night out. You come home drunker than shit. Margarita salt all around your fucking face. [*Laughter.*] Pass out on the bed snoring . . . [*Snores.*] You'd think they would leave you alone. They don't even care if you suck back. They just wanna hold they dick on your lips like a ChapStick. [*Laughter.*] "Hey babe, you sleep?" [*Mimes man bopping penis on lips with microphone, shoving it in woman's mouth. Lots of laughter.*] . . . "Hey, wait a minute, you scared the shit outta me! I thought there was a home invasion, don't do that shit!" [*Much laughter.*]
>
> There are rules about sucking dick. . . . We're not really trying to make you *come*. We're just doing that as foreplay. [*Laughter.*] Seventeen or eighteen sucks and somebody needs to get fucked around here, that's all I'm saying. [*Laughter.*] Twenty-five or thirty sucks if it's Christmas or your birthday. OK? And don't be grabbing the back of our fucking

heads. [*Laughter and applause.*] 'Cause, while you think we're choking on your big fucking dick, you done pushed my head down so far that now your dick is touching that dingily-dangly thing in the back of my throat! [*Makes choking sound. Lots of laughter, people falling over laughing.*]

We must not gloss over the fact that issues of consent in this joke evince the gendered violence of unequal relations of power always present in sexual cultures and practices. I also want to think about what forms of empowerment and agency are possible within those relations, especially when we center Black women's sexual practices the way Luenell does within this bit. Is it possible that, like Black women who perform in pornographic race pornography that arouses "sexual and erotic pleasures in racialization, *even when* (and perhaps *precisely because*) racialization is painful,"[8] as Jennifer Nash claims, Black women might take pleasure in phallic masculine sexual power even when and precisely *because* that phallic power is painful? The expression of desire for and pleasure in phallic masculinity is a site where Black women's sexual subjectivity surfaces in the raunchy aesthetics of the joke's expression. As Kaila Adia Story has argued, "This negotiation with black masculinity . . . is one of the ways in which black feminist women have renegotiated notions of power, sex, and sexual agency that have always been rooted in their own pursuits of pleasure."[9] Raunch is an aesthetic mode for many Black women stand-ups that is about wielding stylistic power in the service of negotiating rather than rejecting the (sometimes fraught) embodied elements of erotic desire and sexual practices, and the explicitness of embodied sass is akin to what L. H. Stallings calls a "guerilla tactic that can be employed in personal and political liberation struggles."[10]

There is an inherent refusal to *be* disgusted in Black women's raunchy sexual humor that privileges imagination and centers ecstasy, and this politics of refusal enacts a radical Black feminist politic. As an enactment of sass onstage at "The Nasty Show," Luenell's raunch aesthetics operated within the context of the history and discourse of slavery that has produced Black women as always already sexually repulsive and simultaneously desirable. The ideology of Black sexual deviance is a bequest of chattel slavery and colonialism that remains with us, and Black women in the public sphere are using sexual guerrilla tactics, as Stallings puts it, "as a rejection of the Western will to truth, or the quest to produce a truth about sexuality, and underscores such truth as a con and joke."[11] Furthermore, and perhaps most importantly, to make use of raunch aesthetics creates a path toward sexual agency for the comic herself. That sense of liberation from the con and refusal to engage in its affective and ideological logics that hold it together leak out into her audience, surfacing in their belly laughter.

Sass as Corporeal Orature

Vulgar language and raunchy humor are ubiquitous in stand-up comedy in general, and in the remainder of this chapter, I focus on their aesthetics and efficacy in Black women's onstage stand-up work. Raunchiness seems simple at first, low-hanging fruit, but as I have watched more and more stand-up and spoken to the comics themselves, it is clear something else is happening. Mireille Miller-Young has discussed the ways some Black women who participate in various forms of sex work engage in what she terms illicit eroticism, which she contends "provides a framework to understand the ways in which black women put hypersexuality to use . . . [and] manipulates and re-presents racialized sexuality—including hypersexuality—in order to assert the value of their erotic capital."[12] Similarly, many Black women stand-ups who marshal raunch in their personae and routines are engaging in illicit erotic labor, making hypersexuality work for them as a subversive comedic and marketing strategy. What is the nature of the laughter and the extent to which Black women's raunchy humor is more than it appears? What kinds of political and intellectual questions arise when we center Black women's sexual desires, pleasures and experiences, and language?

Speaking back to power, even and especially when delivered with the slick of blue humor, has always been a subversive tool for Black women to assert their humanity. The question about sexuality and feminist politics is an old one. I am more interested in thinking about the process by which certain kinds of expressions of desire and pleasure that read aesthetically as raunchy can give the impression that Black women comics are not concerned with the politics of liberation that the sass in their humor leans toward. Feminist philosopher Naomi Zack has targeted blue humor, which she defines as "a public excursion into what is disreputable or forbidden, for its own unmediated sake," when performed by Black women comics as "intrinsically problematic, because both male and female American Blacks have historically been stereotyped as hypersexual and morally degenerate."[13] Moreover, manipulated by mass media and linked to minstrelsy, artistic efforts employing blue humor may be used against working-class Black women to justify and further entrench forms of marginalization. As Zack explains, "The people who might be most directly harmed by unmediated minstrelsy are Black women who can identify with the characters being obscenely mocked in the acts, because these women and characters are at once objects of humor and objects of repulsion."[14] Some people may be made uncomfortable by the hard-core, blue humor of Black women stand-ups. But those Black women comics who are the subjects of this chapter demonstrate the seriousness of "blue stuff."

At the intersection of Black sexual practices and politics one should consider desire and pleasure. Sexual desire, Stallings argues, can be "the context for rebellion from the beginning, as opposed to its presence as afterthought," for Black women comics, a necessary investment in pleasure as a feminist politics of redress.[15] Furthermore, powerful forms of agency have been made available through willful acts of sexual deviance. Humor works on and through the body when Black women comics stage explicit, illicit sexual encounters to titillate and touch their audiences. "Humor indeed is preeminently not a 'saying' but a doing": a "making (someone) laugh," notes Shoshana Felman.[16] When Black women publicly stage and excite erotic pleasure via stand-up comedy, they are making choices where the sensorial and political dimensions of humor become intertwined. There is a fundamental connection between the kind of seduction involved in provoking laughter and the slipperiness of language necessary to accomplish a successful joke. If Felman is correct, and a joke "is not simply a *pleasurable act*" but also, "and especially, a *subversive* act,"[17] Black women comics are uniquely positioned on the stand-up stage to be radically disruptive in a space where "Black women's erotic lives," as Treva B. Lindsey and Jessica Marie Johnson have argued, "do not [have to] stand apart from a project of liberation."[18]

Depending on the audience, developing an intersubjective mood is an especially challenging task for Black women stand-ups. Lawrence Mintz notes intersubjectivity as a critical component of an effective audience-performer relationship. "The comedian must establish *for the audience* that the group is homogenous," he argues, "a community, if the laughter is to come easily."[19] In a comedy club, blue humor can be a means of cultivating an *intimate* community; the universal topic of human sexuality contracts the distance between performer and audience in an environment where sensations of pleasure (from laughter itself and perhaps even from sexual arousal) can flourish. Susan Seizer discusses the use of obscenity by "road warrior comics," those stand-ups who travel across the United States and perform in front of live audiences at a variety of venues, from bars to comedy clubs. According to Seizer, dirty words serve a particular function for performers: "Armed with these non-standard signs, comics enlist everything from pun to parable to bring audiences with them into the wilder reaches of their comedic imaginations."[20] Extravagantly explicit sexual humor creates a playful, "nonofficial" atmosphere where the performer and audience can imagine worlds anew, setting the foundation for deep intersubjective connection.

LaWanda Page is well known for her role as the loudmouth "church lady" on the hit sitcom *Sanford and Son*, starring comedian and fellow chitlin circuit entertainer Redd Foxx. The show ran from 1972 to 1977 on NBC, a period in which Page also released five comedy albums. Page's stand-up comedy broadened what and who a Black woman *could* be in the 1970s, as she publicly rehearsed a version of Black womanhood that referenced and transformed ways of doing gender and sexuality. There is a connection between gender and power in stand-up comedy. As Peter Kunze argues, humor, masculine performance, and power are intimately linked, evidenced in "the masculine comic persona.... [Men] drink, smoke, curse, and womanize. They are cool. To incite laughter is to cause others to lose corporeal control, which empowers *men*."[21] As a Black woman, Page performed renegade comedy, causing her audience to lose bodily control in their laughter, thus becoming empowered herself. Arousing them with explicit, raunchy humor, she snatched a bit of empowerment and pleasure for herself in the moment of performance. Page's hard-core routines publicly mocked norms of sexual propriety with the open celebration of eroticism, vulgarity, and non-heteronormative sexual practices. In a sense, Page embodied coolness in a way that enabled her to transgress social norms through the explicit style of her verbal expression, which helped her fit into the landscape of stand-up where audiences demand to have their expectations shattered.

With campy theatricality, Page catered to working-class Black people, and her comedy was "indubitably soulful,"[22] indexing the accoutrements of Black urban pleasures as defining features of her comic style. Page's comedy provocatively brushed aside middle-class codes of respectability in favor of an erotic politics of public pleasure. Her extravagantly blue material, much of which was written by men—notably her mentor and contemporary Redd Foxx—employed explicit sexual imagery onstage to "remind us of pleasure in the sex act,"[23] and indeed, Page's audience howled with laughter throughout her performances in the bluest moments of transgression. Page's blue material is embodied sass and functions as an unconventional mechanism of social redress where Black women can enjoy and elicit erotic pleasure, marshaling an aspect of their subjectivity—their desire for sexual satisfaction—that has been routinely shamed and maligned in popular culture.

On her 1973 album *Pipe Layin' Dan*, Page tells the humorous, extravagantly explicit tale of "fat fuckin' Suzy Ann . . . the world's only 450-pound virgin."

Page privileges the Black body as both a site and an instrument of erotic pleasure. Suzy Ann's "ass was flat and her teeth was buck," but still, she took out an ad in the paper to "find a good fuckin' dad." She desired and would pay for a specific kind of sexual pleasure. "Cock Sucking Bill [was] fuck outta luck . . . I ain't no freak to have my pussy sucked . . . all I wanna do is live good and fuck," Suzy replied to one potential suitor. The album culminates with the story of "a mean motherfucker called Pipe Layin' Dan," a bit that foregrounds the experience of claiming erotic pleasure as an act of redress. Suzy Ann's ad read, "To any man who'll fuck me or just get it in, I'll give him $10,000 and a new El Dorado." Suzy Ann met and married Pipe Layin' Dan, "the fuckin'est motherfucker the world had ever seen." Thoroughly enraptured, "they fucked for a year and only stopped to piss, shit, and eat."[24]

This raunchy claim on pleasure relies on laughter, which serves both sensorial and cognitive functions in the body. Page marshals those functions to lead her audience to an alternative social reality where the scatological enjoyment of erotic pleasure *publicly* is empowering for Suzy Ann, Page, and perhaps Page's audience, too. The comedy is potentially transformative in the moment her audience experiences it. Not only do Page and her crowd cognitively *recall* sensations of erotic pleasure in talking about sex, but, in the extravagant explicitness of the joke's expression and the laughter it derives, they *experience* it—the aesthetics make the moment *funky*, and "sex [i]s representative of art as experience."[25]

Hyperbolic sexual imagery can liberate the performer and audience to enjoy what is prohibited, and Page delighted in taking language about the sexual body and bodily functions to the extreme, reveling in the transgression, refusing to be disgusted by the discourse of sexual deviance that her vulgarity both signaled and produced. A former stripper, Page had lingered on the margins of sexual propriety early in her career, and the vulgarity of her stand-up comedy brought her audience to the margins with her. They, too, could confront sex as a natural, normal, nasty, pleasurable, and regular part of life that could and *should* be discussed openly. Page often used poetic rhyming bars to describe sexual encounters, staging what I term corporeal orature,[26] a mode of expression in which the eroticism of the body is the focal point of a narrative performance, with a style and intent meant to publicly redress the marginalization of certain sexual practices and sexual subjects. Orature "realizes its fullness in performance," as Ngũgĩ Wa Thiong'o argues, and Page's performances displayed the poetic dimensions of stand-up comedy and the erotic politics of Black women's raunchy humor.[27]

Page begins the 1977 album *Watch It Sucker!* with a tune that may be blues or gospel. Page croons, "My ass is an open door. My secret is no secret anymore."

Calls of "Right on!," "Aw shit!," and "Amen" intertwine the space of the church and the nightclub as Page delivers sexually explicit readings of biblical stories and verses, exciting her congregation to frenzy. "Welcome to the church of the open-door hoes," Page invites her audience. An interpretation of a lesson she learned from "the good book" follows, where she explains the reason why she "don't wear no damn drawers." She continues, "Be ye all so ready," and the congregation breaks up in laughter, anticipating Page's raunchy but accurate conclusion: "'Cause you never know when the son of man is *coming*!" Working in the call-and-response tradition and fashioning it to fit her needs, Page repeatedly calls on the audience to sanction her sexual sermon: "Can I get a amen for the *come* . . . the *lips* . . . the *freaks*?"[28] Using wordplay and pun, the preacher identity is reinterpreted, liberating both Page and her audience/congregation. "The majority of obscene words" used in stand-up, Seizer argues, "come from the source domain of sex and sex talk. . . . Taking these words out of the realm of the senses to use them in public address collapses the expected barrier between these experiential arenas, an incongruity that surprises."[29] Indeed, Page recontextualizes obscene sexual language to impart new, subversive meaning. With a captive and enthusiastic audience, Page ushers her flock into the kind of church where women openly command sexual attention and discuss human processes like seeking out erotic pleasure.

Page enacts corporeal orature as she constructs scenes of the body with layers of imagery, sound, and gesture that open a space where redress is possible for Black women who may inhabit marginalized or shamed sexual identities *in that moment*. The routine "Suck It Dry" on the album *Watch It Sucker!* is another example of stand-up as corporeal orature that accomplishes this more precisely:

> I'll suck it dry, honey. That's what she said. That muthafucka likes it when she give him some head. Her lips are as smooth as a new baby's ass, and suck like a plunger, honey, this bitch got class. Talented is the word, honey, best describing her tongue. It feels like a corkscrew going deep in his buns. His balls how they swell with that hot load of cum. *Yeah, baby*. Then she wraps her lips around it, and then stick it in the bum. Can you dig it? *Whew! Yes honey*, like a dog with [*inaudible*] he lays there and shivers. His pecker is throbbing, honey. And his asshole it quivers. Honey, he faints from the pleasure that she just has given. And she waits there patient, for that son-of-a-bitch to re-stiffen. Now the first drop of juice is there for her to sip. Honey, that's when she back off and just lick the tip. You hip to the tip? *Whew, honey shit!* The head is bright red. And his shaft is all swollen. His guts feel the need to unload the

liquefied colon. So, she cut out the teasing honey, and she works on the pole. And she gently inserts her fingers up and down his asshole. *Haaa! But it hurts so good!* With expert maneuver she sucked hard and fast. Hell, that thrashing and crying tell me that son-of-a-bitch ain't gon' last. And then he goes off honey, and the juice hit her throat. Hell, it's enough of the batter to fill up a boat.[30]

As the routine begins, the audience laughs at Page's titillating, shocking narrative of a sexual bacchanal. Once they become aesthetically barraged with explicit imagery, the audience continues laughing as the evocation of intense sexual pleasure becomes familiar, comfortable, and open in the celebration of its hard-core nature. Page enacts a form of Bakhtinian grotesque realism where "the bodily element is deeply positive. It is presented not in a private, egotistic form, severed from the other spheres of life, but as something universal, representing all the people."[31] The bodily function of sex is foregrounded in Page's corporeal orature and, as a bodily referent, takes the act of sex from the ideological and moral discursive fields that make the hypersexual Black (wo)man stereotype possible into the concrete realm of universal human relation. Page inaugurated carnival time during her performances, like the people in the feudal folk worlds of Rabelais. Page evoked laughter and stimulated (self) pleasure, evidenced on this recording in the guttural ad-libs between the lines: "Whew, honey shit!" she utters, simulating the sounds (and ostensibly gestures) of enraptured sex; *Haaa! But it hurts so good!*[32]

In Page's oration of sex, the audience was invited to engage in an aural sexual feast that was no longer sensational but sensory. Expressions of Black female sexuality became ordinary, and the distance contracted between performer and audience. It could also be the case that LaWanda Page was so explicit in her comedy because of the political and cultural atmosphere at the time of second-wave feminism and in the field of Black feminist thought, when women of many races and ethnicities in the United States began to openly discuss sexuality as a means of pleasure in itself. Moreover, the 1970s moment in the wake of Black Nationalist social and political ideology demanded that Black expressive culture be infused with styles and aesthetics considered to be "authentically" Black, based on the supposed needs and desires of a particularly working-class Black segment of the population. Richard Pryor's outrageous yet poignant pathos evoked unapologetic Black male sexuality as a part of his persona, an ideal of Black urban authenticity that may have helped to generate a market and desire for a Black woman comedian who would, in her own way, "tell it like it T-I-is."[33]

Page's catchphrase, telling it "like it T-I-is," encapsulates the discourse of Black women's sass; its underlying element of truth-telling from the core, no matter to whom one is speaking or the consequences, was the site of her ribald humor. Page's stand-up oeuvre functioned in the realm of entertainment, yet with glaringly political dimensions. The act of speaking from the position of the bottom, as Page did—literally and figuratively—using the discourses of belowness, obliterated forced silence and discipline around Black women's sexuality through which a politics of respectability and cultures of dissemblance played out in the public sphere. Page's raunchy humor was infused with the kind of sass akin to that of her foremothers, enslaved Black women who spoke back to authority as a challenge to unfreedom. Page's sass was about pleasure and as much about the body and sensation as it was about her interiority, interpretation, and expression of her sexual subjectivity.

"Damn It, She Can Talk about It"

By 1985, Black women comics like Thea Vidale, Jane Galvin-Lewis, Marsha Warfield, Alice Arthur, and Shirley Hemphill were performing in mainstream venues across the nation like the famed Comedy Store in Los Angeles. That same year, Michael Williams, a concert promoter turned nonprofit fundraiser, ignited a chain of events that would change the course of stand-up comedy and American popular culture. Williams produced the talent and managed the business of the Comedy Act Theater, which would become the premier venue for Black comedy in Los Angeles. In an interview in 2012 at the Females in Comedy Association Convention in Los Angeles, Williams said he brought in almost anyone who had the guts to go onstage: "Somebody's uncle, somebody's cousin, somebody's brother, somebody's sister. Somebody whose friends would say, 'You're funnier than these people; you need to come on out to this club that's happening for Black folks. . . . You make us laugh at work,' or, 'You make us laugh at school,' or church. 'You need to come on and try it.' Those were the ones who were doing it."[34]

The urban, working-class Black comics of the Comedy Act Theater packed the venue week after week from 1985 into the early '90s, and other venues around the country began to accommodate the new trend of urban Black stand-up. The Black comedy boom produced dozens of women comics between 1985 and 1997, most of them appearing on the popular showcase programs *Def Comedy Jam* on HBO and *Comic View* on BET. Women comics were relatively few compared with the hundreds of male comics, yet a rich comic culture arose among the women. The themes of their humor were not unlike those of other women, focusing on relationships, family life, body image, and current events. However, urban Black women's humor also relished explicit eroticism onstage. Part of what came to constitute Black racial authenticity in the pop cultural imagination of this era was the barrage of mass media images—music videos, television shows, song lyrics, and film—of young Black people openly embracing and talking explicitly about sex and displaying excessive materialism and titillating anti-establishment practices associated with street culture (for example, the rise of the "thug life" ethos embodied in Tupac Shakur's music and inscribed on his body as a tattoo).[35]

According to Williams, the stand-up acts were encouraged to be as vulgar as they saw fit in their routines. "The thing is, nobody was in the position to tell them no. They got yeses. I was told that the industry said, 'Let them be as nasty as they wanna be, because we're making money.'"[36] I am not implying that white women comics do not address taboo topics in their comedy or talk explicitly about sex, but sexual taboos are manifested somewhat differently in their routines.[37] As hard-core rap music rocketed to the mainstream in the 1990s, comics from the same demographic of the urban working class incorporated some of those aesthetic elements into their routines. Williams reflected on the trend in Black stand-up comedy: "All of a sudden, you're hearing the women don't want no soft dude, they want a bad boy or a gangster or a thug. And now guys are thinking they gotta be like that to get women. Now they're starting to believe that all you have to do is cuss everybody out, call everybody 'niggas,' call everybody 'bitch,' tell everybody you're sucking dick and eating pussy and getting fucked all kind of ways, and you *in*."[38]

With representations of deviant yet desirable Black sexuality at a premium in the 1990s, Black women comics reveled in the pleasure of bringing laughter to an audience, creating a space for them to talk publicly about their lives in ways that validated and affirmed their humanity. It makes sense that Black women comics would seek to capitalize on the salaciousness of raunchy humor in that moment, given the potential for exposure to a broader market on cable television outlets. One of the most difficult things to contend with, many comedians have discussed with me, is the way the powerful gatekeepers in the comedy industry and comedy audiences alike peg Black women as a monolith, as all the same, no matter their comedic style—often undergirded by the idea that all Black women overly rely on vulgarity and raunchy humor.

In 2012, I sat for an interview in Los Angeles with comedian and activist Hope Flood, who led a successful strike in the late 1990s of BET's *Comic View*, which eventually ended with comics on the show being compensated for their labor. Flood founded and organized the Females in Comedy Association

Convention (which has subsequently been rebranded the Comics Rock Convention), bringing dozens of comics and industry people together over four days to perform and participate in workshops about becoming successful at the business of stand-up comedy. Over an hour, while comedians were performing onstage in the background, we discussed the artistry and business of stand-up comedy, especially as it pertains to Black women. I asked her what she thought was the biggest barrier for Black women's success in stand-up. "Getting onstage is the easiest part . . . I can get you comics 'til the end of time. It's you [promoters] getting the asses in seats." When I dug deeper, Flood offered the harsh reality that many Black women stand-ups endure as they navigate the profession: "It is there." What's there? I asked. "The preconceived notion that we are all bitches. We all have attitude problems. That we all got that diva mentality; we're all talking about the same thing. We don't have any versatility. We're not diverse with what we're talking about. We're all angry. We're all big and fat. We're all this. We're all that. All of those things are there. So, you walk into a room as a Black female comedian, and they already think that."[39]

In a 1993 routine on *Def Comedy Jam,* Adele Givens told the audience, "I'm sick and tired of people saying what a *lady* can and can't do, can and can't say. I feel like this: if a woman can suck your dick, then damn it, she can talk about it."[40] In another routine, Givens joked, "Last time I came to New York City, met a stupid motherfucker at the airport. Walked up to me like, 'Hey, girl. How you doin', where you from?' I said, 'I'm from *Chicago*.' He like, 'Who you wit?' I said, 'I'm by my *got*damn self.' And he was shocked, y'all. 'Girl, you came all the way to New York *by yourself?* You came by your*self?*' Like it's so unusual for a *real* lady to *come* by herself."[41] Presenting herself as a liberated urban woman with the privilege of mobility, Givens is comfortable in her independence, challenging the idea that men are necessary instruments of erotic pleasure for Black women's full satisfaction. To "come by herself" defies conservative, patriarchal sexual norms to which "proper ladies" must often (publicly) adhere, and in publicly claiming status as a *"real* lady," she includes her ability to satisfy herself as a barometer for meeting that standard. Givens makes use of raunch as a politics of deviance, especially given the fact that her audience is Black and working-class. Her claim on pleasure and insistence on sexual fulfillment as part of what makes her a *real* lady "provides an analytical point of entry into examining the complex circulation and meaning of nonnormative behaviors intraracially *without* presuming that so-called deviant bodies always share the same tactics and motivations for producing autonomy and experiencing pleasure."[42] Givens refuses to engage with the idea that a "proper" lady relies on men or phallic power for her sexual pleasure or that she should be silent about what she desires and how she goes about getting it.

I want to be clear that Givens's speaking back to power does not encompass her identity offstage but happens *in the moment* and in the historical and social context of the joke's delivery. Givens refuses to be affected by tired stereotypes and expectations of Black women in the public sphere: "I'm sick and tired of people saying what a *lady* can and can't do"; "I'm by my *got*damn self." In these comedic moments, Givens asserts her humanity in the way she speaks back to disciplinary structures that dictate the propriety of certain kinds of language in the public sphere. Givens is not a "sassy Black woman" just because she is the kind of Black woman who might deign to publicly utter these transgressions of gender and sexual normativity. No, her audacity to say them *in the moment* is the enactment of sass, the expression of the ideal of freedom that springs from her consciousness of herself as a human being with human desires who wants to talk about them freely in public.

The Pleasure and Politics of Raunch and Hip-Hop Aesthetics in the 1990s

The emergence and eventual mainstreaming of hip-hop culture and the hard-core pornography industries shaped urban comedic performances in the 1990s, at times drawing on the very sexual experiences and practices stereotypically portrayed by the mass media and exploiting ideas about hypersexual "Others." A survey of more than twenty Black women stand-ups' routines on HBO's *Def Comedy Jam* and BET's *Comic View* from the 1990s reveals that explicit sexual disclosure was a major trope of urban working-class Black women's comedy.[43] Comedian Simply Marvelous brought audience members to their feet in July 1992 as she broadcast her sexual desire in her routine on *Def Comedy Jam*: "See, I'm almost forty years old. I'm at the point in my life, I do not wanna make love. Goddamnit, I wanna *fuck*! I wanna fuck 'til I destroy some shit! I wanna fuck 'til the four walls come down! I wanna fuck 'til a bird fly over and shit in my bed!"[44]

Sheryl Underwood, mostly known for her role on the daytime show *The Talk* on CBS, got her start performing stand-up in the early 1990s. Underwood had one of the most brazen sexual disclosures on *Def Comedy Jam*, where abject/subject inversion is in play:

> 'Cause I'm a bitch that love to fuck, you know what I'm sayin'? I love to fuck! 'Cause you know what, my legs be open so much my IUD pick up cable channels, goddamnit. 'Cause that's the kinda bitch I am, you

know, fuck that! Fuck that shit, you know what I'm sayin'? I'll tell you what, I'm fuckin', I love to fuck! I love to fuck more than I love to eat. If you put a dick between two slices of bread, ya got me! You know what I'm sayin'? I love to fuck! Manwich ain't nothin' but a sandwich, but a dick, that's more like a meal, goddamnit. And you know, I'm an easy bitch, too, you can have this pussy from the front, you can have this pussy from the back. Hell, this pussy's like Burger King, you can have it your way, goddamnit!⁴⁵

In this routine, Underwood refers to 1990s cultural touchstones (the IUD signals birth control integrated into the contemporary lifestyle, and Manwich and Burger King indicate the ubiquitous commercialization of fast food) to situate herself as a woman of the times. She illustrates that being a woman of the nineties means sexual mores are a component of cultural competence, and private sex becomes public culture. In this moment, we see the political force of Underwood's explicit enactment of sass. She stalks the stage like a hip-hop emcee engaged in a rap battle. Her free hand grips her crotch in an expression that involves her body in an enactment of corporeal orature. Underwood co-opts the phallic, masculine rhetorical gestures pervading hard-core hip-hop music, displacing herself as a sexual object for Black men's pleasure, claiming them as tools to talk about her own illicit sexual adventures. Even though she is a "bitch that love to fuck," she is also a responsible citizen who uses birth control, the well-placed IUD a subtle aesthetic and political choice in her routine that repudiates the ubiquitous "baby mama" stereotype that came into public discourse during this period. What is more, she elevates the idea of hard-core Black sex from dirty and abject to something that can and should be as satisfying and nourishing as food (even if that food is nasty). In the same move, Underwood underscores the pleasure and anxiety of Black sex, which in her account can be so intense that the lovers threaten to consume one another.

Underwood invites her audience to share in that erotic transformation. Her deployment of Black male hip-hop swagger coupled with her punchy, unapologetic disclosure about her desires is outré, recalling LaWanda Page's raunchy aesthetics. If urban, working-class Black women had been marginalized in liberal Black feminist politics, stand-up comedy is a site where they might make the case for their own incarnation of feminist practices that account for their erotic desires. In form and content, performances like LaWanda Page's and Sheryl Underwood's reflect how Black women comics inhabit and transgress margins. As they engage with their audiences, connecting with them through intersubjective laughter, they make themselves visible as sexual subjects, despite the demonization in the mass media of their sexual practices and politics. Moreover, the shared humor "promises the spectator the revelation of something unknown, of the truth about a difference hidden within the [raunchy] performance" of desire and ecstasy onstage.[46] Perhaps the audience's laughter is also a form of recognition, an awareness of their own potential to be the "Other." Fantasy facilitates this process and plants the seeds of these alternative social relations called up by Black women's sass; there cannot be liberation without a deep subjective (and collective) consciousness of what one desires out of the condition of being free.

"Don't Cussing Feel Good?"

There is no doubt that Black women's practices of self-presentation have been at the heart of cultural debates about gender, class, and sexuality in public culture, and respectability politics as a strategy for circumnavigating problematic discourses of unruly, excessive Black womanhood has historically loomed large. The sexual exploitation and demonization and violation of Black women's bodies has understandably precipitated practices and politics of protection, like what Evelyn Brooks Higginbotham calls the "politics of respectability"[47] or like Darlene Clark Hine's notion that Black women engaged in a "culture of dissemblance"[48] in order to conceal their sexuality in public spaces. Hazel V. Carby traces the discourse of Black women's sexual deviance to slavery. "The links between Black women and illicit sexuality consolidated during the antebellum years," Carby contends, and "had powerful ideological consequences for the next hundred and fifty years."[49] These strategies of publicly preserving their dignity by deemphasizing their sexualities was constructive to the extent that these practices of the self functioned, to a certain degree, as a shield of protection from sexual violence. At the same time, those strategies assumed that Black women, especially working-class Black women who refused to assimilate middle-class sexual and cultural mores, were deviant and in need of protection from both white and Black institutions and organizations.[50] Indeed, the politics of respectability has developed broader discursive and material force and encompasses a set of disciplinary expectations about the way that Black folks should act, speak, dress, and carry ourselves in order to be respected as citizens and human beings. Black women's sartorial choices and language practices have historically been (and are still) one of the main battlegrounds, and comedy is a site where much (respectability) politicking takes place.

Internationally known stand-ups Gina Yashere and Mo'Nique, two Black women with drastically different performance styles and comic personae, both began doing comedy in the 1990s. They are more visible than most Black women comics and tend to shoulder what Kobena Mercer terms the burden of representation, a phenomenon where a few popular images of Black people result in mainstream society believing "all Black people are like that."[51] The desire for self-definition sometimes drives mainstream comics to explicitly differentiate themselves from roles they have played and to distance themselves from the confining and sometimes disrespectful popular discourse that surrounds those performances. After winning an Academy Award in 2009 for her role in *Precious*, Mo'Nique embarked on a national stand-up comedy tour, "Spread the Love," in April 2010, and I saw her perform live at the Paramount Theater in Oakland. Mo'Nique began by declaring her comic persona as the "real" her.

She twerked from behind the velvet curtains, audience members exploding to their feet. In her trademark manner, she began her set by degrading "skinny bitches." As people continued to make their way to their seats in the front row, she welcomed them, "Come on big bitches, sit your fat asses down! [*Laughter*]," ordering the "skinny bitches" not to sit in the front. Her black cocktail dress was strapless, and the tight bodice with a flowing skirt defined her svelte figure. Her toned calves glistened as she sashayed across the stage in her stiletto heels, moving continuously to the beat of the music. Her hair, a dark brown curly lace-front wig, bounced with her motions, and her enormous diamond earrings sparkled under the spotlight. "Fuck y'all, I been workin' the fuck out, trying to get this shit in order! [*Laughter*.] I don't have high blood pressure. *Or* sugar [*diabetes*]. [*Laughter*.]" Weight loss was a personal choice for her, not a health necessity. One day, she explained to the audience, her husband was "fucking her up against a wall," and as he picked her up they fell. "In the sweetest voice," he asked, "How much do you weigh?" "And I said proudly"—the audience, seemingly already knowing the answer, echoed "PROUDLY!"—"262 pounds." "That's too much, baby," her husband replied; "I want you for a lifetime." Mo'Nique performed jumping jacks on the stage, saying, "I got up that night! [*Laughter*.]" The woman sitting next to me shouted words of encouragement to Mo'Nique: "Go in, bitch!" she implored. "If you wanna know about me, ask *me*," Mo'Nique concluded; "don't read the magazines."[52]

Mo'Nique's desire for unfettered self-definition onstage was consequential and illuminates one of the central tropes of Black women's humor and also its most salient—sass. However, Mo'Nique's quest to be defined on her own terms was not without contradictions and a healthy amount of irony. Indeed, in the immediate aftermath of her winning the Academy Award for Best Supporting Actress, she was informed by Lee Daniels, her friend and director of the film

Precious, that she had been blackballed by the Hollywood community for her refusal to "play the game" according to the standards of that community. In 2015, Daniels told the *Hollywood Reporter*, "Mo'Nique is a creative force to be reckoned with. Her demands through *Precious* were not always in line with the campaign. This soured her relationship with the Hollywood community. I consider her a friend. I have and will always think of her for parts that we can collaborate on. However, the consensus among the creative teams and powers thus far were to go another way with these roles."[53] Mo'Nique had apparently flouted the etiquette of campaigning for the film at parties, instead opting to spend time with her family, a breach that is ironic given that she hosted the VH1 show *Flavor of Love Girls: Charm School*, which was a spinoff of the problematic *Flavor of Love*. On *Charm School*, Mo'Nique was tasked with disciplining thirteen contestants to learn the art of "proper" etiquette in order "to be principled," the one showing the most improvement winning $50,000. The consequences for breaking with etiquette—or talking back to "power," as Daniels put it, were steep for Mo'Nique, and she lost out on a host of acting roles. Her stand-up career seemed to suffer less, at least closer in proximity to her Oscars win, and there is some striking material within her performances that highlight the contradictions of raunch as an embodied trope of Black women's sass, enabling her to have certain kinds of conversations about self-definition in that context that are directly challenged by some of her other public discourse on social media.

Throughout her routine in Oakland in 2010, Mo'Nique joked about her proclivity for using vulgar language. Stallings maintains that for Black women comics, blue material develops as a response to racial and gender oppression that marks Black women as either asexual or hypersexual,[54] allowing them an avenue to express desire. "I don't know how to be politically correct, especially in interviews," Mo'Nique began a joke at the Paramount Theater. A journalist once asked, since she was so vulgar onstage, did she curse at her children? Mo'Nique retorted, "Are you out of your motherfucking mind, you son of a whore?" The crowd burst into laughter, loudly cheering. "Don't cussing feel good?" she asked. Mo'Nique's invocation of the affective qualities of raunch captured the ephemerality of her sass here, how it surfaces when necessary to speak back to power, materializing an embodied response and posture of agency. "Cussing will keep your pressure down." As a child, Mo'Nique continued, she knew she "was gonna be a cusser." Later in the bit, she asked rhetorically, "Who the *fuck* are we behaving for? This is who we are!" Mo'Nique had a drawn-out series of jokes about Oprah Winfrey, Michelle Obama, and Harriet Tubman, Black women in the American cultural imaginary who have been alternately praised as Black feminist heroes and subjected to demeaning stereotypes. These women, Mo'Nique joked, also "wanna cuss a motherfucker out." The desire to use vulgar and raunchy language, gesture, and style in the way Mo'Nique uses them highlights the continuing and shifting legacy of Black women's sass as the backbone of their humor. "Cussing a motherfucker out" is about claiming voice in the face of the discourse of respectability, refusing to be silenced no matter what consequences may come in that moment. This enactment of sass drew Mo'Nique's audience to her, seemingly inspiring them judging by the long, robust applause and laughter her language and posture garnered.

Mo'Nique is different about respectability politics in her real life. In a May 2022 post on Instagram, the "real" Mo'Nique, draped in her bathrobe in her hotel room in Mississippi where she would perform stand-up that night, admonished her followers:

> It took me a minute to say what I'm getting ready to say because I wanna make sure I'm not saying it in judgment [but] saying it from a place of love. Some of y'all have given me the title of auntie . . . but there are times when auntie gotta talk to her babies and say some real shit. Yesterday, I was in the airport in Atlanta. . . . I was excited. . . . As we begin to walk through the airport . . . I saw too many for me to count . . . too many for me to tap . . . so many of our young sisters in head bonnets, scarves, slippers, pajamas, blankets wrapped around 'em. And this is how they're showing up, to the airport . . . not just at the airport. I've been seeing it at the store. At the mall . . . and the question that I'm having to you, my sweet babies, when did we lose pride in representing ourselves? When did we step away of "let me make sure I'm presentable when I leave my home" . . . so that if I'm out in the street, I look like I have pride? . . . All I'm saying is, could you please comb your hair? . . . Please listen to auntie.[55]

As the comic persona Mo'Nique, she makes use of sass to undercut respectability politics that have disciplined Black women like herself into believing and acting in the world as if their presentation of self holds the keys to the kingdom. "Cussing" is her way of expressing her humanity, the will she has to be the person she wants to be and to say what needs to be said as that human being. Onstage, raunch is an aesthetic mode through which she is unbound to the politics of respectability—they simply do not apply. Mo'Nique enacts sass in that moment and not a second after, which is not a contradiction of her character at all. On her Instagram post, there is no pressing need to speak back to power, no need for Mo'Nique to lay claim to her humanity—only to exert a judgmental posture that holds Black women to artificial standards of behavior to satisfy her own need to validate herself as a legitimate subject. To her followers *she* is the authority, the auntie, who Black women need to speak back to in order to lay claim to their own humanity, and the act of sporting a bonnet or blanket in public—or wearing one's hair in a style not meant for the public, as Brittney Cooper claimed Michelle Obama had done at Donald Trump's inauguration— might just be the act of sass to accomplish it. And to those literate in the art, aesthetics, and politics of sass, it might be funny.

"Meat Is Cock, Mateo!"

I first met British Nigerian Gina Yashere at the Just for Laughs festival in 2015, where I saw her perform in two shows at Club Soda, "The Nasty Show" and "The Ethnic Show." In 2016, I watched her perform a set for "The British Show," which featured only stand-ups from the UK. While she was one of the only comedians on any of the shows to do political commentary, with a series of Black Lives Matter jokes on "The British Show," Yashere did not offer much raunchy material in the traditional sense. Yashere, who has been doing stand-up since the 1990s and now stars in the hit CBS sitcom *Bob Hearts Abishola*, which she cocreated, reflected on her stand-up comedy career in Britain versus in the United States. Some of the most difficult things to contend with when she moved to the United States were the ideas about Black American women that circulate in pop cultural discourse. She told the crowd at "The Ethnic Show" in 2015, "So, I live in America now. It's awesome, I like it. I live in New York. I used to live in Los Angeles. But I left 'cause I had to leave. I'm not Hollywood. I don't fit into that Hollywood industry. I haven't got that Hollywood look. Look at me. LOOK AT ME! [*Laughter*.] I haven't got that look. There are two looks for women in Hollywood. You either look like Halle Berry [*pause*] or Precious. [*Laughter*.] I could possibly play someone who robbed Beyonce's mom's friend. [*Laughter*.]" Yashere has become a mainstay of the American stand-up circuit, and in her transition from the scene in the UK to the United States, she found ways to distinguish herself from other acts. One tactic was to do less raunchy material. When I watched her perform live sets, I noticed that her gruff, punctuating tone sets her apart from most American Black comics, a tone that, along with her accent, underscores her Britishness.

Yashere is not Black American and does not pretend to be, and typical discursive markers that distinguish "urban" stand-up, especially those that are sexually explicit and delivered with a specific style, simply do not seem to be Yashere's bag. Yet, in places like "The Ethnic Show" at Just for Laughs in Montreal, where expectations for Black women's raunchy humor are more expansive, raunch really did work for her in a different way, aesthetically nuanced, to express her sexuality and desires. Yashere has recently begun to integrate more material about sex in her act, especially after coming out as a lesbian later in her career. Given the reputation of "The Nasty Show," I would have expected Yashere to come raunchy, but that set was relatively tame compared with those of the other comics. She certainly used a lot of vulgarity, as is typical in her stand-up. However, it was at "The Ethnic Show" in 2015 that Yashere luxuriated in the art and aesthetics of raunchy humor. Before she appeared onstage for her set, the host of the show did an audience poll and found that most in the crowd were Montreal natives. He noticed that there was a young boy in the audience, and it turned out that Mateo was twelve years old, watching the show with his mother. The rest of the audience appreciated the moment, laughing at the prospect of the boy hearing some age-inappropriate humor. "I don't know if you can tell from the outfit," Yashere said in a bit toward the middle of her set, looking herself up and down. "But I'm not a fan of the penis." Almost ten seconds of light laughter and clapping ensued. "I don't like cock, Mateo. I don't." The crowd roared with laughter, applause, and whistling. "J'aime le vagin" (I love vagina), she said, low and sly. There were almost eighteen seconds of shocked delight, and someone within earshot gasped, "Oh my god!"

Yashere moved on to discuss coming out to her Nigerian mother. "When I came out to my mum many years ago, I had to tell her something more shocking to dilute the shock. So, I told her I was a vegan. She was like, 'What?! You don't eat *meat*? And you don't eat *meat*?' [*Laughter.*] 'Cause meat is cock, Mateo, it's penis. Cock. [*Laughter.*]" Audience members were overcome by laughter at Yashere's raunchy ad-libbed work, inspired by the presence of a hapless and out-of-place twelve-year-old in their midst. "Mateo is gonna leave here the oldest twelve-year-old." Yashere felt welcome in Montreal, she told us, because she could tell there were a lot of lesbians in town. "You know how I know this? I'll tell you how. 'Cause every building I've gone to in Montreal, you guys have got signs on the door that say 'Poussez.' [*Laughter.*] . . . So 'Poussez' Mateo . . . *vagin*." The crowd had come to laugh at Yashere's ethnic humor at "The Ethnic Show," and what they ended up laughing at most was the raunchy humor that emanated from the interaction between the comic and twelve-year-old Mateo. The laughter at this series of jokes was long and visceral. You could feel the delighted shock in the room. "I think you should tell that one at school. Teachers will love you." Yashere was bold and vulgar. This set was raunchy as Mateo's presence rendered Yashere's language excessive. Yet the comedic crescendo did not strike as extravagant in the way that many other Black women comics' raunchy humor does.

Gina Yashere and Mo'Nique have two wildly different styles, but what unites them as Black women comedians is the inherent desire to speak their truths, authority and discipline be damned. They share the desire to "cuss a motherfucker out," in terms of those who deign to tell them what they should and should not say publicly for the benefit of others. What they both convey explicitly is that their comedy, first and foremost, is for *them*—which is the element of sass that is the foundation of Black women's humor, across time and geographical space. Naomi Zack claims that working-class Black women comics cannot effectively use blue material to "go beyond performing unmediated Black-on-Black minstrelsy about Black women."[56] Yet, when Black women engage in raunchy humor to publicly express the desire for and erotic pleasure in sex, there is more at stake than the simple, uncritical reinforcement of stereotypes just for easy laughs. Such articulations turn the abjection of Black sexuality, in particular Black women's expressions of sexual desire and pleasure, upside down. Comics like the ones examined in this chapter revel in their ability to elicit (erotic) pleasure, even if fleetingly, by writing their own scripts about the function of comedy, demanding we imagine laughter as the intense pleasure of human connection.

What are the implications of moving studies of Black women's humor toward an analysis of erotic pleasure? Political discourse can obfuscate the supple poetic and sensuous achievements Black women accomplish when they express their pleasures and desires to their audiences. Shoshana Felman reminds us, "If laughter is, literally, a sort of explosion of the speaking body, the act of exploding—with laughter—becomes an explosive performance in every sense of the word."[57] More precisely, the erotic dimension of explicit sexual joking in public—the way it feels good deep down in your body to recall and recount the pleasure of sex in the intimate space of a stand-up routine—is the means and the end of these comedic events.

It seems that Black women's raunchy humor involves a fair amount of risk, in terms of misinterpretation and outright dismissal, but the reward is both right on the surface in the explosion of laughter and fundamentally deep when we consider what laughter can signify, "a sense of satisfaction and completion."[58] To return to "WAP," the anthem at the beginning of this book, we can appreciate the way Black women's sass, dripping with raunch (pun intended), can be explicitly enacted to pointedly political ends. The way the song was called forth in the wake of the 2020 US presidential election speaks to the overt political efficacy of Black women's raunchy humor. The pleasure and desire evoked in the song is first and foremost for the Black woman speaking subject. The raunchy humor emanating from "WAP" is a Trojan horse with the *potential* to shock hegemonic sensibilities, delight with erotic sensation, and transform social relations with its audacious inversion—possibilities for a complete kind of subjectivity conveyed in the song's powerful last few lines, "If he fuck me and ask 'Whose is it?' / When I ride the dick, I'ma spell my name." What does it mean that Black women's raunchy humor has come up from the basement where LaWanda Page's party records use to live, that it is now by way of this performance event at the White House in 2020 as publicly present as possible? When I consume, take pleasure in, and take part in Black women's raunchy humor, it feels to me like what the rapper Nicki Minaj expressed in 2010: "In this very moment I'm king. / In this very moment I slayed Goliath with a sling." Performing live stand-up gives me that same feeling, which is the subject of the next chapter.

CHAPTER 3

BUTCH LIVES MATTER

SASS, MASCULINITY, AND FAILURE

> My granddaughter here, is choosing to be . . . lesbian. And this little girl needs to understand the consequences of that choice, in the real world. I'm not saying I have any problem with it. Love is love. But Laila needs to understand that she was born Black. She was born a woman. And all that is hard enough without this other thing on top of it. You see the news. The gays and the lesbians are at higher risk for everything. Failure. Depression. Addiction. *Failure*. And that, Laila here, is just too good for all of that.
>
> —In Treatment, season 4, episode 3

The chapter's epigraph is from an episode of the HBO drama *In Treatment* where a grandmother seeks therapy for her granddaughter, Laila, who has just come out as a lesbian. I foreground this scene considering my own experience of what life is like on the margins of Black womanhood. It seems Laila's grandmother may be on to something. Perhaps Black lesbians are more likely to suffer from *failure* in many of life's dimensions. Yet Laila, unlike me and the women who are the subjects of this chapter, has an outwardly feminine gender presentation. My masculinity as a woman, which I label *butch*, and which others have historically named (or been named) otherwise—bulldagger, stud, aggressive (or AG), bull dyke, to list a few—is a gender presentation signifying deviation from established norms of female femininity within mainstream and intraracial institutional spaces. Butchness, along with other identities that reflect embodied expressions of female masculinity, is a broad spectrum that encompasses a variety of outward presentations and cannot be simply reduced to "she who is most masculine," nor is it always in fundamental conflict with traditional tropes of femininity.

Gayle Rubin has noted that even though most butch women are comfortable with some degree of masculinity, not all want to be men. As Rubin puts it, "Most butches enjoy combining expressions of masculinity with a female body. The coexistence of masculine traits with a female anatomy is a fundamental characteristic of 'butch' and is a highly charged, eroticized, and consequential lesbian signal."[1] As this chapter bears out, Black female masculinity is an important site where we can think about how Black women comics navigate ideas about Black womanhood through humor. In examining the comedic performances and experiences of Black masculine-presenting women, we gain a deeper understanding about the way sass functions in Black women's humor, especially how it enables comics and spectators alike to expand their ideas of what Black womanhood means and how enacting sass involves nuanced and fundamentally political ways of claiming humanity.

"It's Not Relatable"

I paced the stage nervously. I had chosen to wear brown patterned slacks and a blue polo shirt with a slick matching tie to perform what I considered my first "professional" stand-up set at the J Spot Comedy Club in Los Angeles in 2012. I had been performing at open mics periodically for a couple of years at this point, but this was the first time I had the opportunity to grace the stage of an actual comedy club. In the audience were internationally known comedians like Luenell and Thea Vidale. Also in attendance were comedy producers like Michael Williams, who founded the famed Comedy Act Theater, which put most of the well-known Black comics of the 1990s on the pop cultural map, and Tina Graham, who was a producer for *Def Comedy Jam*, one of the most significant sites of contemporary Black stand-up. I was doing ethnographic fieldwork and conducting interviews at the first Females in Comedy Association (FICA) Convention at the time, and I was given the opportunity to perform a five-minute set, organized by conference founder Hope Flood. In the weeks leading up, I had performed a couple of times at open mics to get my set as tight as possible. There's nothing like hearing your name called to the stage when you know it is about to get *real*. "Coming to

The author performing stand-up comedy in 2023. Image courtesy of Marie-Jeanne Féthière.

the stage from Oakland, California, it's J Finley!" Eve's "Tambourine" blasted as I mounted the stage and gripped the microphone: "Shake your tambourine go and get yourself a whistlin'!" I'm not sure this song cast the vibe I had envisioned. I bopped to it nonetheless, head freshly shaved, comfortable in my butchness.

"Have you ever accidentally bought scented tampons?" I asked the audience. "No one ever goes into a store to intentionally buy scented tampons. It's always an accident. You get home [*sniffing and rummaging through a bag*] — did I get dryer sheets, too?" I heard a few laughs. "I look in the bag and see that pink band, and I'm like, AW, DAMN! But I'm not going back, so I'm just gonna use 'em; hell it's just a week. I hate scented tampons. They say they're 'Spring Rain' scented. Try Spring Rain *Shrimp Salad*. Or Jasmine Rain. No. How about Jasmine Rain *Trout*." It took a few seconds, but the laughter from the crowd said they got it, releasing a roll of chuckles and a bit of applause.

The next day, the comedians at the convention with whom I had been interacting and having a good time showed me love, complimenting me on my set and repeating the punch line of my closing joke. It was exhilarating to feel a part of this community, even if only marginally. I sat down that night to interview FICA organizer Hope Flood. A comedy show went on in the background at the J Spot. I had gone back and forth about whether to ask her what she thought of my set, which would have been the first time a professional comedian would

BUTCH LIVES MATTER

comment on my performance. I finally asked, and Flood's opinion of my act shocked me. "It was more mainstream to me," she said, to which I laughed. "So, I'm white mainstream, that's how you would describe me?" I responded, half joking, half knowing how I am perceived by Black folks, considering my presentation of self as very butch, an unapologetic code-switcher when I speak. "I think so," Flood explained politely, with a playful tone. "You ain't ghetto Black. It's not relatable, some of that stuff you were talking about. You were talking about periods. I know you have one, but I didn't expect you to get up there and talk about it. If you would have gone on Sunday night, the kids' [gay] night . . . I think it's a gay act. I think you would kill kids' night." I felt flattered, because indeed, my act was a "gay act." Yet, to Flood, it was unintelligible as also and inseparably a Black act and a woman's act. My masculine embodiment seemed to nullify my womanhood, which I intended to convey via jokes about my period that referenced it. My butchness signified a failed performance of womanhood. It also indexed a failed Blackness too, failure made concrete in the collision of the period joke coming from a Black butch body. Even my joke "Soul Titties," the closer, did not sway Flood.

In the fall of 2011 I was sitting in on a graduate course, Feminist Ethnographies, at the University of Pennsylvania. We had to present our doctoral research as part of the final project, and for this I decided to write a feminist joke. I wanted to take my body image humor deeper and workshop a joke that used my body to speak my politics. "Susan G. Komen is racist," the joke starts. The professor and students smiled and nodded knowingly, right there with me. I wanted to unmask the seemingly innocuous yet discursive prejudice of the ubiquitously pink breast cancer awareness industry. "How does the color pink represent *everybody's* titties?" A few people started snapping as if we were at a poetry reading. "Right?!" someone cosigned. "I mean, just once, I wanna see one of those wristbands or a Yoplait yogurt top that's brownish purple." Giggles squeaked out from the audience, and I was slightly flushed with embarrassment but continued, "Maybe some of those little bumps on it." The class cracked up. "'Cause me"—pausing for a few silent seconds—"I got sooooooooooooooul titties! You raise up *my* shirt and look at *my* areolas, and you'll be like, 'Is that an Al Green record?' [*Singing*] 'I'm so tired of being alone . . .'"

This is my favorite joke. It embodies *me*, from my ambivalent insecurity with and appreciation of my womanhood to my commitment to a Black feminist ethos in my life and work. This joke is intended as a political performance; I want to continue the conversation about the hegemonic representation of white women's bodies as *all* women's bodies in mainstream feminist politics and beyond. In short, my Black feminist politics expressed in the joke materialize the corporeality of my feminism. "Soul Titties" is a way of coming to terms with the difference of my Black butch body and affirming its value in a world that constantly produces images and ideas that Black masculine women's bodies are dangerous, excessive, or failed. This is the joke I used to close out my FICA set, a joke in which my Blackness was foregrounded in the content of the joke with the reference to and performance of Don Cornelius's iconic catchphrase on the show *Soul Train*, but also with the nonstandard linguistic register of Black English. This was a joke about affirming my Black womanhood—indeed, my humanity—and even though the joke worked well in front of my classmates and at the comedy club, to at least one other Black woman in the audience, that part of my act did not quite make my general performance a "Black woman's act" that night in Los Angeles.

Recent literature on stand-up, marginality, and affect explores humor as a mechanism to reveal or circumvent the body as a site of injury. John Limon has put stand-up comedy on the couch, so to speak, in *Stand-Up Comedy in Theory, or, Abjection in America*, arguing that abjection has become its central motif since the early 1960s. Limon offers a theory of stand-up comedy *as* abjection. "What is stood up in stand-up comedy is abjection. . . . All a stand-up's life feels abject to him or her, and stand-ups try to escape it by living it as an act."[2] Limon's theory of stand-up engenders one of the four most common ways of understanding the function of humor, the theory most associated with Freud: humor is a means to release tension and a direct expression of forbidden urges, be they sexual or excremental. For Freud and Limon, humor is fundamentally a coping mechanism, a subversive kind of escapism from the tragic to the comic. Cynthia Willet and Julie Willett, however, are not satisfied with this theory, nor with the other three familiar theories of humor: the superiority theory, the humor of incongruity, and the ludic function of humor. Willett and Willett challenge us to rethink the way we conceptualize humor and its functions, centering those people who live life on the margins and perhaps need more than escape from marginality, more avenues for certain kinds of connection than the ones in current circulation.

Not satisfied with the adage "comic relief," Willett and Willett offer an alternative reading of the function of humor. Tig Notaro and Hannah Gadsby, queer, genre-bending stand-up comics, are two of Willett and Willett's points of departure, given that both have used the public stage to reveal and address their traumatic experiences head-on in their comedic material. "Instead of fostering an attitude of adaptation that rises above a fraught situation," empathetic, embodied humor "serves as a catalyst . . . break[ing] open the social circle of belonging," Willett and Willett argue, "widening the sphere of amity and offering the potential for political realignments along with social and psychic change."³ Black butch women are many times invisible as legitimate subjects, and Willett and Willett's theory of empathetic humor offers a way to see how public comedy proffers a challenge to institutional regimes that give rise to marginality—disciplinary structures and discourses like race, gender, and sexuality.

There is something interesting Willett and Willett bring up in *Uproarious* about revelation and interiority in stand-up. What is the nature of this "soul-baring" that is at the heart of their theory of tragicomedy—what does it mean to bare one's soul? Does it simply mean to make oneself vulnerable before a public audience? In the bits Willett and Willet analyze, Notaro and Gadsby are first and foremost baring their bodies, each articulating how her body has been the site of injury and trauma. Notaro comedically discusses her mastectomies and then literally bares her chest before her audience. Gadsby moves from jokes about the way she formerly dealt with incidents of homophobia to a frank revelation of the violence she was subjected to as a lesbian. Notaro and Gadsby both reveal the ways their bodies have failed them—how their bodies have been discursively produced and materially vulnerable because of this production. It seems that as marginal comics—queer women who perform womanhood at the edges of cultural norms, engaging in a politics of failure on the stand-up stage—there is comedic currency in a particular kind of visibility of their bodies as failed.⁴ This aesthetic of failure is central to my analysis of Black butch comics. Moments of failure frame the perception of vulnerability, cluing in the audience to the fact that each comic is becoming vulnerable in baring her body because the audience demands this failure to be imagined anew in the performance. Indeed, the women of this chapter invite the audience to gaze at them as they have gazed upon themselves: their bodies becoming sites of empowerment and moving toward an otherwise sociality—transcending trauma and grief—inviting serious contemplation of new norms of identity and embodiment.

Mignon Moore's groundbreaking empirical study of Black lesbian gender styles offers insight into the way gender presentation is a crucial framework that organizes social life. Moore argues that we must think beyond the registers of play and performance when we investigate Black lesbian gender presentation and its social and cultural functions. There is a seriousness and gravity that we must account for, specifically "whether or how gender presentation structures relationships in contemporary gay communities."⁵ We must treat Black lesbian gender styles seriously, and I want to push Moore's argument further to think about the seriousness of Black masculine gender presentation outside of the way it structures social and interpersonal relationships in gay communities. It functions for Black women comics to produce meaning in transformative ways—specifically, dealing with the physicality of butchness onstage, claiming humanity, and understanding the politics of sass that have always been in play in Black women's comedy.

Besides Mignon Moore's study, numerous creative and critical works, including fictional literature, poetry, documentary, and dramatic films, have engaged with Black lesbian cultures, specifically butchness and female masculinity in terms of how they are experienced, represented, and mobilized as an embodied politic. Sharon Bridgforth's *Bull-Jean Stories* offers a fictionalized, poetic narrative of

> rural
> southern working-class black bulldaggas
> who were aunty-momma-sister-friend
> pillars of the church

who experience love, erotic longing, and rhythms of everyday Black life.[6] In the story/poem "bull-jean & that wo'mn," the speaker describes the disparity between how she sees herself and the way she is perceived by those in her community:

> Na/I's a wo'mn
> Whats Lovved many wy'mns.
> me/they call bull-dog-jeani say
> thats cause i works lik somekinda ole dog
> trying to git a bone or two
> they say it's cause i be sniffing after wy'mns
> down-low/begging and thangs
> whatever.[7]

In a similar vein but through the medium of poetry, Cheryl Clarke's collection *Living as a Lesbian* poignantly recalls experiences of being politically active and self-possessed as a Black lesbian in Washington, DC. Poetry is a powerful tool for Clarke, who says she uses it to "explore the politics of the time," and gender and sexuality are political sites that Clarke examines.[8] Both scathing and subtle, Clarke's poetry evokes butchness as outcast in the "orientation" of a hat, as in "wearing my cap backwards," the second poem in *Living as a Lesbian*. Invoking witches and poets, Clarke calls up a class of women who are dismissed by society because of their speech and likens them to butch lesbians, whose self-presentation has the same effect; "wearing [her] cap backwards" marks the butch, or as she is described in another poem, "the plain one," she is someone who refuses to be bound by normative codes.[9] Furthermore, Debra A. Wilson's 2003 documentary, *Butch Mystique*, uses interviews to provide an intimate account of the experiences of several Black butch women living in the Bay Area, examining how historical gender norms, family and Black cultural expectations, and social pressures affect their lives. The film's trailer hints at the ambivalent, sometimes agonizing experience of butchness as the narrators offer vulnerable stories of being forced into dresses as children, being wary of entering women's restrooms, and feeling invisible. One woman sounded almost in tears: "It hurts me so much when men look at me in a way of hatred, because they only hate me because I'm not making myself available to them."[10]

This chapter builds on this body of work, centering the Black butch's voice and perspective within what it means to embody and experience female masculinity. The nature of stand-up comedy as a form of public performance as epistemology crucially reveals what one can do in and through performance—as Black masculine women set the terms with which our butchness will be engaged, sometimes reaching toward the familiar in the process. To put a finer point on it, even while we tell stories onstage that upset traditional racial and gender common senses, Black butch comics make space for an expansive notion of Black womanhood and Black butchness at the same time. This chapter attempts to move toward the socio-perceptual arena that takes seriously the minutiae of living as a Black butch woman, calling upon the subjective experiences of female masculinity, especially its apparent expression in everyday life and what it means and feels like to be butch.

Butch comics hit on "seemingly universal topics that are by no means exclusive to lesbian experience, ranging from food, fashion, family and relatives, to politics, psychotherapy, and sexuality."[11] Janet Bing and Dana Heller's categorization of lesbian humor does important work in helping us think about the way comedy enables community and self-making for lesbian comics. However, their study misses an important opportunity to take the intersectionality of Black lesbian women's experiences seriously, especially how those dynamics filter into their comedy. For example, they argue, "for the most part there are no references to heterosexuality, to harassment or to oppression, but many references to a self-empowering, self-conscious community based on cooperative principles."[12] This claim does not align with the material of the Black women comics under investigation here. In fact, several interconnected sets of issues arose in my ethnography of Black masculine women's comedy: butch body politics, affirmation of womanhood and female embodiment, violence and misogyny, gender performativity and politics, and empowerment. Black butch comics inhabit the trickster role, slipping in and out of legibility, in their daily lives and before public audiences. One major theme surfaced as I examined my own comedy writing and performance and that of other Black butch comics that directly contradicts Bing and Heller's account of lesbian humor: *failure*, and the extent to which butch sass fits and functions in a Black queer framework.

Furthermore, drawing on scholarship interrogating the conditions of Black queer embodiment, I argue that Black butch comics use the stage as a site on which they embody the possibility of liberation in new ways—namely, as what I term *fantasy-bound subjects*, they illuminate pathways toward a radical gender freedom. This fantasy-bound subject is a remix of GerShun Avilez's "injury-bound subject," who, marked by the risky embodiment of nonnormative gender expression, moves through space navigating threats of various kinds of injury but risks injury nonetheless in the pursuit of "affection, unrestrained pleasure, freedom of movement, self-definition, and unencumbered embodiment."[13] Black butch comics are somewhat restricted by the material reality of an embodiment that is a "space of injury," as Avilez puts it, such that when they get up onstage or in everyday life, they must "recognize the possibility of injury in all locations and resist the desired belief that certain places may be assumed to be safe."[14] Yet their comedic material and unapologetic presentation of self as masculine on the public stage connect their risky embodiment to the kinds of acts of imagination that reach toward the utopian elsewhere called forth by the project of radical Black feminism. As the Combahee River Collective so powerfully put it in 1977, still undeniably relevant, "If Black women were free, it would mean that everyone else would have to be free since our freedom would necessitate the destruction of all the systems of oppression."[15]

The Black butch comic is the fantasy-bound subject who calls up that radical futurity because she disturbs Black gender common sense. There is a tendency in Black cultural discourse, as Marlon M. Bailey and Matt Richardson explain, to regulate "black gender and sexuality," which "produce a common discourse about black culture,"[16] and the Black butch comics of this chapter make use of and explode this common sense by embracing a masculine sartorial repertoire that invokes the performativity of gender and a politics of deviance—their dress, style, and comedic material taken together are sites of risk, fantasy, and subversion. Black butch embodiment onstage "reaches for the otherwise-genders [as] an undoing of fundamental bedrock of whom we have come to believe we are," to offer an answer to Marquis Bey, who asked, "Is there room for one to clutch at cis womanhood while aiding the insurgent politics to abolish the deleterious effects of gender's regime?"[17] While this embodied politics of deviance, based on indeterminacy, risk, contingency, and imagination,[18] looks like "a radical politics of the personal" and may "not necessarily [be] made with explicitly political motives in mind," it does "demonstrate that people will challenge established norms and rules and face negative consequences in pursuit of goals important to them, often basic human goals such as pleasure, desire, recognition, and respect."[19]

The fantasy-bound subject engages dialectics of failure and freedom; her unruly embodiment signals failed womanhood and lays her open to the danger of "a beatdown," while that same failure conjures what Avilez calls aesthetic redress, "or paths to freedom and pleasure that *imagine* ways through but never fully move beyond threat."[20] The dialectic of failure and freedom is held together by the strands of vulnerability and imagination woven by the comics, and besides being rooted in a radical imaginary that makes liberation possible, there is also an element of mourning, for "redress is itself an articulation of loss and a longing for remedy and reparation."[21] In other words, the Black butch comics under investigation here materialize a fantastical freedom—what cannot possibly be but at the same time *is*.

For this chapter, I rely on ethnographic fieldwork, interviews collected at comedy venues around North America, close readings of recorded comedy performances and interviews, and my own stand-up practice, focusing on how humor enables comedians and spectators alike to probe the materiality of Black butch bodies and the interiority of our experiences in them. Stand-up comedy requires our attention to the mutual imbrication of the body and mind, and the seams become obvious when a joke calls up the relations of power that frame liminal embodied subjectivity like Black butchness. Black masculine women comics reveal and contest those relations of power in ways that have not before been explored.

Butch Body Politics in the Public Sphere

By the time the Great Depression rolled around, blues women like Gertrude "Ma" Rainey, Bessie Smith, and Ida Cox had cemented the classic blues into the most popular genre of American music.[22] Black women had entered the pop cultural marketplace in new and profitable ways, mostly as singers, dancers, comic actresses, and combinations thereof. Emancipation, Angela Y. Davis argues, precipitated new freedoms for Black Americans who had previously been tied to the land on which they had forcibly toiled. These new forms of freedom generated novel forms of consciousness and cultural material that reflected them.

Supplanting the spirituals, blues music offered Black people the opportunity to explore more personal ideals of freedom; most germane here were the new opportunities Black women had to discuss aspects of their lives that had not previously been publicly expressed. Black women's interpersonal relationships and sexuality came to the surface in early classic blues music, revealing not only the ways that sass came to define how Black womanhood was popularly understood but also how Black women made use of it as a discursive means of laying claim to their humanity, entertaining their audiences at the same time.

I have discussed how the meaning of sass came to cohere around the turn of the century as a Black woman self-possessed, "a Black woman who commanded above all intelligence and competency,"[23] and the expression of that self-possession—sass—became as varied as the experiences of the Black women who often humorously enacted it. The kind of embodied performances that women in the early twentieth-century entertainment industry engaged in, which included women cross-dressing, can complicate the reductive notion that the discourse of sass exclusively requires femininity or the deployment of feminine codes and gestures to be understood as such. The presentation of Black female masculinity may indeed have been part of the discourse of sass since Black women began entering the arena of popular culture in the early twentieth century.

Take Gladys Bentley, for example. Bentley was a majorly influential personality during the Harlem Renaissance and, like Zora Neale Hurston, fell into obscurity behind her unconventional and impudent attitude toward racial, gender, and sexual norms. Yet, Bentley and Hurston have both been resurrected as bastions of Black feminist politics in the mid- to late twentieth century.[24] Bentley was well known as a gifted singer, pianist, and scandalous humorist who famously reinterpreted popular songs with a vulgar twist. James F. Wilson wrote of Bentley's ribaldly outrageous performances of corporeal orature, "She would take popular songs of the day and just put the filthiest lyrics possible. She took the songs 'Sweet Alice Blue Gown' and 'Georgia Brown,' and combined them and it became a song about anal sex."[25]

> And he said "Dearie please turn around!"
> And he shoved that big thing up my brown.
> He tore it. I bored it. Lord how I adored it.
> My sweet little Alice Blue Gown.[26]

Bentley was a lesbian, and as historian Eric Garber noted, "A large part of Bentley's popularity [during the Harlem Renaissance] was due to her novel appearance." Bentley personified the one identifiable Black lesbian stereotype of the period: the tough-talking, masculine acting, cross-dressing, and sexually worldly "bull dagger." Bentley "had insisted on being herself during a time when others hid their difference,"[27] Garber claimed. Furthermore, "There was nothing feminine about *him*," Saidiya Hartman intimated in her critical description of Bentley's nonnormative gender; "it was more than glamour drag, more than a woman outfitted as a man, as several of his wives, both white and colored could attest ... an exemplary architecture of black possibility."[28] Bentley's butch gender was an embodiment of and fantasy of freedom from the strictures of the day that dictated how Black women could present themselves in public. That embodiment of course came with the risk of violence and other forms of injury, as Avilez suggests of Black otherwise-genders. Yet as the image of Bentley that has become iconic attests, Black female masculinity on the public stage also materializes a utopian elsewhere: what cannot be but at the same time *is*.

Bentley's unapologetic presentation of female masculinity during the early twentieth century might be understood as an enactment of butch sass that emphasizes the idea that for Black women, especially those in the realm of popular culture, presentation of self and indifference to gender norms are a manifestation of sass. To embrace masculinity onstage as a Black woman is a way of claiming bodily autonomy in that moment, daring to speak back to hegemonic authority that frames how the embodiment of Black womanhood gets understood and accepted as "normal." Both Bentley and her contemporary Moms Mabley were humorists, and both had something to say. While Mabley cloaked her social satire in granny drag, Bentley dressed to the nines in formal attire associated with men and masculinity. The reason that Bentley could walk the world inhabiting her female masculinity with such confidence and aplomb while Mabley needed the garb of another character is complex, but what we know is that genre matters.

Both women were virtuosic performers who delighted audiences with humor. For Bentley, though, humor was not the primary language with which she spoke to the crowd, and the musicality of her raunchy remakes rendered her performances unserious in a way. Mabley, on the other hand, spoke directly to her audience in style that could be perceived as political speech if unadorned with the granny gear that visually and discursively disguised it. This generic difference in their approach to public performance could account for the reason Mabley's drag was different than Bentley's. We must also remember that considering the political landscape and Black women's ongoing vulnerability to social and political violence, their sartorial choices were much more meaningful, especially when they decided to flout norms that might have ordinarily offered relative protection.[29] It is in this context of the threat of violence and

Gladys Bentley, circa 1930s. Collection of the Smithsonian National Museum of African American History and Culture, www.si.edu/object/gladys-bentley-americas-greatest-sepia-player-brown-bomber-sophisticated-songs:nmaahc_2011.57.25.1.

injury, given the ways that butch embodiment shatters the illusion of gender as a natural order, that butch sass functions primarily as an embodied enactment that undercuts normative, disciplinary narratives about who is and who cannot be a *real* Black woman. The unique combination of dressing and acting "like a man" in public enabled Bentley to portray herself as a woman fully confident and in control, and both aspects played heavily into her ability to use raunch to entertain and amuse her audiences. Moreover, Bentley's style and subversive gender practice historicizes the way Black women's sass becomes the primary means through which we understand the particularity of their humor in an interesting way.

We ought to trouble the idea that sass is only a recognizably Black *feminine* discourse. Articulating a *butch sass* sensibility demonstrates that Black women who embrace masculine elements of gender performance in their onstage personae and comedic material reveal the porous, elastic boundaries of Black womanhood. I present the concept of butch sass, which highlights the experiential and performative elements at play in contemporary gender presentation. More specifically, butch sass, like that which Gladys Bentley deployed during the Harlem Renaissance, is about how Black womanhood is done in practice by women with masculine presentations of self and the (tragi)comedic commentary on it. In other words, we do not always or only find Black women's sass where it is expected, convenient, or compatible with gendered norms and aesthetics or in neoliberal marketing strategies for the commodification of Black cultural products.

Butch sass is articulated within the broader discourse of sass and functions, through language, style, gesture, and intention, as a means for Black masculine-presenting women to claim humanity by undermining the authority that might threaten their subjectivity at a given moment in time. When comics enact butch sass, they do so within the temporal frame of contingency, as Avilez beautifully theorizes, a state that recognizes how the threat of injury and constant surveillance structure the way butch subjects navigate public space, but at the same time this state of possibility "leaves open space for evasion along with play, pleasure, and desire within the context of threat."[30] Butch sass emphasizes and incorporates female masculinity as a focal point, and the central critique of the gesture circulates around standards of gender normativity to which the Black woman refuses, in one way or another, to comply. In this sense, female masculinity is disambiguated *and* legitimized as "other," by way of the humorous meaning produced in enactments of butch sass. It thereby calls into question, affirms, and expands on the historical meanings attached to Black womanhood. Butch sass acknowledges gender variance by illuminating experiences of Black women in a new way that foregrounds that variance. In this way, comics can lay bare the pleasures, anxieties, and politics of inhabiting a Black female masculine body.

What does claiming one's humanity look or sound like for Black masculine women comics onstage? Like most other marginal comics, Black masculine women comics marshal their experiences of belittlement, ostracization, and vulnerability—experiences that are often sites of trauma—to animate the range of their affective states and ultimately propel conversations about a politics of failure, which many times butch comics embrace as the soul of their comedy. Butch sass disturbs normative sensibilities and awakens social and political consciousness, manifesting the dialectic of freedom and failure that is the condition of the fantasy-bound subject. The way Black butch comics engage with failure and freedom onstage has significant implications for how we think about Black womanhood, sass, and humor in this historical moment.

The Unacknowledged

"I used to wanna be a singer," begins comedian Marsha Warfield in a set from the early 1980s, recorded in the 1984 documentary *I Be Done Been Was Is*. "What stopped me is that I grew up in the sixties. And most of the Black women singers in the sixties were tongue-tied. And I wasn't fortunate enough to have a speech impediment, so I couldn't be a singer." The audience is hushed, awaiting the punch line. "You remember those old songs, don't you?" Warfield smiles and giggles to herself before getting a laugh. She sings the nasally, garbled lyrics of "A Lover's Concerto," the 1965 pop song by the girl group the Toys, "How gentle is the rain, that falls softly on the meadow . . . ," continuing into another tune after a chuckle. "Tonight you're mine, completely," she coos, mocking the Shirelles song "Will You Love Me Tomorrow."[31]

Warfield distances herself from the African American girl groups of the sixties, because even though they helped integrate mainstream popular culture and signaled new expressive possibilities for Black women, their jumbled speech represented a murky incoherence of their voices. Warfield refers to this incoherence as a "speech impediment," pointing to the emerging commercialization of the ultrafeminine, saccharine brand of Black womanhood in sixties girl group recordings as a form of silence that she simply refuses to replicate. During this routine Warfield calls attention to and parodies race and gender politics when it was still customary for women to be seen and not heard. Warfield's mockery of girl groups opens a conversation about the Black woman's social and political location within the context of the civil rights era, when she was present but, at some critical moments, voiceless. During the 1980s, the tongue-tied Black woman is troubled and obliterated as Marsha Warfield brings her to light and then rejects her with her comedy.

Stand-up comedy became a space that allowed Warfield, who got her start doing stand-up at the famed Comedy Store in Los Angeles with iconic male comedians like Richard Pryor, Robin Williams, David Letterman, and Jay Leno, to fulfill her desire to be a performer whose words and ideas were heard. Despite popular ideas about who a Black woman was and could be in the 1980s, Warfield envisioned and performed the kind of Black woman she *wanted to be*, and stand-up had a great impact on her identity. "The person I wanna be is the person I project onstage, a strong individual who can handle anything that's thrown at her," she explains in *I Be Done Been Was Is*. This desire to *be* her comic persona is highlighted in a joke Warfield ended her set with in a 1987 show in San Francisco, after having just done a joke where she mimicked fellatio on the microphone. "Some people say I have a dirty act," she said, pausing a beat to pick up her drink. "But fuck 'em. [*Laughter and applause.*]"[32] The confident self-possession in this moment both belies and low-key redresses Warfield's troubled existence as a closeted lesbian. Upon coming out to her mother, Warfield promised to not publicly disclose her sexuality until after her mother had passed away. This painful tension between her public coolness and private agony comes through as she finishes her thought in the documentary. "The person I am," she confesses, "is like, sickening. It's the person like, 'I love you, don't leave me.'"[33]

Unlike contemporary Black lesbian comics who address sex, sexuality, and gender politics directly in their acts and are not "closeted" in their public lives, Warfield did not have the space, opportunity, or convenience to speak her truth, which to her felt "sickening." When she officially came out as a lesbian through a Facebook post in 2017 after a period of retirement from stage and onscreen appearances, Warfield said her being gay was not actually a "secret" but instead "an uncomfortably kept promise to my mother." Moreover, she went on, "everybody who knew me, knew I was gay. The people I didn't tell knew anyway and tacitly agreed to pretend that the unacknowledged had been acknowledged and accepted."[34] In other words, she did not shy away from ambivalence but wore it as a cloak that enabled her to be both seen and not seen, depending on the circumstance.

Warfield's stand-up act conjured Dick Gregory onstage. She smoked cigarettes and stood still while she wryly delivered her jokes, an entertainer to be sure, but she was not theatrically oriented. L. H. Stallings sums Warfield's image up as gender-neutral, "wearing pants, a natural afro, and a less-than-soft demeanor coupled with a polished and made-up face. She conveys soft butch."[35]

An observational comic with a set of personal experiences she wished to share with her audience, Warfield sought onstage to "strike a human chord,"[36] which led to her role on the NBC sitcom *Night Court* (1986–92) as Roz Russell, a no-nonsense bailiff with a dry sense of humor. In *Night Court* and in her stand-up act, ambivalence is right on the surface—there is an unasked question posed by her appearance and demeanor left deliberately unanswered, which makes sense in the context of the 1980s, a period in which her gender and sexual transgressions could have cost her both a relationship with her mother and opportunities to work in mainstream entertainment. Warfield's laid-back, soft masculinity was an uneasy site of ambivalence and possibility, a fraught expression of butchness that frames and historicizes how contemporary comics on the spectrum of female masculinity engage with gender and sexuality onstage to enact their humanity. To put a finer point on it, there are genealogical traces of Black female masculinity and butch sass in the broader tradition of Black women's comic culture to which Mabley and Bentley belong, but also within the stand-up of later comics like Warfield, whose gender variance and sexuality were unacknowledged and in plain sight.

"White People Are Looking at You!"

Ideas about the work of sass and Black women's historical and affective relationship with it are complicated; sass has at times been embraced as a marker of Black authenticity and discursive power while at others rejected as retrograde and demeaning for the way it has been positioned as a commodity and harmful stereotyping device in popular culture. Wanda Sykes, one of the most popular Black women comics of the twenty-first century, who also openly identifies as a lesbian, rejects the stereotypical "sassy Black woman," even though in a 2004 interview she seemingly condemns the *idea* of sass writ large: "No one calls Ellen DeGeneres sassy. Sassy is all attitude and no content. And I've got something to say."[37] It is interesting that Sykes explicitly discusses the way discourses of the "sassy Black woman" have the potential to politically defang and silence Black women. In fact, we could say that Black women are often constrained by the same kind of vulnerability that GerShun Avilez argues marks Black queer people as injury-bound subjects when they are perpetually perceived and reduced to the "sassy Black woman," because that perception renders Black women subject to violence, both from the state and interpersonally. Black men might get away with murdering Black women, Sykes claims in her 2004 memoir, because "judges are sympathetic. They know how a Black woman can drive you to murder with all our 'attitude and sassiness.'"[38]

Sykes wears a dark, three-piece leather suit, and her signature Afro brings together her butch presentation in her 2009 special, *I'ma Be Me*, taped in Washington, DC, right on the heels of Barack Obama's historic presidential election. In one of her first jokes, she covertly criticizes the "sassy Black woman." She begins, "Gotta get used to having a Black First Lady. . . . That's why we had all those articles when they first got in office, like, 'Who is the *real* Michelle Obama?' 'When will we see the *real* Michelle Obama?' You know what they're sayin'? When are we gon' see *this*?" For a full twenty seconds, Sykes performs wild, finger-snapping, hip-swirling, talk-to-the-hand gestures, finally punctuated with a repeated exclamation, Maury Povich–style, "YOU NEED TO TAKE CARE OF YOUR BABY!"[39] Several more seconds of "sassy" gestures ensue to the delight of the audience, who have been clapping and laughing throughout the bit. In a final motion, before exasperatedly shaking her head at the idea she has heretofore been performing, Sykes delivers a long, slow cut-eye, drawing intense applause. "Well, you're not gonna see that from Michelle Obama," she scoffs, "and we all don't do that," garnering even more applause. Sykes drags the universalized idea of the "sassy Black woman" represented in her exaggerated gestures and words and simultaneously punctuates her final utterance with a more subtle, slow roll of the eyes that enacts the discourse of sass that is such an important element of Black women's humor—its audacious critique of power—"we all don't do that."

Michelle Obama as faux daytime talk show guest is an image of sassiness as an *inherent quality* to which all Black women can be reduced and summarily dismissed. It is this representation that draws Sykes's ire, apparent in the words that her "sassy" Michelle Obama utters: it screams (literally and figuratively) *Maury*. Sykes invokes the iconography of Black women out of control as an entertainment commodity, the idea of sass that flourishes in the pop cultural imaginary. There is some irony in Sykes's takedown of the archetypical "sassy Black woman." The crowd is both amused at Sykes's accurate rendition of it, evidenced in their copious laughter; yet they are also attuned to the political critique that is the center of her performance, as the longest and loudest applause comes with Sykes's sincere if subtler cut-eye after she says, "And we all don't do that."

As the scene plays out, Sykes makes it clear that Michelle Obama (and Sykes herself) in fact *does* want to enact the discourse of sass. "I happen to know for a fact that during the campaign she had rods implanted in her neck," Sykes continues to the delight of spectators; "she is *incapable* of doing that." There are certain situations in which she strongly desires to claim her humanity, or as Mo'Nique colorfully put it, "cuss a motherfucker out." Sykes continues, "You see, sometimes she wants to, but she *can't.*" Like Sykes, Obama has something of substance *to say*, but she had better watch how she says it, how she enacts it with her body language, because "white people are looking at you," as Obama's live-in mother chides her at the end of the bit. Sykes's deployment of cut-eye was an enactment of sass, or more to the point, a deviant practice of freedom, ambivalent to be sure given that what made her feel fleetingly free was a sense of liberation *from* the idea of the "sassy Black woman" trope.[40] This ambivalence of contemporary Black women comics toward the *idea of sass* is clear given its propensity to objectify and silence Black women in the contemporary moment and its discursive ability to speak truth to power.

Armed with the discourse of sass, Sykes demonstrates that Black women, though kaleidoscopically connected by history[41]—subject to it, even—are not a monolith, especially a monolith created and maintained by the white racial imaginary. Since 2012, I have attended a handful of comedy festivals and conventions as an ethnographer and participant. These festivals share a central goal in giving Black women a platform to share their art and insights about the comedy industry in spaces that are safer and more open to seeing them as individuals. Centering Black masculine women comics is in service of that goal, showing that not all Black women comics are the same, but many times they pull on some of the same discursive tools to make their claims and do their comedic work.

Just Don't Call Her a *Dude*

Sam Jay is an Emmy-nominated comedy writer and stand-up who has worked as a writer for *Saturday Night Live* since 2017. She is also a Black masculine-presenting lesbian, and in August 2020 her hour-long comedy special, *3 in the Morning*, debuted on Netflix. The buzz of hair clippers opens the film with a close-up shot of the back and sides of Sam Jay's head. A Black man appears, carving a part into her closely cropped hair. This mise-en-scène is the initial frame through which we interpret the comic; the barbershop backdrop evokes a Black masculine space and disposition, registering both her intimacy with Black cultural rituals and the affirmation of her masculine womanhood. About to go onstage after she gets sharp in the barber's chair, Sam Jay presents a short behind-the-scenes look of a comic preparing for her moment, walking in a dingy, nondescript hallway toward the stage as a melancholy jazz tune plays. She wears a navy blue and yellow designer polo shirt, fitted jeans, and white sneakers. "Wow. This shit really hit me today," she tells her audience in a voice-over. "I was walking to the venue, and you know, all the emotions, you know," she continues as a silhouette of her girlfriend and her embracing appears. "This is my fucking special. I'm here. I'm doing the shit that I set out to do the whole fucking time." The sadness in the trumpet belies the upbeat energy with which she mounts the stage. "Holy shit! What the fuck is up, Atlanta!? This shit is fucking amazing, man!"[42]

The comic is clearly conscious of her nonconformity with racialized gender norms, and she embraces this embodied difference. The deliberate acknowledgment and acceptance of one's gender nonconformity at the beginning of stand-up sets is a common way Black masculine-presenting women frame themselves at the outset for their audiences, making sure spectators understand that their presentation of self is intentional, even if it goes against the grain. Indeed, Kara Keeling offers one of the most robust theories of Black butchness in *The Witch's Flight*, especially her engagement with the 1996 film *Set It Off* and the way she works through the cinematic processes through which the character Cleo's Black butchness inaugurates what she calls a "ghettocentric" Black gender common sense.

Especially compelling for Keeling is the representation of the character Cleo's relationship with her girlfriend, a Black femme named Ursula, and the way the first encounter we have with the pair is when we see them kissing, a scene Keeling describes as having a kind of cinematic power to establish the terms through which Black lesbian sexuality is incorporated and marketed to audiences who are attuned to hegemonic ways of consuming and understanding gender common senses. "Sexy and alluring," Keeling argues, "Ursula's relationship to Cleo calls forth a ghettocentric common-sense version of masculinity and makes Cleo's female masculinity recognizable according to ghettocentric masculinity's contours." Furthermore, "Like gangsta rap's thug, Cleo possesses a fine lady."[43] In cinematic and other creative representations of Black lesbian sociality, representations of sexuality structure how Black gender norms and identities are made visible and function as currency in certain markets, and in these cases, Black butchness's proximity to and relationship with Black femmeness is a crucial mode of rendering this visibility, especially the representation of sexuality between them. Keeling might read the opening scene of *3 in the Morning* as a cinematic process through which Sam Jay's butchness is rendered legible by way of the Black femme woman whom she embraces in the opening scene. Their butch-femme hug, she might argue, signifies the sexual relationship necessary, beyond Sam Jay's apparent female masculinity, to frame and authorize the commonsense understanding of Black gender sociality.

As I see it, Sam Jay explodes the idea of Black butchness being coherent based only on the butch-femme sexual schema, as it reaches into a more affective register early in the routine. As they embrace one another, Sam Jay does not possess her partner but leans on her as she is feeling "all the emotions." Perhaps Black butchness needs Black femmeness and commonsense Black gender codes to cohere at certain points in a comedy routine, but this relationship serves a different purpose than in fictionalized accounts that rely on ghettocentric tropes to produce the intended narratives. Sam Jay and other Black butch comics discussed here do this by noting specific aspects of failure they experience, and many times, that feeling of failure is activated in relationship to Black femmeness and invocations of hegemonic (Black) gender common sense. Indeed, as we will see later in this chapter, Black gender common sense (of which Black femmeness is a constitutive element) haunts and harasses Sam Jay, trying to delegitimize her womanhood via her masculinity and render it more proximate to traditional commonsense masculinity. The jokes make it clear that Black butch women do not want to approximate "real" men but want something different. In Sam Jay's stand-up special in particular, it becomes clear that it is not Black femmeness that authorizes and makes visible Black female masculinity or Black butchness as legible; the Black butch's proximity to violence and her expression of the dialectic of her failure and the fantasy of liberation her butch body invokes makes her butchness cohere. Apparent failure and simultaneous embrace of womanhood are the modes of affectivity that hold together Black butch subjectivity, and this dialectic is often expressed as a form of butch sass in contemporary stand-up comedy.

At the Females in Comedy Association Convention in 2012, the audience had the opportunity to ask a panel of several professional comics about building a successful career. One of the comics rattled off a few bits of advice about naming practices. "Nobody really makes it with nicknames," she said. Following up on physical appearance, the comic went on, almost scolding, "Let's glam it up, people. You dress like a star, you get treated like one. . . . You can't wear jeans and T-shirts. You aren't Dane Cook." This exchange about dress and public performance (and success) showed stand-up comedy to be a sociocultural institution that produces a Black gender common sense. This kind of disciplinary advice within the FICA was understandable, given the benchmarks of performance (always compared with white men as the standard) are always higher for Black women. This panel of Black women comics was speaking to a mostly Black audience of aspiring comedians, but I got bristly when I heard this advice. If this was true, Sam Jay was doomed to fail (and so was I). The prefatory moments in the beginning of Black masculine women's stand-up are significant for the way they convey butch body politics and the way they make use of their body—both the surface corporeality in their stage personae and the stories they tell about themselves as masculine women—to produce positive meaning about the varied experiences and instantiations of Black masculine womanhood. In other words, Black masculine women comics' unapologetic presentation of self as both masculine *and* womanly is seriously of consequence—it is a personally and politically charged means through which they speak back to authority and enact their humanity.

Stand-up comic Shep Kelly embraces the "butch" moniker, sometimes donning self-designed "Butch Lives Matter" apparel while she performs. I first met Kelly at the FICA Convention in 2012 in Los Angeles. In 2019, I attended the Black Girl Giggles Comedy Festival, an event Kelly cofounded, and I got a chance to watch her host and perform at LGBTQ+ night at a bar/nightclub called Hi-Ho Lounge in New Orleans's Marigny neighborhood. For now, I want to focus on a portion of an online performance Kelly did during the COVID pandemic because in it, she enacts sass in a somewhat unconventional way that demonstrates its complexity.

Kelly is introduced at the "Cosmic Comedy: A Celebration of Life" online event by her friend and comedian Onika McClain.[44] "She gon' make y'all laugh, she gon' make y'all think. Don't call her a *dude*. Just don't call her a *dude*. Because I be defending her all the time! And she be like, 'Bitch, I *got* this, relax.'" McClain's opening caveat immediately sets Kelly's masculinity up as a focal point and site of vulnerability. It also frames her as a woman who can handle her business and is adept at defending herself against those who would misgender or mistreat her. The screen toggles to Kelly, and with a smile on her face and in her voice she begins her set. "I'm tryna give people some time to take this in." She gestures toward herself, smiling. Kelly's opening stance, "take this in," offers a pathway toward that elsewhere that Hartman invokes in her figuration of the free state, a moment to imagine butch as the norm; one must "take this in" as a fantasy because that state of freedom, in this moment of expression, is so far from the reality Kelly presents before her audience.

Kelly's skin is a deep, chocolate brown, and she wears a closely cropped fade. Her countenance is very masculine, and it is this masculinity that we as spectators are given time to "take in." She continues, "'Cause I know it's still people watching like, 'Well, where she *at*? I don't see *her* nowhere. This is crazy. Onika said it's gon' be a girl. I mean, I seen butch bitches before, but not like *this*!'" Kelly has set herself apart, especially in her adamant framing of herself as a "butch bitch" and the demand that the audience let her embodiment sink in. This is a critical moment in her set that has only just begun. Kelly *does* a version of Black womanhood that chafes against norms of femininity; she appropriates and owns two epithets that have historically defeminized and dehumanized Black women, the "butch bitch," and she asks the audience to engage with both the idea and the materiality of her version of Black womanhood.

"I know I look extra strong in the face. And this quarantine ain't helping. It's all good. I'm just a woman with a deep voice. That's all there is to it. . . . Now the thing is, people be picking at me. They be like, 'You can't be no woman 'cause you got a deep voice.'" Kelly's voice does not sound particularly deep to *me*, but I interpret her invocation of her "deep voice" as a metaphor for her general female masculinity and the way it interpolates her into the public sphere. It is a background signifier of her butchness that brings her corporeal masculinity to the fore, forcing a confrontation. Kelly's entire set is a metonymic expression of the purpose of Avilez's *Black Queer Freedom*; it is "a consideration of how life gets lived and how desire gets expressed within the context of serial, encircling injury."[45] It illuminates Kelly as the fantasy-bound subject whose liberation through humor is produced through its dialectic relation to queer failure. As Tina Takemoto argues, this epistemological register "can engage the psychic and emotional dimensions of loss, failure, disappointment, and shame that accompany LGBTQ+ existence as well as the utopian potentialities of failure as a mode of resistance, intervention, speculation, and queer world making."[46] Kelly continues, "I be like, 'First of all, God blessed me with this voice. And I'mma use *this* voice to the best of my ability.'" Kelly's interjection is an enactment of butch sass, a moment where she lays claim to her humanity—her voice and the will to use it despite bullying that threatens to silence her or force her to conform to norms to be heard.

Kelly simultaneously embraces her masculinity and affirms her womanhood. Not only does she have something to say with her voice, but crucially her "deep voice," the masculinity emanating from her womanly body, is also saying something, producing meaning in that act of making itself known. "I never pay a bill, ever. Bill collectors call my house, I be like, [*deeper voice*] 'She ain't here.'" The punch line unmasks the discursive power of masculinity, and the humor here lies in Kelly's appropriation of that power while simultaneously announcing and embracing her womanhood.

Comedian D. Lo speaks with a heavy Baltimore accent, and I watched her perform at the LGBTQ+ show at Black Girl Giggles in New Orleans. She wore long locs and a white button-down shirt with black slacks. The room was cozy and warm, and as she got onstage, she opened with, "It's hot as shit down here. I got all kinds of titty sweat down here," setting up her first laugh. "I'm all the way gay . . . if you couldn't tell. [*Laughter.*]" D. Lo located her female body and its masculine presentation as the centerpiece of her set. Her female masculinity structured her experience in the world materially and metaphysically, and this feature of her life was the dominant theme of her jokes. Her masculinity and her womanhood are equally important, evidenced in her reference to her "titty sweat" at the beginning of her set, indexing her womanhood, and the fact that she is "all the way gay," signaling her butchness. "And then I'm a nonthreatening old bitch. I'm from the suburbs," she quipped. "I'm not fighting nobody! Don't let none of this fool you! I'm hiding behind *her*, OK!?" D. Lo's invocation of hiding from danger gestured toward the ongoing conditions of her Black queer subjectivity, that "what is often at stake for . . . unconventional gender expression [is] a beatdown,"[47] as Avilez puts it. The audience let out an enormous laugh, indicating their attunement with the comic, especially with how she put the discourse of gender in the spotlight.

At this point, D. Lo made an explicit distinction between what it means to personify the butch aesthetic and the kind of "toxic masculinity" associated with violence, fighting, and "being a man." She pointed toward herself when she said, "Don't let none of this fool you," using her body to convey that distinction to the audience. D. Lo is not a man, a fact often belied by the masculinity she presents in the world. When Black butch women invoke this theme in their stand-up comedy, which they very often do from the beginning of their sets and throughout for emphasis, they enact sass in ways politically and affectively similar to, yet aesthetically distinct from, other Black women comics. Building on Avilez, we might think of butch sass as a form of "aesthetic redress," which offers "the queer body the space to unfold in many directions"[48] within conditions of limited agency. It is in the *intention* to speak back to authority by enacting one's humanity where we can understand Black masculine women as prolific sass artists working in the same spirit as other Black women who make use of the discursive registers of sass in ways that are legible in the sense of racialized gender normativity.

"I Got the *Real* Dick!"

The dialectic of failure and freedom looms large in the comedy of Black butch lesbians, including my own work. We must engage with that tension as a Black queer method for managing the indeterminacy of living Black female masculinity, which, in the current cultural moment, feels ambivalent: politically progressive and personally brave on the one hand, while on the other hand outdated, apolitical, and risking bodily and psychic injury. J. Jack Halberstam sums up butch embodiment and subjectivity as both failure and a threat: "She threatens the male viewer with the horrifying spectacle of the uncastrated woman and challenges the straight female viewer because she refuses to participate in the conventional masquerade of heterofemininity as weak, unskilled, and unthreatening."[49] For me specifically, failure is the special, awful position of being asked what my pronoun is over and over—which feels like being repeatedly "sirred." It is the experience of perennial overdetermination, the insinuation of or outright declaration that butch women want to be men or that we are what Bailey and Richardson term "penis pretenders/frauds" in their genderqueer-phobic taxonomy.[50] We subsequently fail to adequately perform that overdetermination, "You aren't a *real* man." Butch failure encompasses the idea that somehow our gender variation renders us unintelligible in one way or another.

Sam Jay spotlights this issue in *3 in the Morning*. Riffing on the universal experience of bickering with one's significant other in public, Jay tells the story of being at the airport with her girlfriend, who has brought too many bags, when a man comes to offer help. "When men see a masculine woman. That's their favorite shit. They try to come in [*stomping, grimacing like a super-masculine man*], 'I got the real dick!' Goofy fucks! 'I got the *real* dick, where you want the dick?! What bag my dick gotta pick up?!' [*Laughter.*]" Jay slightly chuckles to herself. "And he jacks up the bag and looks at me like 'Now what?!' . . . Like, nigga, get mine too! [*Huge laugh.*] You getting bags, [get] *all* the bitches' bags! [*Laughter.*] The fuck do you think? I'm a lady, carry my shit. Be a fucking gentleman. [*Laughter.*]" Jay leans into failure, enlivening it and forcing spectators to contend with the interconnections between fear, discipline, and hegemonic power. This sets up a liberatory collision between their ideas about Black womanhood. What is the role of failure in Black butch women's stand-up, and how do they strategically use its dialectical relationship with freedom as pathway toward an otherwise-world where at the very least there is an alternative to the disciplinary norms of gender?

When D. Lo hit the stage at the Hi-Ho Lounge in New Orleans for the Black Girl Giggles LGBTQ+ show, her audience was in many ways prepared for her masculine presentation of self. She performed a series of jokes for which her masculinity was the main theme, especially the way it signals her desire for women and revulsion toward sexual relationships with men. "I could never be with a dude. Picture me and a guy together," she joked. "We laying in the bed. We done split a pack of wife beaters and boxer briefs and shit." The crowd was already laughing. "He want me to shape up his beard, and I'm like, 'Can you hit me off, too?' That's gay, I can't do it. [*Laughter.*]" This bit came off somewhat self-deprecatory toward her own masculinity, but D. Lo purposefully took what was seemingly a lack (of femininity, given her comedic facial hair) and turned that lack into a celebratory flex.

Instead of being inadequate at meeting the standards of proper femininity, D. Lo flipped inadequacy on its head, instilling a sense of confidence and self-compassion as she told the joke. Her failure to meet the standard of female femininity—of not being enough—was inverted, and her masculinity was not only affirmed but transformed into a new norm (that some women do not mind having features associated with masculinity) that created a space for personal vulnerability, sociopolitical consciousness, and a sense of liberation from hegemonic norms. When Black butch self-deprecation turns into the flex, it can become an enactment of butch sass wherein comics instrumentalize failure to speak back to disciplinary powers that constrain the fullness of their humanity. In so doing, D. Lo was the fantasy-bound subject who created a new avenue for understanding Black womanhood as a highly nuanced, dynamic category of existence, which was the surprise of the joke that inspired connection and laughter.

A sense of feminine inadequacy is prominent in my own comedy, and many times I have used the public stage as a space to be vulnerable and talk about my experiences and feelings about my masculine gender expression. "Whenever I'm not in a city, I start to feel like such a big dyke. I really notice how different I look. So dykey!" This is how I began my set at an open mic comedy show at Bucknell University in 2017. "Any dykier, I'd be Rob Gronkowski." Gronkowski is a highly decorated tight end in the NFL who is popularly known for his incredible athleticism on the field but also for his viral antics off it in which he performs a form of hypermasculinity that is flamboyant, bordering on campy. For example, when he caught a touchdown pass, he performed the "Gronk Spike," where he spiked the ball with incredible force in the end zone to celebrate scoring. The setup of my joke hinged on the self-deprecatory construction of myself as "such a big dyke" and the implication that my butchness is somehow a personal flaw. Of course, it is not actually a flaw; my butchness is, however, highly visible, regularly commented on by strangers, and a site of ongoing internal and external struggle. Yet in the punch line of my joke, my goal was to flip the script and turn that fraught dykiness, my seeming failure of femininity, into a send-up of (Gronk's) extravagant masculinity and an open flex of the way my masculinity goes right up to the edge but does not become something of a caricature.

"I Got Titties, Too!"

"My best friends are straight," D. Lo joked in her Black Girls Giggle show, setting herself up as the foil to proper feminine womanhood (straight). "They be calling me when they be having man problems and shit. Like I'm the one you should call when you need to handle your man problems. And they always call me like 'Bitch, you need to get over here, Tyrone is fucking up! You need to come whip his ass!' And I'm like, 'Bitch *why*, I got titties, *too*! He gon' whip my ass like he whip yours!' Excuse me, pass me my bonnet please." D. Lo's reference to her titties signaled her comfort with and affirmation of her womanhood, an invocation of butch sass in action—in a way, D. Lo talked back to the sites of discipline that would cast her as an illegitimate woman (her straight friends who see her masculinity as serving their femininity at the expense of D. Lo's own womanhood). The way she made explicit reference to her titties was like giving the middle finger to those who would cast her as an illegible woman and shed light on her condition as a Black queer subject—she perpetually walks through life marked by multiple forms of embodiment (Blackness, femaleness, butchness) that render her subject to an ass-whipping. It seems like Black butch women endure a kind of tripartite condition of injury-bound subjectivity.

Similarly, Sam Jay calls on her titties to invite a conversation about how butches fit within and exhaust existing ideas of Black womanhood. A running joke in Jay's *3 in the Morning* special is the way her girlfriend engages with Jay's masculinity, for better or for worse.[51] "The other day I was in the shower. She went to the store, and she didn't lock the fucking door. That's how I know she thinks I can handle everything." Here, because of her butch appearance, the supposed traditional qualities of femininity (the assumption of physical vulnerability, entitlement of protection, and the like) are not afforded to Jay, a predicament she challenges head-on. "That's crazy, to leave a woman in the shower. Titties soaped up . . . I'm in the shower, my titties is soapy! I got soapy titties in the shower. And my shits is perky. . . . These is good titties. Not a lot of wear and tear 'cause I don't take dick. [*Laughter.*] They not bouncing around." Over and over, Jay utters the word "titties," drawing a connection between her female body and her gender as a woman. We once again see the Black butch comic oscillate between the injury-bound and fantasy-bound subject—the tension between Jay's apparent failed femininity creates space for the imagination of womanhood and masculinity to coexist, and it is not in the shower but in the figure of the butch openly laying bare (no pun intended) her vulnerability as "a woman in the shower. Titties soaped up."

"I get out the shower, I check the door, it was unlocked. I was livid. I was like yo! That's fucked up. She was like, 'How did you even know it was unlocked?' I'm like, 'Bitch 'cause I'm a bitch and I checked. I'm petty. . . . Whenever you're in the house and I leave the house I lock up the house.' 'Cause that's the rules of pussy. When there's pussy in the house, lock it up. [*Laughter.*]" Jay's use of the terms "titties" and "pussy" are critical, insurgent even. They are the utterances that performatively enact her womanhood and speak back to her partner, who has explicitly marked her womanhood as illegitimate vis-à-vis her butch appearance. Furthermore, her invocation of her titties and pussy signify a calculated disrespect toward her girlfriend and hegemonic discourses of Black womanhood that cast butch women out of the fold.

The last part of this bit is challenging and painful because it illuminates the fear and anxiety that many Black masculine women face about being subject to sexual violence yet not taken seriously as targets of that violence on account of our masculinity. "She left me ass-naked in the shower as if the rapist is gonna come in and be like, [*peers into the shower*] 'Nah, she got a fade, I ain't gon' do it.' [*Big laugh.*] What I *don't* do is take fade pussy. [*Laughter.*] That's what I don't do. I take all types of ass, but not the one that's faded. [*Laughter.*]" Her "fade pussy" is an affirmation of her masculine womanhood, a site of butch sass where Sam Jay enacts her humanity as she speaks truth to power and enables a path toward liberation from hegemonic disciplinary structures that instantiate some women as gender failures or unworthy of certain kinds of rights, privileges, protections, and care.

Sam Jay's shower bit stretches and adds nuance to Keeling's theorization of Black butchness and is aimed at undoing some of the work of ghettocentric common sense where Black female masculinity is visible only via the silencing and sexualization she would force onto a Black femme. She does this by insisting that her womanhood is commensurate with her "fine lady's," to use Keeling's term, and that her masculinity does not in fact "consolidate hegemonic heterosexual sociality."[52] The way Sam Jay makes space in the Black lesbian commonsense dyad of butch-femme for Black female masculinity that embraces certain aspects of femininity undercuts commonsense assumptions. In the process, Sam Jay also reincorporates some forms of hegemonic common sense in the way her jokes about trans women seem to draw a distinction between trans women and "real" or "regular" women: "What are we gonna do when trans women start beatin' up regular bitches? [*Laughter.*] As a regular bitch, I'm a tad bit concerned. [*Laughter.*] . . . I don't wanna be in a fight with one of these motherfuckers . . . let them fight! No, get this nigga off me! [*Laughter and applause.*]" At this point, Sam Jay performs some cut-eye, calling to her competency in the feminine tropes of sass that almost says that there *is* a distinction between "trans bitches" and "regular bitches," the latter of which she aligns herself with. "This motherfucker is strong in ways I did not expect. [*Laughter and applause.*] Please help. [*Laughter.*]" To be generous, even if Sam Jay calls on hegemonic common sense to frame her legitimate womanhood, could it be that her bit that has been lambasted as transphobic raises the question, What do we do when the concerns (however so contested or problematic) of two marginalized groups might be in conflict with each other? And how might butch sass, which is what Sam Jay is enacting, enable us to grapple with questions of power, authenticity, and what it means to be "free" to be who you are?

One thing I learned about writing jokes has been to try to find problems that can be "solved" in the joke work. I knew I was going to get a lot of mileage out of my experience with men trying to hit on me. Like most of the other Black butch comics I have seen, I have a whole set of jokes reserved for the unwanted sexual advances of men. Many times, these experiences are comical, but they often veer into and overlap with a sense of fear about physical safety and anger at the insults that often accompany or precede the come-ons. "A woman with a shaved head is like a closed KFC," I told an audience at my first comedy show in Oakland, California. "You can see all the breasts and thighs inside, but the door is locked tight." Earlier that day I had gotten my head shaved at the barber college that used to be on Telegraph Avenue in Oakland. The clippers vibrated over my skull, and the barber asked, "Does this *feel* right to you?" I caught his eye in the mirror, and I knew he was not talking about the way the clippers felt on my head. He was referring to my masculinity and to the way him cutting my hair inaugurated a sense in *him* that *he* was an instrument of my failed female femininity. He was going against Black gender common sense, the disciplinary logics he had learned and internalized about what and who Black women are, what they should look like, and what hairstyles are appropriate for us.

My bald head rendered me inappropriate, and it made him uncomfortable. "Yeah, usually I do it myself." The crowd was laughing. I became more comfortable. "I mean, I'm shaving my head, not my whole pussy off!" There was no ambivalence here; the remark about my pussy was a political act. It was not simply vulgarity for the sake of cheap laughs. This joke was about asserting my humanity before the barber and before the audience. If the barber was uncomfortable by my act of upholding my masculine womanhood by asking him to shave my head bald, perhaps the audience was too with the explicit reference to my pussy—my womanhood in that moment.

I opened this chapter discussing a set I did in Los Angeles where I had a joke about scented tampons and a professional comic expressed that the discussion of my period was unexpected given my butch appearance. To that comic, I was illegible as a woman, and therefore there were certain aspects of womanhood that would be unlikely for me to touch on in my comedy. This is convenient for a comic because it allows space to create jokes that both are surprising and do a certain kind of political work in the revelation of logics of discipline that constrain ideas about what womanhood should look like and talk about. People of various genders and bodies experience menstruation, but most of the masculine women comics I have observed invoke menstrual periods and the language around periods (for example, "feminine products") to affirm womanhood and create a surprising way to humorously challenge audiences to examine their conceptions of masculine womanhood.

Just before she began her position as a *Saturday Night Live* cast member, Punkie Johnson, a comic from New Orleans, took the stage at the Black Girl Giggles LGBTQ+ show. It is not surprising that Johnson took as a major theme of her set the way she is perceived in the world as a masculine woman. "I'm a grown-ass dyke out here in these streets," Johnson told us. "Like, these young dykes look up to me. I can't be out here changing no *pad*, nigga that shit is *gay*! I can't be out here having no *period*, nigga." The crowd was laughing and applauding. "I'm all in the middle of a conversation with my boys and then I gotta excuse myself 'cause I gotta go to the bathroom. You know what I'm saying? We talking about Drew Brees hitting a record and shit. . . . I'll be right back, player, I gotta go to the bathroom. . . . I gotta change my pad, nigga. One of y'all got a *super*? I left the tamps at the crib." There was no single punch line of this joke, but clearly the setup was Johnson's masculinity, and the way she talked about having a period in such a familiar way served as the gag that destroyed any expectations that Johnson was not a "real" woman.

When Johnson uttered the words associated with her period with such comfort and familiarity, the crowd laughed hardest. In those moments when Johnson countered the idea that butch women were *unwomen*, she spoke back to those who might consider her version of womanhood illegitimate. When she claimed, "These young dykes look up to me" and then went on to talk about how her "boys" might react to her having a period, she was embracing her masculinity and locating it as a site of ambivalences, which produced the laughter. This kind of ambivalent humor is an antidote to the way female masculinity is often surveilled and disciplined.

The butch body politics that came out were about not hiding and refusing to accept illegibility. Afterall, Johnson could have been going to the bathroom to perform a variety of functions, yet she chose to explicitly discuss her period. This was about challenging the idea that Black butch women do not *want to be* women or have the impulse to hide their womanhood in response to a variety of social, cultural, and interpersonal pressures. Johnson's joke and others of its kind traffic and delight in ambivalence. They often enact butch sass from the ambiguous, marginal position of female masculinity, bringing butch embodiment to the center of the conversation about sass as a genre of discourse, even and especially if it makes audiences uncomfortable, and opens space to imagine otherwise-genders as a social norm. The interaction between failure and freedom is the hallmark of butch sass that highlights its political and affective work.

"This Is a *Uniform*"

The experience of being a Black butch is not all about the trauma of not being seen or always being gawked at. However, the fear, anxiety, and worry about public humiliation and being subject to physical violence are no small annoyances.[53] This fear is taken up by many Black butch comics, and I want to focus here on the rest of Shep Kelly's online set during the COVID-19 pandemic to illustrate the ways Black butch corporeality produces certain kinds of anxieties about female masculinity that may put Black women in danger of, at best, being constantly surveilled and, at worst, being subjected to bodily harm. During her almost twenty-minute-long set, Kelly at times veers into a mode of performance akin to the comic monologue. She achingly animates her body as a "space of injury"—her masculinity constrains her and provokes fear and anger in equal measure (in terms of herself, as well as of those who misunderstand or hate her).[54] She challenges her audience to engage with her as a Black woman, to read her embodiment against the grain, and to confront how certain kinds of Black women are treated when they exceed and fall short of the norms that are deeply embedded in that treatment.

Kelly is a resident of New Orleans, a city hit hard at the beginning of the pandemic in March 2020. "I miss outside," Kelly begins the online set. "The one thing I don't miss is trying to go to public restrooms looking like a straight *dude* having to pee." Kelly acknowledges the depth of her masculinity and spotlights one of the most common sites—the bathroom—for which people are surveilled and policed based on their gender presentation. "I go in the women's restroom. Because that's where I'm *supposed. to. go.*" The last sentence is staccato, each word emphasized with a head nod on the syllable. Kelly herself is a disciplined woman. That is the gag, the punch line to the almost tragic bit that is about to play out.

"That's where I'm *supposed* to go," conveys Kelly's sense of indeterminacy. She does not dress the way she is "*supposed* to" dress. Therefore, we are entreated to "take this in," "this" being her masculinity, at the beginning of her set. She does not present herself as she is "*supposed* to" present herself, yet the way she frames herself as a woman with this turn of phrase suggests that she sees herself as reducible to her genitalia, a common way that sex and gender are disciplinarily conflated at the door of the bathroom—a prime spot for acts of interruption, as Avilez terms these interactions, which means a person may "hav[e] access to public facilities (such as bathrooms) limited."[55] At its core, why does one use the women's restroom? Because one has "female" genitalia. Anatomy is all that matters in conservative bathroom discourse that seeks to regulate the boundaries of gender based on arbitrary (and not so arbitrary) identifiers of womanhood. Kelly's joke insists yes, but the existence of female genitalia is not adequate to determine one's identity or entry into the vaunted space of the women's restroom.

This part of Kelly's set calls up Phillip Brian Harper's reading of Black queer life in which a constant state of indeterminacy is a persistent feature, a lens through which Black queer subjects must see and walk through the world speculatively, "for not to proceed speculatively is, to speak plainly, not to live."[56] Furthermore, "amid such indeterminacy, incessantly encountering new unknown persons whose reactions to one cannot be predicted and very likely will throw one yet again into a state of confusion that, because it cannot be resolved, feels profoundly debilitating ... this [is a] matter of indeterminacy."[57] Kelly's comedic narrative speaks back to regulatory forces, explicitly pointing to her failure to meet standards of womanhood in some ways (her butchness) yet to her success at meeting the sexual standards by subtly pointing to the fact that she has female genitalia, boldly inhabiting the controlled space of womanhood anyway.

"I remember one time I was peeing." The next part of the bit takes the audience inside the bathroom to the literal interior of what her failed womanhood looks and feels like. "I guess the girl just wasn't thinking about it. ... So I'm peeing. I'm hovering over the stool. Because that's what we do." Again, Kelly insists on her womanhood and her genitals as the primary site of it. "You know, if you a *lady*, like myself, you know, with all these boy clothes on, you hover ... so I'm peeing." Not only is she a woman, but Kelly snatches the title of lady for herself, an explicit performance of butch sass through which Kelly demands from the audience a new way of seeing and treating her—with all the respect, rights, and privileges of a lady, "boy clothes" be damned.

"And I looked at the bottom of my stall door and I seen her feet stop. And I was like, I know the fuck she didn't! And I leaned my head to the side. And both me and her eyeballing the crack of the stall. Now this is uncomfortable. Like, I ain't do nothing. I just came to pee. You came in here *actin'* like security."

Kelly's set bares the soul of tragicomedy. She is surely a talented storyteller and jokester, bringing spectators into her world with charming wit and attention to detail. Yet, the humor is nested in a narrative with pain and mourning at its core. "I really do miss the gym though," Kelly continues, musing on her pandemic woes. "But I don't miss going to the gym bathroom neither. Like, I literally plan out holding it. . . . When I got to the gym locker room, I was tiptoeing around making sure I didn't hear anybody or see anybody. . . . I ain't trying to startle someone in a towel. 'Cause at that point it's nothing left to say. I don't care what your excuse is. Somebody will beat your ass buck-ed nekkid if they think you a man in the women's gym locker room."

The fear of being misgendered and publicly humiliated leads Kelly to transform the way she travels about the world, curbing her movement and forcing her to anticipate the extent to which her illegitimate womanhood may threaten her safety. This portion of Kelly's set has shades of Hannah Gadsby's *Nanette*, a laying bare so brutal of the homophobia and gender panic that often characterizes the embodied experience of nonnormative gender presentation. Are there certain experiences that may be beyond the realm of laughter? Must stand-up comedy's endgame be laughter in the first place, or can it do more, politically and personally—especially for comics on the margins who, like Wanda Sykes, "have something to say"?

Thematically, the way cisgender men treat masculine women is at the top of the list—from seemingly benign experiences to the more intense ones—of Black butch comedy. Mignon Moore's examination of Black lesbian gender presentation reveals this issue to be a salient feature of Black gender-transgressive women's lives. One of her interlocuters, a Black gender-transgressive woman, discussed the underlying gender ideology of anti-butch violence. "People call us out [of] our names, threaten us, all because of who we are and what we look like, what we represent. . . . [Men have] spent their whole lives with one idea of who they are, and then they look at us with our men's shirts, our men's shoes, and realize *gender is something that is taught.*"[58] The idea that a woman might be in competition with heterosexual men for romantic/sexual relationships with women is ripe for humor, especially feminist humor that strikes at the heart of gender as a discursive construct and the inversion of power that comes with men "losing" their notions of sexual superiority. "Another thing that I just don't miss," Kelly continues in her online set, "sometimes, dudes can't handle butch chicks. . . . They think that we wanna fuck all the girls. . . . I have standards. It's not *every* bitch, my nigga." The anxiety that butch women provoke in men is funny here, until it takes a frightening turn.

"Some dudes, they get real, real mad," Kelly continues, keying the audience in to the not-so-funny aspects of these anxieties and how they play out in real life. "And they threaten me." Her eyebrows are furrowed in an injured scowl, and she takes a few seconds to continue. "Like one time I got offstage and this dude said to me, 'Since you, uh, look like a nigga, I'mma fight you like a nigga.' And I'm like, 'Wait a minute, sir. This is a *uniform*. I totally don't wanna fight a *real* dude. I don't even have an issue with you. You just gon' beat me up 'cause you don't like the way I look?!' It's crazy, I'm not even a threat." Kelly adeptly highlights the "feedback loop" Avilez argues threatens Black otherwise-gendered people's lives, "the circular thinking that makes minority groups be perceived as perpetual threats,"[59] and sends up the absurdity of a common misconception about masculine Black women, which is that we want to "be" men and that our self-presentation renders us unfeminine, subject to the same kinds of brutality and violence usually reserved for men in the social and cultural imaginary. Kelly's invocation of her "uniform" demonstrates the performativity of gender in action.

In *3 in the Morning*, Sam Jay mostly discusses her experiences of inhabiting a nonnormative gender presentation in relation to the people with whom she interacts, primarily her girlfriend. While it comes off as playful bickering between the two, the humor emanates seriousness and gestures toward the cultural and political efficacy of butch sass. While on a flight, the couple has a squabble. "Her main thing is, she likes to fuck with me," Jay jokes; "she likes to say shit to me like, [*pointing, miming being poked by her girlfriend*] reminding me that I'm a woman. I fucking know that, you know." The crowd is laughing, but the conversation is darkly humorous. "But she likes to, [*pointy prodding*] because of my outfits and shit. 'Cause of how I dress she's like, [*jabbing*] 'I'mma break you down and remind you that you a whole bitch.' I'm like, 'Bitch, I got a *pad* in these boxer briefs, I know what's happening. I don't need this energy from you. Goofy ass.'" Jay's maxi-pad punch line is punctuated with a talk-to-the-hand gesture with some cut-eye. I end this chapter with this bit because it emphasizes the ways butch sass functions within the broader discourse genre to center Black masculine women and enables the affirmation of their humanity. Sam Jay's sass forces us to contend with the way Black masculine women's enactments of it can be particular to their experiences of nonnormative embodiment and conventional—pulling on its traditional gestural repertoire to make their claims and critical intent known.

Sam Jay's joke about her exchange with her girlfriend exemplifies how contemporary Black women stand-ups, especially those who are gender-variant, engage with the many discursive registers of sass to affirm their humanity and challenge their audiences to grapple with them, too. The stories Black masculine women comics tell about ourselves as failed feminine subjects enable audiences and critics to fantasize about what Black womanhood and sass mean and can be anew and gestures toward the elasticity of their boundaries.

CHAPTER 4

FROM AWKWARD TO DOPE

SASS, INTERIORITY, AND BLACK WOMEN'S ALTERNATIVE COMEDY

> What do we learn when we pause at sites of contradiction where Black creativity complicates and resists what Blackness is "supposed" to be?
>
> —ELIZABETH ALEXANDER, *The Black Interior*

It was late April 2012, and comedian Hope Flood was hosting the first annual Females in Comedy Association Convention at the J Spot Comedy Club, about a minute-long drive from Los Angeles International Airport. I was about twenty minutes late to the first event, a roundtable discussion called "Meet Me in the Ladies Room, Cuz We Gotta Talk." I hurried in and took my seat, scanning the room. Nearly all the comics who had showed up for the convention were Black or women of color, with a few white women sprinkled in. The space was dark, the atmosphere comfortable and warm. Bowls of peppermints lay scattered about and assorted snacks and bottled water were at the bar area. Convention participants had just been invited to ask the panel of headlining professional comedians—Luenell, Thea Vidale, and Miss Laura Hayes—any question, about anything. A woman stood and directed her question at Miss Laura, who, besides her recurring role on the sitcom *Martin* as Cole's mom

(1992–97), was the popular cohost of BET's *Comic View* throughout the 1990s. "How did you come up with your 'wig bit' from *The Queens of Comedy*?" Miss Laura offered us an explanation: "I was on the stage and this guy kept interrupting. And then, I don't know what he said, I think he called me a something, something bitch. And next thing you know, I snatched my wig off and it was me and him! Tables and drinks . . . they were trying to pull us apart. And after it was over, my manager said, 'Oh, that was *funny*!' And I was like, 'What?' And he said, 'That *wig thing* you did,' and I said, 'Nigga, that was *real*!'"[1]

Life on the margins deeply influenced Miss Laura's comedy. She conveyed to me in an interview that she had literally lived the life of a "bad girl" from the streets, doing the kind of "dirt" associated with street life. At one point she felt lonely and excluded from the activities of her pimp/drug dealer husband, so Miss Laura learned how to "boost"—to steal and sell merchandise on the black market—to free herself from the boredom and unhappiness of street life.

> The only thing I ever wanted to be in life was a wife and mother. I thought I was on my way to that dream. So, I got my little boyfriend, I was thirteen; he was eighteen. We moved out, lived together. . . . I was on my way to this white house with the picket fence. He worked at the post office. He comes home one day and announced to me that he was about to be a pimp. I had no idea what that really entailed. But I wound up following him because I figured he was going through some kind of crisis. . . . Being a box of rocks at the time, I went along with it. Well, eventually, he kept going on and on. . . . I felt left out. They was all in the living room having fun, smoking cigarettes, bagging dope. And I'm in the room by myself. So, I wound up following him into the street life, and there was a couple of girls who were friends of mine who would sell me clothes. And they were boosters. And I talked them into teaching me how to boost and from that point on, I was kinda just in that life.[2]

The way she delivered stories onstage about her personal experiences created a special kind of connection with her target audience, which was mostly Black women. Miss Laura was deft at evoking feelings of familiarity as she recounted her life in the form of humorous stories. Miss Laura's comedy was fundamentally informed by the fact that she grew up in the Bay Area, where life could be tough for Black girls and women. Indeed, this environment was shaped by class stratification, racial segregation, and unstable gender dynamics, making it necessary and possible for Miss Laura to adopt collective and unwavering tactics for keeping herself and her family safe. More importantly, it was a conduit through which she expressed her inner life. As Elizabeth Alexander put it in her canonical work on Black interiority, "Art is where and how we speak to each other in tongues audible when 'official' language fails."[3] Comedy was the art form, like boosting, that enabled Miss Laura to feel a sense of belonging; furthermore, it was an intimate means through which she opened her interiority to her audiences.

In the 2000 film *The Queens of Comedy*, Miss Laura performs a rendition of the "wig bit" about growing up "in a big family of girls," with a father who "raised us tough."

> He taught us to stick together; you marry one of us, you marry *all of us*. [*Laughter.*] And when there's a problem, we get *together*, baby. And Moms is the dispatcher. My little sister got in trouble, she had to call Mama. "Mama, [*crying*] this nigga hit me." Woo! Mama was cool though. She was like, "Don't worry about it, baby." Moms hung up the phone and dialed one number; *all* our phones rang. [*Laughter.*] "Bertha, Laura, Ula, Ruthie, get on over to Alice's house; that nigga done gone crazy!" That's all we needed, we jumped in the car, we rollin'. We slappin' fives over the seat. . . . Get to the house, screech up real fast, walk in the door, the nigga just about to hit my sister. We go "AW, *naw* [*snatches wig off*], not tonight, motherfucker! [*Laughter and standing ovation.*][4]

The expression of the collectivity of Black feminist sociality conveyed in this bit is a point of connection between Miss Laura and her audience, chiefly Black women. The Black mother is the center around which the corrective action takes place, and Miss Laura takes us through the process of learning the cooperative nature of Black feminist action. Yet cooperation is not the only element of Miss Laura's Black feminist ethos; it also, and equally importantly, involves a struggle—violent if necessary—beginning with the recognition in the self that one is worthy of the struggle that is about to ensue.

As their sister is about to take a beating, Miss Laura (and ostensibly each sister) removes her wig and forcefully intervenes in her violation, a performative act of disrobing, and in so doing exceeding norms of femininity in the service of protecting the targeted sister. Kristin Denise Rowe has argued that the televisual use of wig snatching "produces a kind of vulnerability . . . that eventually leads the character to a different place mentally and emotionally. By depicting these moments of 'undoing' cinematically, Black women directors, producers, and actresses converge to create moments that Black women viewers actively mark as intimate and authentic, as they relate to the scenes in particular ways."[5] When she snatches her wig off before her audience, Miss Laura creates a sense of intimacy as she becomes vulnerable enough to reveal her "true self," materialized as her natural hair, which, as Rowe argues, "is meant to be private—hair that is matted, tangled, unstyled, or dry is not fit to be seen."[6] Miss Laura's vulnerability is a means for accessing and enacting a form of authenticity on the stage, and she explicitly links her life experience to the character she brings to life onstage. This fighter ethos is an expression of her humanity, the primary impetus for her enactment of sass in the wig bit.

One of Miss Laura's earlier versions of the "wig bit" appears in her "realimentary," *2 Bees from Oakland*, a multimedia project Miss Laura and her good friend comedian Luenell produced about their personal and professional trials and tribulations. Before a series of clips illuminate how the wig bit became her signature act, a text screen reads, "Long before it was part of my comedy, it was a part of my life."[7] In one clip of Miss Laura performing stand-up, she discusses the regressive (and violent) gender politics in Shahrazad Ali's infamous and well-lambasted text from 1989, *The Blackman's Guide to Understanding the Blackwoman*. "Talking that shit . . . 'If she don't act right, then just slap her in the mouth.'" Someone in the audience recognizes the ideas of that book with a call of "That's right," to which Miss Laura directly responds, "Oh, that's right? [*Snatches off her wig.*] Well then take your best shot!"[8] The audience erupts in laughter and applause.

Miss Laura's life and her full claim on her subjectivity are reference points for her signature wig bit, but as Peggy Phelan has importantly argued, "The document of a performance . . . is only a spur to memory, an encouragement of memory to become present."[9] The wig bit's selection, scripting, and mediation underline it *as* a performance, a rendition of the "truth." The autobiographical impulse in contemporary Black women's comedy underlines the link between performance, interiority, and the subterranean politics of contemporary Black women's sass, which is the subject of this chapter. There are of course drawbacks for Black women using public performance, as Deirdre Heddon notes, as a means of "dislodging dominant cultural representations by showing other representations drawn from experience, whilst understanding that these experiences are themselves culturally and socially contingent."[10] When they publicly share stories about themselves in their comedic material, Black women face the challenge of essentialism, where "the relation between life and its performed representation"[11] can congeal into the appearance of a coherent, static representation of Black womanhood.

Luenell and Miss Laura regard the documentary camera in 2 *Bees from Oakland* as the "one-eyed therapist," taking us into the trials and tribulations of the comedy industry and their personal experiences of loss and longing in their collaborative work. Miss Laura and Luenell revel in the disclosure of moments in their lives that might otherwise have been private—histories of incarceration, rape, and abuse; trouble paying the rent; longing for their AWOL husbands. These narratives are captured to provide an account of what it means to be a professional comic for a wider audience, but at the same time they are humorous and intimate descriptions about what it means to live as Black women in America. In one moment of vulnerability, Luenell reveals to her two friends in a conversation over drinks, "Yeah, my titties got me raped." Her small audience is momentarily shocked before Miss Laura, amused now, breaks the tension with "Oh, heavens!" and the three women double over laughing.

Bringing her experience of rape to the foreground in this tragicomic moment is risqué and outré, a moment of feminist humor that "is not about just escaping such toxins [as rape] or simply cleaning them up." As Cynthia Willet and Julie Willet contend, feminist humor "is about transforming, deep down, negative energy into a political tour de force."[12] Luenell is not merely trying to shock. She is attempting to create a kind of intimacy, a moment of connection and grief sharing that belies the gravity of her revelation. Perhaps Black women's raunchy humor, whether erotic or traumatic, enables us to "have a glimpse of an alternative formula for humor based not on detachment or distance, but on sharing one's emotions and on felt connection," a formula for feminist humor that Willet and Willett offer up and that makes sense as a lens through which to examine the Black women of this study.[13] Luenell is unwavering and more pointed about the role of her professional success as a comic in bringing her from the margin to the center: "I'm the eighth of eight children. Nobody really listened [then] to me."[14] Stand-up comedy was a forum where she could turn her difficult situation on its head and literally stand up, she explained; "I don't have to write anything. It writes itself. . . . Everything I talk about onstage is 100 percent true."[15] It is in this spirit that I take up Joyce West Stevens's charge: "We need to know more about those phenomena [like sass] that take place between the psychic-physical space of self-regard and that of social context."[16] In *The Black Interior,* Elizabeth Alexander focuses on the Black interior as a space where Black artists trouble mainstream expectations of Blackness, primarily in visual art and literature and film. What happens if we interrogate the Black interior as it relates to stand-up and podcast comedy and examine how humor enables contemporary Black women comics to play with vulnerability?

Throughout this book I have discussed sass as a genre of discourse that enables Black women to assert their humanity and speak back to authority. Sass, in fact, is an art form that creates space for a revelation of the performer's interiority. Sass responds and shape-shifts depending on historical, cultural, and social conditions that dictate what it looks like for individuals based on what forms of power and authority need a clapback. I draw on ethnographic data and close readings of podcasts and recorded performances to think about contemporary enactments of Black women's sass as revealing interiority, exploring some of the aesthetics and sensibilities taken up by Black women performing in the alternative comedy scene. How does their comedic material foster more nuanced understandings of Black women's identities, experiences, and perspectives—perspectives that have historically been elided, trivialized, or, perhaps worse, universalized? This chapter explores the aesthetics and efficacy of sass as it travels through bodies, across genres and audiences.

Black Women and Alternative Comedy

> If you, as a comic who is Black, don't perform that [*Def Comedy Jam*] kind of comedy then you lose your Black title and you're called alt-comedy.
>
> —AMANDA SEALES, *VH1 Presents: All Jokes Aside: Black Women in Comedy*

"Black alternative comedy" is twenty-first-century nomenclature, but the tradition of Black comic misfits is long. Scholars have chronicled the struggle for Black humorists to both create and perform content that not only is in their own voices and in keeping with their cultural experiences but also is marketable and accessible to audiences beyond Black communal spaces. Yvonne Orji commented in the 2017 documentary *VH1 Presents: All Jokes Aside: Black Women in Comedy*, "I want to . . . almost be all things to all people. . . . Let's figure out a way to connect." Jessie Fauset's formative 1925 essay "The Gift of Laughter" pays tribute to the richness and versatility of Black folk humor in the first decades of the twentieth century. Fauset documented the sheer effort required of Black comic actors to gain a foothold in "legitimate" theater in dramatic roles in the early twentieth century, to transcend the common roles of shuffling, mindless buffoons—roles they were often forced to perform during an era when blackface minstrelsy was the most popular comedic genre in the United States.

"The Gift of Laughter" sheds light on the long quest of Black humorists to move into what Fauset called "universal roles," unbound by racial caricature.[17]

There is a tradition of Black humorists attempting to work outside of conventional representations of Blackness and Black life; however, a difficult conundrum was on the horizon when, until the mid-1950s, mainstream (white) audiences accepted only Black comedic performances that reinforced long-established stereotypes. When Black comics have dared to produce and perform outside of stock roles and scripts, there has been a risk, ironically, of not being taken seriously and of being cast out from Black cultural institutions.[18] The alternative comedy scene is a contemporary site where Black comics have been able to take risks with their style and approaches to forge new ways of understanding the many registers of Black life and experience.

The alternative bent to Black women's comedy has always been present. In the groundbreaking 1984 documentary *I Be Done Been Was Is*, the first film to chronicle the struggles and triumphs of Black women comedians, director Debra Robinson presents a discourse of Black women's subjectivity without homogenizing their experiences. Instead, she lets the four women guide a narrative of difference. Each of the comics—Marsha Warfield, Jane Galvin-Lewis, Alice Arthur, and Rhonda Hansome—perform before racially mixed crowds in nightclubs, bars, and even at a public park. Galvin-Lewis remarks in the film, "I've never had an all-Black house."[19] There were very few "Black rooms" in the 1980s where Black comics could showcase their talent to Black audiences, so most worked white or mixed rooms.

Thea Vidale began performing in the 1980s, honing her act before mostly white audiences in Texas before gaining mainstream success on her eponymous ABC sitcom, *Thea* (1993–94). Vidale became a headlining stand-up act in small towns at any venue where she could get stage time, from bars to hotels. She crafted her act in ways that distanced her, before the eyes and consciousness of her white audiences, from stereotypical images of Black womanhood, which you could argue was a strategy for succeeding in a mostly white profession. Onstage at the first Females in Comedy Association Convention in Los Angeles in 2012, Vidale sat in a chair almost at the level of the audience, rather than above them. She rarely raised her voice and almost never moved beyond gesturing with her hands for emphasis. Vidale's stillness and non-theatricality were acts of what Signithia Fordham terms "gender passing," employed by Black women in the academy to "be taken seriously," thereby increasing their chances of academic success.[20] Building on Fordham's line of argument about gender passing, Vidale's quietude and stillness in her stage presence can be read as "an act of defiance, a refusal on the part of high-achieving females to consume the image of 'nothingness.'"[21] Vidale worked hard to avoid being pigeonholed, forced into a ready-made mold, instead calling attention to the struggle contemporary Black women comics face to gain legitimacy while producing and performing comedy that reflects the specificity of their experiences without the intervention of gatekeepers of the status quo.

Today, there is a network of Black women comics who appreciate and are literate in styles and aesthetics of traditional tropes of Black humor but also exceed the boundaries of the genre, aesthetically and politically. These comics include Michelle Buteau, Chloe Hilliard, Calise Hawkins, Gina Yashere, Zainab Johnson, Rae Sanni, Dulce Sloan, Amanda Seales, Yvonne Orji, Issa Rae, Jessica Williams, Phoebe Robinson, Naomi Ekperigin, Marina Franklin, Sasheer Zamata, and Nicole Byer. Along with others, these women are producing and performing innovative, self-reflexive comedy in alternative spaces like dive bars, random apartments,[22] the Upright Citizens Brigade Theatre, and Union Hall in Brooklyn. Yet it would be naive and ill advised to cast them outside of the realm of the Black comic tradition. There is no easy distinction between Black women's urban and alternative comedy, no essential bifurcation between the cultural production of Miss Laura and Luenell and the alternative Black women comics listed above. However, the aesthetic and stylistic approaches of Black women's alt-comedy is worth exploring because we can find important insights regarding how Black women are engaging in comedic practices that lay bare the heterogeneity of their experiences and, more importantly, Black women's desire to be regarded as complex, complicated, and thinking human beings.

When I use the term "alternative comedy" or the "alt scene," I am referring to the alternative comedy scene in the United States since the mid-1990s, not the alternative scene that emerged in the United Kingdom in the late 1970s. UnCabaret, a weekly comedy showcase that takes place at Au Lac in downtown Los Angeles, launched in 1993 and claims to be "the first alternative comedy show." UnCabaret's website characterizes alternative comedy as "soul baring, mind bending, intimate, conversational, idiosyncratic comedy," a style associated with comedy stars like Patton Oswalt, Kathy Griffin, Margaret Cho, David Cross, Janeane Garofalo, Andy Dick, among many others.[23] As Emily Hertz puts it, alternative comedy "denote[s] comedians that challenge the boundaries of the field through innovation, pastiche and reflexive provocation."[24] E. Alex Jung described the aesthetics of the new wave of Black *male* alternative comics in an April 2015 article on the website Vulture. "Their jokes are *oddball* and sometimes *experimental*, occasionally *detouring* into the *self-referential* and the *surreal*, and they have popularized a more *playful, introverted* version of Black masculinity."[25] We could extend these descriptors to contemporary Black women comics in the alternative scene. I would like to go further and discuss how much of their comedic material embraces individuality, celebrates awkwardness, and rewards racial transgression. Furthermore, what is the extent to which this genre of comedy—that which embraces the awkward—can incorporate sass as a technique?

David V. Gillota describes the "Black nerd" as a new comic persona in the landscape of twenty-first-century American comedy, arguing that this figure constitutes a class apart from "contemporary African American humorists [who] tend to reinforce their ties to Black communities and concepts of Black authenticity by aligning themselves with recognizable signifiers of Black culture."[26] Black (male) nerd comics are emerging in the mainstream, many of whom are in the highly educated Black middle class, with "new" styles, aesthetics, and source material. The humor of these Black nerd comics "contrasts sharply with the hip, loose, and stylish visions of Black masculinity that are most often represented in popular culture."[27] The cool and the intellectual collide in the Black nerd comic persona, a sort of reconciliation of the classic Du Boisian condition of double-consciousness, "this sense of always looking at one's self through the eyes of others, of measuring one's soul by the tape of a world that looks on in amused contempt and pity. One ever feels his two-ness, an American, a Negro; two souls, two thoughts, two unreconciled strivings; two warring ideals in one dark body, whose dogged strength alone keeps it from being torn asunder."[28] The Black nerd comic is the ultimate embodiment of intelligent, Black middle-class cool; the divided experience of being both Black and American are finally united, the metaphorical veil lifted via African American alternative comedy—two-ness become one—precipitated by the ascension of President Barack Obama, argues Gillota. Black men who perform in the alt scene work against the veil of stereotypes of what Gillota characterizes as "the violent, hypersexualized 'Black buck' or the comic, lazy 'coon,'"[29] while Black women comics raise the veil of deeply held cultural beliefs that Black (funny) women are endowed with bottomless reserves of strength, resilience, and indignant self-assurance—the specter of the "sassy Black woman."

This condition of double-consciousness manifests differently for Black women comics as racial ambivalence, lacking the neat resolution we see for Black men in the figure of the "Black nerd." If the Du Boisian "veil" can be understood in the words of Judith R. Blau and Eric S. Brown as "the color line that divides and separates . . . an essential aspect of perceptions and communications between those divided,"[30] we might say for Black women comics the veil materializes as the web of stereotypes, images, representations, and discursive assumptions about "authentic" Black womanhood. Lisa B. Thompson has demonstrated that in the post–civil rights cultural milieu, Black women use visual and narrative strategies to expand ideas of who Black middle-class women are and can be in the pop cultural imaginary. While many introduce elements of sex and sexuality, "the performance of middle-class black womanhood . . . relies heavily upon aggressive shielding of the body; concealing sexuality; and foregrounding morality, intelligence, and civility as a way to counter negative stereotypes."[31] It is this web of signifiers about sex, sexuality, and the Black female body that comes under fire in the routines of contemporary Black women comics, especially those who perform in the alt scene, in ways that can work paradoxically to upend hegemonic ideology that circulates around what it means to be a Black woman—and at the same time, these routines might buttress the moralistic logic of the existence of "good" and "bad" Black people. Indeed, the way sex, the sexual body, and feminist politics get talked about is a site for a more thorough interrogation of economic class antagonisms as an inflection point in contemporary Black women's humor.

"Shake-a-Dang-Dang!"

When I first met Naomi Ekperigin in 2011, she was twenty-seven years old and living in New York City. She grew up in Harlem and got her start doing improv theater at Wesleyan University in Connecticut. Ekperigin was one of the few African Americans in her improv group, yet she was able to develop her talent because of the "loosey-goosey" atmosphere of her small liberal arts college. "Everyone was about owning their differences, their otherness," she explained. When she performs stand-up, she uses her own life as the foundation of her routine: "I don't wanna go up on that stage and alienate you, 'cause then it's gonna be awkward."[32] Ekperigin's own awkwardness was the subject of her earlier humor, in which she illuminated her experiences of alienation. She aggressively does so in her stand-up, but without being aggressive toward her audience. This strategy enables her to focus her humor sharply while at the same time creating a distinction between her as a Black woman and confining stereotypes of Black women comics.

"I'm doing what they call the *alt scene*," Ekperigin told me back in 2011, which was the first time I had encountered this term. The alt scene, she explained, "is basically bar shows, writers, guys from *The Onion, Funny or Die. That* alt scene. You have that, and then you have the club comic, kind of the everyman. The alt comic is more of a personality. Usually, they're like, weird, neurotic, awkward." The alternative comedy scene thrives on awkwardness and the quirky and is well matched with Ekperigin's experience as someone who has felt like an outsider. Alternative comedy's anti-traditionalist celebration of edginess seems a suitable scene for Ekperigin to come to terms with her history of alienation. "Stand-up is the only place where you can be subversive. Stand-up is where you go when you don't fit anywhere . . . that idea of observational humor, and just sort of picking out the weirdness in life that comes when you're standing on the outside. You just kinda watch how people work."[33] There are very few opportunities in the entertainment industry for Black women to address their affective states, especially feelings of vulnerability and anxiety, yet for Ekperigin and a host of other Black women in the alt scene, comedy in this genre opens space for them to stage a radical interiority.

The Awkward Comedy Show (2010) is a documentary produced and directed by Victor Varnado, showcasing the comedic talents and experiences of five African Americans who consider themselves alternative comics: Varnado, Hannibal Buress, Eric André, Baron Vaughn, and Marina Franklin. The comics are described as "nerds who don't need any revenge, just a mic and an audience who cares about smart comedy from a personal perspective. . . . *The Awkward Comedy Show* will show the world doofy jokesters are to be laughed at on their own terms."[34] From the outset, the comedians attempt to draw some distance between themselves and their styles and sensibilities and those of other African American stand-ups. The trope of naming Black comedy that does not "fully" embrace traditional tropes and aesthetics as "smart," "nerdy," and "intelligent" is problematic given that this division assumes "traditionally Black" comedic productions, producers, and audiences *do not* possess those qualities.

Given pervasive stereotypes associated with Blackness and Black comedy, it is understandable that comics would want to mitigate confining categories. Rebecca Wanzo has described a millennial genre of comedy she terms "precarious-girl comedy," which hinges on an intractable sense of alienation. Awkwardness is a comedic trope through which abjection is mitigated, and Wanzo's description of "awkward" is germane. "The complexity of affects that make up the 'awkward' is ephemeral: inappropriate speech, bodily movements, social interaction, and emotion."[35] The labels "smart," "nerdy," and "intelligent" perform some of that work of modifying abjection in Black alt-comedy, "lessening its power to wound."[36] Marina Franklin, the lone woman spotlighted in *The Awkward Comedy Show*, discusses the tension and anxiety of being subject to a set of aesthetic and stylistic expectations. "When I first started," Franklin explains, "I tried to go into what someone said was a 'Sheniqua voice.' I would end every joke with that 'Mm hmm.' It actually worked for me. They seemed to like it. [*Eric André chimes in, "For a white audience?"*] Yeah, I was doing more of it than I did in front of a Black audience."[37] Franklin immediately goes into a bit about rejecting the expectation of playing the "sassy Black woman," a bit that has become a staple of her live comedy shows.

I caught Franklin headlining a show at the Vermont Comedy Club in Burlington in June 2016, and she prefaced the joke by providing the audience with some context. "I'm from Chicago," she reported. "I grew up in Highland Park, a white neighborhood. I was the only Black kid in a white school. . . . Then we moved to the South Side. But it was too late. I was white. I didn't have any skills. I didn't know how to fight. I didn't know double Dutch." She moved through a series of jokes about getting beat up by an "ugly girl" and discussed some of the ways her grandmother kept her close to her Black cultural roots, despite having been raised in mostly white spaces, setting up her "sassy Black woman" joke:

> I'm not, like, a sassy comic onstage . . . some people like that from a Black female comic. They like that "Mmh! Mm hmm! Yeeah! Mm hmm! Shit! [*Laughter.*] Hell yeah motherfucker! Mm hmm! Shit! [*Laughter and applause.*] Shake-a-dang-dang! [*Swiveling her hips.*] I'm exhausted. I'm exhausted. [*Laughter.*] It's too much work. I put that on my Weight Watchers as an activity. [*Laughter.*] Being a sassy Black woman for half a second. [*Laughter.*] And now I can eat cake. . . . When I first started doing comedy, I would do that, and I would just say the wrong thing. 'Cause you know, if you're not being yourself, you'll mess it up. So, I would get up there and I would be like, "I got a big pussy!" [*Raucous laughter.*] "Who got a big pussy?!" [*Laughter.*] That's not really a compliment.[38]

Onstage, Franklin's liminal status was clear, as was the anxiety and ambivalence wrought by her awareness of a supposedly authentic Black subject and the comic sensibilities expected of "Black female comics." She expertly cited and then symbolically punished the "sassy Black woman" image. Franklin's accurate representation of the stereotype, in word and gesture, signified her literacy in traditional tropes of Black women's expressive culture. At the beginning she faithfully mimicked the gestural repertoire of the "sassy Black woman," "Mm hmm! Yeeah!" She rolled her eyes, swerved her hips, and looked her object up and down. However, Franklin's awkward and grossly caricatured tagline, "Shake-a-dang-dang!," reminded her audience that just in case they had been fooled by the accuracy of her "sassy Black woman" impression, she was something of an impostor, in spirit if not in gesture.

Franklin's commentary on the evolution of her comic sensibility confirmed the underlying anxiety and ultimate revelry in racial transgression that marks Black women's alternative comedy. Regina N. Bradley argues that "Black girl awkwardness" is a particular identity that Black women have claimed to move beyond stereotypes. Specifically, Bradley discusses Issa Rae's mobilization of

"Black girl awkwardness," how enacting and celebrating this postmodern subjectivity "humanizes, visualizes and pushes back against standard performances of (comedic) femininity." Furthermore, "awkwardness signifies the shifts in how Black women in twenty-first-century popular culture navigate interlocking discourses of *race* and *gender* that dictate our day-to-day lives."[39] The trope of "Black girl awkwardness" signals some of the ways Black women work within and push against established norms of Blackness and femininity and how they engage with the sexuality of the Black female body in public discourse.

It is also important not to downplay the role of socioeconomic class when we think about the work "Black girl awkwardness" does or the way Franklin's "Mm hmm"s, expletives, vulgarity, and rejection of the "sassy Black woman" identity signifies a will to punish, if not purge, a distinctly working-class image of Black women that in popular culture can be easily reduced to a roll of the eyes, a sucking of the teeth, and a swivel of the hips—and Franklin's off delivery of "shake-a-dang-dang!" The way Franklin signaled her class status by repudiating the language of the sensuous Black female body, asking satirically, "Who got a big pussy?!," solidified a working-class "sassy Black woman" who was constituted by her sexualized body and a middle-class version who comedically shamed her. This "sassy Black woman" was a one-dimensional representation that could be understood in this context *as* the Du Boisian veil Franklin was working to pull back to reveal Black women as thinking, feeling human beings as opposed to expressive objects for "a world that looks on in amused contempt and pity."[40] This repudiation of the "sassy Black woman" was an outward expression of Franklin's interiority—her anxiety about meeting the standards of norms and her desire to fully share her experiences without certain aesthetic expectations tied to her embodiment—how she should speak about and move her body in public.

Franklin has embraced her "Black girl awkwardness" and uses this misfit status as a primary source of humor. When I saw Franklin perform live in Vermont, the punch line of her joke about the altercation with the ugly (and "sassy") girl ended with Franklin getting beaten up, thereby symbolically punishing *herself* for not conforming to conventional norms of working-class Black womanhood. In *The Awkward Comedy Show*, however, it is the ugly girl who is punished as the school principal comes to Franklin's rescue, enabling Franklin to employ some trickster tactics of racial transgression. In the latter version, Franklin tells the audience, "I'm bilingual. I'mma use my white voice," and with an accent that skillfully indexes a white Valley girl, or what sociolinguist Penelope Eckert calls the "Northern California shift,"[41] Franklin reports to the principal, "I don't really know what *happened*. Oh my god. That *Negro* hit me!" Franklin is a Black woman, yet in this version of her joke the performative distinction between the ugly "Negro" girl and herself sets up Franklin's multivoiced-ness as both a tactic of racial transgression and a comedic embrace of "Black girl awkwardness," with all the contradictions and irony it entails, embodied in her clever alternation between multiple discursive registers.

"Do Some Impressions"

Prior to the 2014 season of NBC's *Saturday Night Live*, pioneering sketch and comedic actress Maya Rudolph was the sole mixed-race woman (her mother is Black American and her father is Jewish) repertory player during the early aughts, appearing from 2000 to 2007. Rudolph enjoyed a highly successful run not least because of the range of characters she was able to portray and the vast array of celebrity impersonations she brought off successfully. During her time on *SNL*, she rendered fourteen distinct characters and did impressions of nearly fifty celebrities, including but not limited to Black superstars like Oprah, Beyoncé, and Michelle Obama. Valerie M. Lo argues that Rudolph's "ability to transcend race is unique and also relies on her ambiguous appearance," which has enabled her to convincingly impersonate celebrities across the racial and ethnic spectrum including "Jennifer Lopez, Lucy Liu, Barbara Streisand, Donatella Versace, Liza Minnelli, and Paris Hilton—all due, at least in part, to her ambiguous appearance."[42] Racially ambiguous appearance aside for a minute, Rudolph is a comic who does not disavow her Blackness and is regularly accorded celebratory accolades from Black cultural institutions, having received a handful of NAACP Image Awards for her work in sketch and film.

Rudolph does not reject or underplay her Blackness in her sketch roles per se, but she has foregrounded her comedic craft and rejected racial labels often attributed to comedians who are not white. "Because I never thought of myself one way or another [Black or otherwise], I think it helped my performances. I never think of the characters I play based on race. Ever. It doesn't come into my head," Rudolph told *The Guardian* in 2015.[43] In short, Rudolph has been able to cultivate a broad fan base and enjoy success as a sketch comedian and in both independent and mainstream film roles because of the versatility and range of her comedic talent, as well as her racial fluidity through which she "transcends racial boundaries by being known apart from her racial background."[44]

After Maya Rudolph, the next Black woman to enjoy success as a repertory player on *SNL* (2014–17) was Sasheer Zamata, another comic with an improvisation background who brought a measure of diversity to mainstream productions and an aptitude for comedic impressions. Rudolph is clearly a stand-out in this regard given the wide range of, public demand for, and generally positive critical reception of her impressions. Zamata, on the other hand, has generally sent up only Black celebrities and portrayed characters who are racially coded as Black, which is not limiting on its own. Rather, the expectations from audiences and the narrow character and celebrity pool are constraining, obscuring and moderating the comedic talent of the art of impersonations for which Zamata has become known.

Sasheer Zamata got her start doing long-form improv at the University of Virginia and regularly performs stand-up comedy in both clubs and alternative spaces. She has hosted a comedy/variety show, *Sasheer Zamata Party Time!*, at established alternative spots like Union Hall and the Bell House in Brooklyn and has also performed in the Brooklyn Comedy Festival, which bills itself as "NYC's Premier Alternative Event."[45] Along with *SNL*, Zamata is known for her comedic impersonation clips on YouTube. I caught a stand-up show of hers at the Vermont Comedy Club in 2016, and one joke stood out that seemed to typify the aesthetic and stylistic qualities performed by Black women in the alt scene—the tendency toward irony, absurdity, self-reflexivity, bitter emotional affect, and multivoiced-ness. The content of Zamata's joke was about becoming a well-known comic and how suffocating it is to be expected to be able to "do Black womanhood" on command.

Zamata began the joke speaking directly to the mostly white audience, remarking that many of them might know of her because of her role in the cast of *SNL*, to which there was some applause. She related that a woman came up to her after a show at a comedy club and said, "Aw, I was hoping you'd do some impressions . . . maybe Michelle Obama or Beyoncé." Zamata replied,

> Maybe next time . . . but what I should have said was [*with a mocking, nasally tone*] "Aw, I was hoping you'd do some impressions . . ." [*Laughter.*] That was my impression of *you.* That's what *you* sound like. [*Laughter.*] [*Same mocking tone*] "Aw, I was hoping you'd do some impressions." Tell your friends this is how you sound. [*Laughter.*] [*Even more nasally and shrill*] "Aw, I was hoping you'd do some impressions." [*Mimicking chasing the woman as she walks to her car*] Where are you going, I'm not done yet! [*Laughter.*] "Aw, I was hoping you'd do some impressions!" [*Woman:*] "Get outta my car!" [*Zamata, almost incomprehensibly screeching*] "Aw, I was hoping you'd do some impressions!" [*Laughter and applause.*][46]

Zamata challenged the woman's call to do an impersonation of a universalized idea of Black womanhood embodied in Michelle Obama and Beyoncé, refracting that call back on the white woman who initiated the call itself. Her mockery showcased her expertise at performing impressions, but instead of mimicking an idealized image of Black womanhood, Zamata performed an incisive caricature of the white woman that, in form and content, laid bare the ambivalence and bitterness of what it feels like to be a Black woman comic and continuously expected to embody not oneself but an *idea* of who one has become legible as in American cultural discourse. Zamata does not own the privilege of racial ambiguity enjoyed by Maya Rudolph, and as such Rudolph rarely if ever has to make this joke—she simply performs and is critically acclaimed for her adept cross-racial impersonations. Meanwhile, Zamata's joke delivered the same message. Chasing the white woman with a shrill, nasally impression of her own self, Zamata captured for her audience the effect of being subject to a shallow representational pool—it gets more and more annoying as it is cited and reiterated.

The humor of this bit is borne by the sense of being chased figuratively by the specter of "Black womanhood" and then literally as Zamata's subversive fantasy plays out. Repetition is key when it comes to how the humor functions. Citation and recitation bring out the absurdity inherent in the racial script played out in the joke—and ostensibly, as a fixture of everyday life when Black people interact with people who see Blackness as a monolith that can be turned on and off at will. Instead of performing what is expected of a "sassy Black woman," like Franklin's anti-sass character who got beat up by the ugly "Negro," Zamata remained awkward in the "real" interaction, evidenced in her response to the woman, "Maybe next time." Strikingly, what seems to be a salient trope in both Franklin's and Zamata's comedy is a politics of racial transgression where we see them embracing and skillfully enacting their Black cultural identities while at the same time comically lifting the dusty veil of stereotypes to demonstrate to their audiences that Black people, though perhaps "bound by ties of blood," are often "separated by training and tradition."[47] In sketch and stand-up performed by Black women in alternative venues, enactments of sass such as Franklin's "sassy Black Woman" and Zamata's "impressions" bits use satire as a mechanism to externalize interiority—they render humorous and ridiculous normative ideas of Black womanhood and the Black body. In these scenarios, a comedic aesthetic prevails where the symbolic destruction of those representations and the expectations to meet them are foregrounded in the joke work.

"Be Blacker"

I have argued elsewhere that Black women's postmodern satire is citational and marked by personal experience and emotion, and this is particularly true when contemporary Black women comics like Franklin and Zamata cite and then reject the "sassy Black woman" character. In this dynamic process, the goal is not the repudiation of Black womanhood per se but a will on the part of the comics to enact one's individuality and articulate their interiority without being reduced or pigeonholed into roles that reify Black women as aggressive, overly expressive simpletons whose humor shakes out (pun intended) to mere buffoonery. Nicole Byer is a comic whose cultural production spans multiple media, from a web series with Sasheer Zamata (*Pursuit of Sexiness*) to a scripted comedy on MTV that was canceled after one season (*Loosely Exactly Nicole*), improv appearances at the Upright Citizens Brigade, and many stand-up comedy performances, including a Primetime Emmy Award–nominated Netflix special (*BBW*). Byer is perhaps most well known as the cohost of the Netflix reality baking competition show *Nailed It!*, which was also nominated for a handful of Primetime Emmys, and she is at the time of this book's writing a cohost of the TBS game show *Wipeout*. I will turn to a sketch early in Byer's career, "Be Blacker," that she cowrote with Sasheer Zamata and performed in a UCB comedy skit for YouTube. As will become clear, this sketch exemplifies the process of citation and rejection of the "sassy Black woman" that underscores how Black women in the alternative scene use sass to expose and subvert this popular trope.

Directed by Zamata, the skit begins with a director—a young white woman with thick, red-rimmed glasses and bright pink lipstick, fashionably draped with a scarf—welcoming Byer to an acting audition.[48] A young white man with a Justin Bieber–style swooped haircut is an assistant and acts as Byer's reading partner and foil, and the director instructs Byer to "play everything to him." "LaShwanda, did you get those clams I asked for?" the assistant asks. Byer quickly responds in a style and diction consistent with Standard English, dismissively but pleasantly gesturing with her hand: "Ooh child, I got them clams; I got everything on that list you gave me." This is a mundane scene that does not appear to have or need any reference to Black life or culture, beyond identifying that the actress will be played by a Black woman because of the culturally specific name. Yet it becomes clear that the "sassy Black woman" has become the only legible persona for Black women comics, a veil of stereotypes through which society views and expects Byer to conform, despite her first reading for the part seemingly as her authentic Black self. The director stops Byer in the middle of the read: "Ok great, I love what you're doing. I *love* what you're doing. I have an adjustment if that's OK." Byer nods awkwardly. "How can I say this? Um, I need you to be more urban." Byer chuckles, cocking her head perplexedly. "Um, what?" "This role calls for a really urban, *ethnic* Black person," the director insists. "Can you be that for me?"

The role is predicated on the existence of racial difference, but Byer's version of Black womanhood is insufficiently legible and must be forcibly heightened to play up the supposed fact of that racial difference. Indeed, she is called upon to engage in an act of racial transgression to inhabit the "sassy Black woman," which suffuses every part of her being as she adjusts her performance—in word, gesture, and attitude—which subsumes her personality, reducing it to a completely absurd caricature. The assistant begins again: "LaShwanda, did you get those clams I asked for?" In the second read, Byer's response includes exactly the same words, but she affects a guttural voice quality and sing-song cadence that harks back to Mammy scolding Scarlett for not eating when she's trying to fit into a corset in a famous scene from *Gone with the Wind*. Her neck rolls, and her body shimmies with each syllable.

Byer switches between the "sassy Black woman" representation and her true voice between the reads, inviting the audience to grapple with her ambivalent mood. This is most noticeable in the commentary between scenes. The director stops her once more: "Hey Nicole, I need you to be Blacker. Do you understand what I mean when I say Blacker?" Byer responds with an uncomfortable smile. "No, I'm sorry I don't." In this moment, Byer's authentic voice materializes her interiority, a voice that deviates from normative assumptions of how Black people should (be able to) talk, and in her speaking back to the woman in her own voice, bookended by her readings as the "sassy Black woman," she at once cites and rejects the trope, a humorous reconciliation that lays bare the fallacy of an essentialized, authentic Blackness and the idea that "sassy" is a static racialized gender trait. "Do you know how to be [*snaps finger to the side*] sassy?" the director asks. Byer responds by repeating the snapping gesture, nodding her head to indicate that she is willing to give "sassy" a try.

In the next reading, Byer repeats her response, snapping now with each syllable, dancing with deep, boisterous movements: "Ooooh chile, I *got* them *clams*! I got everything on that *list* you *gave* me!" "Blacker," the director insists, entreating Byer to give her Spike Lee, *In Living Color*, Steve Urkel, and Oprah. In the end, Byer moves back into what seems like her authentic voice and asks the director, "Sooo, did I get the part?" and the director informs her that she is being considered as an option among many but assures Byer that she feels good about her performance. Ultimately, as the sketch closes, we see a blonde white woman in the role of a character now named "LaShanda" on the faux big screen, even though "this role call[ed] for a really urban, ethnic Black person," as the director mentioned after Byer's first read. This skit indicates a capacity on the part of Byer to demonstrate her literacy and mastery of Black pop cultural references and the long tradition of Black comics satirizing the mainstream entertainment industry's treatment of Black cultural material, as well as her ability to transgress racial norms in ways that are equally authentic. This juxtaposition of styles is ultimately a desire for reconciliation of the enduring condition of double-consciousness—a site where we can truly see the false dichotomy of traditional Black comedy and Black alt-comedy.

If we take Amy Becker's assessment of parody as functioning to "offer an interpretation of a text that is really just a likeness of an original form, a copy that is infused with a critical perspective or take on a preexisting genre,"[49] Byer's parody of the "sassy Black woman" is an enactment of sass that flies under the radar, and the reconciliation that Byer engenders has political implications. "The parodic copy," as Robert Hariman argues, "is far removed from the serious discourse by a series of displacements, each of them involving another drop in legitimacy, and yet it also directly points toward the center of its target."[50] The delegitimization of the "sassy Black woman" trope by way of exposing it and rendering it absurd is a means of enacting sass that strikes at the heart of the stereotype.

"I'm Jamaican. But My Name Is Sarah."

In late 2021, riding a fresh meteoric rise from her TikTok lip-synch parodies of Donald Trump, comedian Sarah Cooper embarked on a stand-up tour across the United States. In mid-September, Cooper kicked off the tour at Largo at the Coronet in Los Angeles, a small, well-trod theater that feels like a high school auditorium. There is an old-school comedy vibe there; images of performers like Margaret Cho and Patton Oswalt ring the room, framed in black and white, intimate and cozy. I arrived early, double-masked amid the coronavirus pandemic, and took a seat near the middle of the theater. The red curtains were lit up by stylish sconces and orangish icicle Christmas lights. A familiar stool and microphone sat on the stage, and the mostly white, mostly millennial crowd trickled in to fill the seats at about 80 percent capacity. When Cooper mounted the stage, she let us know that this was the first time she would be doing a full stand-up set.

Circling back to the Donald Trump parodies that were her claim to fame, Cooper seemed ambivalent about her status as a "celebrity," highlighting the way she perceived her humor and its audience. She self-deprecatingly joked about being recognized by young and old people who have seen her viral lip synchs. "I have become that joke at the end of the email [*Laughter.*] . . . That was me now. I didn't wanna be that. I didn't wanna be if dad humor was a person . . . I didn't wanna be that. [*Laughter.*]" Cooper's set dripped with ambivalence and was striking in how a mood of vulnerability hovered. "I'm Jamaican. But my name is Sarah," she began her bit about the nexus of her racial and cultural identities. "So those things cancel each other out. [*Laughter*.]" Cooper moved through a few jokes about wanting but failing to live up to popular assumptions about Jamaican-ness, being "chill" and "irie." Building an atmosphere of intimacy, she went back to her birth to reveal how she came to inhabit this uncertain identity and experience of Blackness:

> When I was three months old, a family friend picked me up and instinctively called me Sarah. And at that moment, I think, the ghost of a white woman jumped into my body [*laughter*] and gentrified my whole personality. [*Laughter*.] ... My mom would cook *amazing* jerk chicken when I was growing up. At least I *think* it was amazing. I couldn't eat it! [*Laughter*.] It was *way* too spicy. [*Laughter*.] My friends would all be like "Oh my god, your mom is an amazing Jamaican cook!" And I'm like, "So I hear! [*Laughter*.] ... I don't know ..." [*Mom, with Jamaican accent*] "Sarah, why you no eating?" And I would take a little bite of the jerk chicken, and I'd be like, "My mouth is on fire!" [*Laughter*.] And she'd be like, "Sarah, you know there are children around the world, all they get for dinner is bread and water." And I'd be like, [*whispering*] "That actually sounds really good. [*Laughter*.] Can I go get a scone and a chai tea latte?" [*Laughter*.][51]

Cooper laid bare her interiority, the way Blackness is both a site of cultural identification that is aspirational and out of reach. Jerk chicken is at once a token of Jamaican pride *and* racialized shame that signifies Coopers inability to fit into proper registers of Blackness. The joke enabled Cooper to delve into and express her interiority in a way that brought her closer to her audience and forced us to grapple with the nature of Blackness in concrete terms. "I think the weirdest part about being Jamaican in America," Cooper continued, "is that ... I *am* Black. But then again, *am I*? [*Laughter, applause*.] I'm Black? No, I'm not Black. I'm *Black*? Question. Question." The audience laughed with her, also feeling the dizzying oscillation between ideas of Blackness and that which was presented to us onstage—a misfit Blackness that sought nonetheless to be recognized and understood.

"I moved here when I was three. I didn't realize I was Black until I was eight." Cooper used time travel to bring the audience on a journey where we got a glimpse of her inner life such that we might recognize and understand her experience of racial ambivalence and the ways it affects how she sees herself now. We might also imagine a future where Blackness is unlimited by the constraints of racial hegemony. "I was walking home from the bus stop with my best friend Stacey. She's Jewish. . . . [*Laughter.*] These white high school students drove by and yelled out the N-word. And I turned to Stacey, and I was like, 'How can they call you that?' [*Long laughter.*]" Cooper emptied the N-word of its power to harm her by the way she turned it on her white friend. "She was like, 'They aren't talking to me!' [*laughter*] and I was like, 'Who were they talking about?' Then I went home to my parents, and I was like, [*crying*] 'Mama, Papa, I think I'm Black.' [*Laughter.*] And they were like, 'No mon, you're Jamaican!' [*Laughter.*]" Cooper's parents wanted distance for their child, not from Blackness but from the racial discourse of Blackness that renders Black people "N-words," proximate to all the horrors that the epithet entails. Cooper humorously leaned into her ambivalence to engage her audience to ponder the questions What is Black, and how do I know? It is these kinds of questions in contemporary Black women's stand-up comedy that give us insight about what Rebecca Wanzo claims is "the comedic potential of abjection [to] escape the shadow of Black humiliation shaped by white supremacy."[52]

Cooper continued her journey through racial ambivalence and anxiety. "I'm Black enough to be called the N-word but I'm not Black enough to say it. [*Laughter.*] I don't wanna say it; when would I say it? While I'm shopping at Ann Taylor's Loft?" Cooper finally offered the audience, and perhaps more importantly herself, some relief. "'Can I get this blouse in a medium, nigga?' [*Raucous laughter.*]" The fact that she named Ann Taylor's Loft as a shopping destination rendered her awkwardly Black, as did her uncomfortable utterance of the N-word. The N-word/"nigga" conundrum reflected Cooper's alienation from mainstream ideas of authentic Blackness and her claim on it, too.

Wanzo was referring to Issa Rae's character J from the web series *Misadventures of Awkward Black Girl* when she unpacked the function of awkwardness, describing it as a quality "grounded in her African American subject position. . . . She is between being unrecognizable to others as Black and being unassimilable as abject. Thus, Black abjection itself becomes a joke in *Awkward Black Girl* and a refusal of the categorizations allotted to Black people in entertainment (and in the world more broadly)."[53] Cooper inhabits a similarly situated subject position of awkwardness as abjection. Her alienation is part of her interiority that she wishes to bring into the world, expressed as her desire to reconcile being a Sarah and a Jamaican. Stand-up is the vehicle to explore and grapple with this interiority and reveal it. To do so publicly requires a specific kind of vulnerability. There is a sense of relief for her, a resolution to her alienated subjectivity, and that resolution is important because it points to the boundaries of sass as a genre of discourse and to how we understand the aesthetic and stylistic elements of contemporary Black women speaking back to power and enacting their humanity—especially how it interacts with tropes of awkwardness.

"Jan, You a Bad Bitch . . . I See You!"

In 2021 Naomi Ekperigin recorded a half-hour stand-up special for the Netflix comedy series *The Standups*. This performance demonstrates the power, reach, and versatility of Black women's sass, especially how its aesthetics shift over time to accommodate the varied experiences of sass's subjects. "This feels right. This feels right for all of us," she greets the audience members, who are clapping enthusiastically. Now a transplant from New York City to Los Angeles, Ekperigin runs through a series of jokes to her NYC audience about not enjoying life in the hot Los Angeles sun. But her visit to Palm Springs was different—this was a place Ekperigin did appreciate, and Palm Springs functions as a subversive site of critique. "I went to Palm Springs . . . I loved it, turns out. And the reason why I love Palm Springs is because when I . . . hmm, how do I put this? When I wanna practice self-care . . . when I want to get away from it all, I like to imagine I'm a protagonist in a Nancy Meyers movie." Palm Springs is "Caucasian decadence," Ekperigin explains.

> First, imagine I'm a WHite WHoman. [*Laughter.*] . . . I'm in my fifties. I'm in my sixties. I'm living *in* the hot flash, okay? [*Laughter.*] I'm in a moment in time. My name is Margot, with a *T*. [*Laughter.*] And I'm wearing taupe. I'm wearing cream. I'm wearing beige . . . eggshell, ecru. [*Laughter.*] And whatever I'm wearing is loose, but also fitted. [*Laughter.*] And at some point in the movie, I will be sitting with my best friend drinking a California WHite wine. And I'll say, "His new wife is *how* old?" And that's every Nancy Meyers movie in a nutshell. [*Laughter and applause.*][54]

Ekperigin imagines herself as this character in a Nancy Meyers film, living this relaxed, luxurious life in a purportedly fictional world. She brings it to the historical present, forcing the fantasy of a Black woman inhabiting it onto her audience in the here and now. Ekperigin continues talking about the time she spent in Palm Springs, telling the story of meeting Susan and Jan, two middle-aged white women who evoked the Nancy Meyers filmic metanarrative. "Jan *lived* in Maui, Hawaii, and was on *vacation* in Palm Springs. . . . At one point we chit-chatting and Jan says to me dead serious, [*with an exaggerated, high-pitched voice*] 'Well, I know people go to *Maui* for a vacation, but sometimes *I* need a *vacation* from Maui!'" Ekperigin is incredulous, throwing her hands up, pacing the stage in disbelief. "Whaaaaat?!? Y'all, that is the Jan-est shit I ever heard. I said 'Jan, you a bad bitch . . . I see you!'" The "Jan-est shit" is a stand-in for unapologetic entitlement to luxury, relaxation, and unproblematic existence encompassed in the whiteness Susan and Jan represent. It is Ekperigin's next line that is the most cutting, revealing the structure of power that is the site of her critique. "I see you, Jan, talking to me like I'm not Black in America."

Rather than sending up the "sassy Black woman," Ekperigin enacts sass in a unique way—a racial critique to be sure—that does not include the gestural repertoire generally associated with its performance. She brings her exclusion to the foreground in an offbeat move. "I'm tryna be a Jan in this life. . . . How do I be the Jan I wanna see in this world?" she asks, the audience's laughter remaining steady. Her purported desire to *be* a "Jan" is actually a send-up of the "Jan-ness" (aloof entitlement) and forces a recognition of Jan as an illegitimate site of power. "Jan is doing it. . . . Jan is out here *thriving,* and I like to sit in the shower. [*Laughter*]."

It is racist and reductive to understand sass as simply the gestures associated with it or as an identity. Ekperigin locates power in whiteness and directly speaks back to it to assert her humanity by way of indexing Jan's ridiculousness—she is thriving—against her own sense of abjection, conveyed as a person who enjoys sitting in the shower. This joke is an enactment of sass that does not rely on stereotype and engages a critique of power (whiteness and the sense of entitlement attached to it). She imagines a world where Black women are entitled to rest, relaxation, and luxury in equal measure to white people. This is the dream space Elizabeth Alexander conjures, "imagining the racial self unfettered, racialized but not delimited. What I am calling dream space is to my mind the great hopeful space of African American creativity."[55] In other words, awkwardness and sass *can* coexist in contexts where Black women endeavor to assert their humanity by speaking truth to power. Even without the gestural references of cut-eye, suck-teeth, neck rolling, and finger snapping that often punctuate enactments of sass, we must locate and understand its efficacy in its historical and cultural context.

The Neoliberal Turn

Airing on the radio station WNYC from April 2016 to November 2018, *2 Dope Queens* (2DQ) had become one of the most popular comedy podcasts, with millions of downloads and a loyal fan base, both virtual and those who regularly attended the show's live recordings at Union Hall in Brooklyn and elsewhere across the nation. Former *Daily Show* correspondent Jessica Williams and staff writer for MTV's *Girl Code* Phoebe Robinson are the hosts, and both got their starts performing in various comedic genres. *2DQ* features a hip, at times cacophonous vibe of conversations about race, sex, pop culture, and politics with a mix of quick-witted banter and guests who perform stand-up comedy. Coming from the Upright Citizens Brigade improv tradition, Robinson and Williams use the podcast medium to push and blur the boundaries of what Black women's comedic performance sounds like, tapping into the podcast as an alternative comedy space for their brand of humor.

The duo have described their vision as having a podcast that showcases and celebrates a diverse array of voices and experiences, especially people of color and LGBTQ+ people. In a *Glamour* magazine interview, Jessica Williams discussed the surprising popularity of *2DQ*, which "just showed there was like a hunger for new stories because we have alternative comics on our show that wouldn't normally be featured on, like, a white guy's comedy show. We like to have a lot of women and women of color. We like to have people of different sexual orientations. I was, for some reason, surprised by that popularity. I don't know why I was. The old stories are boring."[56] *2 Dope Queens*, both the podcast and the comics themselves, demonstrate the eminently political nature of these "new stories" in terms of how Black women's voices (both literally and figuratively) have been (under)represented in popular media. These new stories indicate some of the ways that representations of a Black middle-class sensibility are shifting, and the podcast opens fresh terrain for Black women humorists to explore issues of race and racism, gender politics, and expressions of sexuality and desire. Engaging with *2DQ* enables us to expand the possibilities and track the limitations of sass in the context of millennial humor and new technologies for its dissemination.

Stylistically, *2DQ* has been described as "irreverent, goofy, incisive, and unapologetically Black and female."[57] Yes, Williams and Robinson bring a Black woman comedic perspective, but race, gender, class, and sexuality explicitly give shape to their identities and their brand. In a Vulture article about Black male nerd comics, Robinson discussed some of the stylistic and thematic differences between Black comedy of old and contemporary material. "Back in the day I think there was a lot of 'white people do this and Black people do that' jokes, which has been done to death a million times over.... There's more that we can talk about."[58] The implication here is that Black people can also do the things white people do—and use it for joke fodder, too.

Several Black women comics are featured guests on *2 Dope Queens*, including Naomi Ekperigin, Calise Hawkins, Michelle Buteau, Sam Jay, and Rae Sanni: women who work (although not exclusively) in the alternative comedy scene. Not only do Williams and Robinson engage in cutting-edge comedic production as podcasters, but they have also given a platform to a cohort of other Black women comics who are bringing "alternative" styles and sensibilities to the mainstream. Vince Meserko explores the contours of what he calls the "the UCB [Upright Citizens Brigade] alternative comedy scene," noting the ways new technological mediums like podcasts enable alternative comics, whose material "navigates along the periphery of mainstream sensibilities,"[59] to build broad (and virtual) communities around that style of comedy. We are living in a golden age of comedy and podcasting that is enabling women and "otherwise" people to get their voices out on the airwaves in new and exciting ways. Phoebe Robinson was featured as a guest on the WNYC podcast *Note to Self* in a segment "about how digital media is changing political discourse," which lauded a feminist politics of podcasting, "giving women a special kind of platform in media to express their ideas, their perspectives, and have a place to be unfiltered. To quite literally, be heard. And there is real power in that, particularly for Black women like Phoebe Robinson."[60]

Williams and Robinson come off as trendy and friendly in *2DQ*, telling meandering and entertaining stories about twenty-first-century millennial living. They use Lyft and Uber; they shop at Anthropologie; they drink rosé; and sometimes they refer to themselves as "Khaleesis."[61] They often discuss their privileged upbringings, as in one episode from 2017:

> PR: If you are a Black person, if you grow up in a middle-class or an upper-middle-class situation, you have to learn about white shit. Like, I have to know what a keratin treatment is. We have to know about barre class.
>
> JW: You've gotta get the canon shit for white people.[62]

By way of being featured on WNYC, *2DQ* pitches its humor to "discerning listeners," those who are "educated, affluent, and culturally active."[63] Williams and Robinson are conscious of and celebrate their identities as Black middle-class women, and they appeal to an audience with an appetite for marginal comedy and with relatively progressive politics, but at the same time they reflect a cultural mood and posture that is inoffensive and easily understandable to white people. In today's comedy marketplace, Black women are making use of technologies like the podcast to evoke the currency of Black middle-class status, reflecting the multiplicity of the Black experience.

The queens are up on the latest Coachella performances, shop on Amazon.com, "try to get bottle service at the fucking Tao," make zoodles (zucchini noodles), love the band U2, and talk obsessively about their sexual attraction to Canada's prime minister Justin Trudeau. Robinson and Williams share the experiences of their everyday lives, facilitating a mood of intersubjectivity and intimacy. In the neoliberal gestalt, those experiences and perspectives become cultural currency. The two comics offer material that is deeply imbued with a middle- class orientation—sensibilities and aesthetics that are performatively borne out in the constellation of products, everyday experiences, pop cultural references, and registers of connection by which they communicate with their audience. As George Scialabba puts it, neoliberalism in culture "means untrammeled marketing and the commoditization of everyday life, including the intimate sphere."[64] Lisa B. Thompson examines the shifting representational terrain of post–civil rights Black middle-class women's cultural production, arguing that Black women have rearticulated "the black female subject . . . to consciously expand the possibilities of middle-class black performance and identity . . . beyond the image of the black lady."[65] While Thompson looks at Black women's narratives mostly in autobiography, fiction, drama, and an assortment of pop cultural moments, 2DQ offers insight into how millennial Black women comics like Williams and Robinson use the podcast as a site to expand, if at times problematically, the ways Black womanhood and Black women's humor get articulated and put to work.

On the last episode of season 2, "Who Is Jeff Tweedy?," Williams and Robinson open with a back-and-forth about the anxieties of getting their hair done at photo shoots—how vulnerable it makes them feel to have their bodies subject to people who may not be schooled in the art of doing Black hair. Throughout each season Williams and Robinson use stories about their hair as a synecdoche for their rootedness (no pun intended) in Black culture, talking about styling it and its sometimes "unruly" texture. The experience of having their hair styled by white people is comedic fodder, even though Williams describes her experience at photo shoots as "soul crushing and horrific." The audience laughs at this description—perhaps responding to the tone in which the line is delivered—rather than at its content. To say that a situation has been "soul crushing and horrific" is an expression of emotional vulnerability characteristic of Black women's contemporary comedy. Like in Marina Franklin's material, this vulnerability signals to the audience that the relative privilege indicated by their classed, racially coded touchstones belie the material, historical status as Black women subject to racialized injury. This sense of being "of one" with the audience engenders a kind of racial absolution for both the comics and some people in their audience. Williams and Robinson gain access to whiteness (or, recognition as human beings) by virtue of their literacy in middle-class, millennial whiteness and their sharing of cultural material consistent with it, solidifying the individuality and diversity that makes them appealing to various audiences. Specifically, white audience members get to pat themselves on the back for not being like the fantasies of "bad" white people played out by the comics.

The duo then moves into a conversation about the moment they entered the photo shoot. It was like the AMC drama *Breaking Bad* as the stylists anxiously shuffled around wondering, "What's the formula, how do I get it exact?" Robinson, in characteristic satirical fashion, sends up the idea of wooden, ignorant white folks, after which she relays a story about a positive experience of having her hair styled by a white person, an exemplary moment of potential racial transcendence. "My edges are jacked," she explained, and the stylist "knew what *edges* are!"[66] This interaction is a moment to once again understand a reconciliation of double-consciousness. What is more interesting, though, is how Williams and Robinson give their audience permission to laugh at a *fantasy* of racial transcendence whereby white folks in the audience get to participate in seeing themselves as not of a piece with the ignorant white people trying to figure out how Black bodies work. This banter about white hands in Black hair projects a fantasy of what "bad, racist" white people are—they are willfully ignorant or do not care enough to learn how to interact with Black hair textures and styles.

In blackface minstrelsy performances, there was a projection of fantasies of Blackness for white consumption, and in this bit, we can see a marked projection of fantasies of whiteness for white consumption. The laughter at these kinds of fantasies of whiteness signifies a white disidentification with this type of "bad" (clueless, ignorant, racist) white person. The communal aspect of a "community of laughter" gets hijacked into the individualism that is the salient, meaning-giving feature of neoliberalism. By engaging in this laughter, the audience is "free" to pursue their otherwise remunerative and neoliberal pursuits, exculpated from the worries of being part of the suffocating and inescapable structures of racial domination that constrain and circumscribe certain people's position and opportunities in society. Wendy Brown's thoughts on neoliberalism beautifully sum up the point I am making here: "Neoliberal subjects are controlled *through* their freedom—not simply, as thinkers from the Frankfurt School through Foucault have argued, because freedom within an order of domination can be an instrument of that domination, but because of neoliberalism's *moralization* of the consequences of this freedom."[67]

"This is how the show flows," writes Allison P. Davis, "two friends flipping from the dire (Black Lives Matter) to the ridiculous (the technicalities of FaceTiming your BFF during anal sex) to the sublime (Michael Fassbender). Sometimes they pelvic thrust in unison. Sometimes they get serious. On this occasion, they did all that in the first seven minutes of the show."[68] However, while historical racial injustice is a regular topic on the show, it is often drawn to an ironic distance via jokes that highlight the deeply individualistic, neoliberal orientation that their podcast takes up, where "there is no mention of collective solutions to historic injustices: indeed, the neoliberal feminist subject is divested of any orientation toward the common good."[69] During the opening set of the "Thank You, Harriet Tubman" episode, the pair generate some intrigue. "This show is gonna get political. We're gonna make the case for reparations." Williams goes into a story about using the Internet to find a home organizer to come to her apartment to help declutter her life. "I got a home organizer to come to my place last week," she says. "I'm like a hoarder-lite. . . . So I found these ladies online, and then get this: these two older white ladies showed up to my apartment and they re-did my whole apartment!"

> PR: Yooo, that's *reparations* right there!
>
> JW: I was like, this is what we did it for!
>
> PR: Yaaas!
>
> JW: Thank you Rosa!
>
> PR: Thank you, Harriet!
>
> JW: Thanks Sojourner! . . . This other white lady was like, folding my clothes, like my intimate underwear, she was folding everything. . . . At one point I hit a wall and I was like, "Ugh, I'm tired." And she was like, "Why don't you go sit down and like, order some food for yourself and I'll just take care of this." And I was like, "Wait, really?" She was like, "Yeah, just go ahead." And I was like, "Damn, this is definitely my reparations."[70]

2DQ's humor is imaginative and absurdist, offering a complex set of images and experiences of Black women navigating multiple worlds in the twenty-first century, and the genre of podcasting enables the production and consumption of this brand of comedy. In another episode a white audience member hits on guest Kevin Bacon, an infraction with which Robinson and Williams were none too pleased.

> JW: What did you say? You tryna get in?
> ... 'Cause this is already taken.
>
> PR: So just, fuckin', nope.
>
> JW: Mmm, you respect what we puttin' down up here.
>
> PR: Back off. This is reparations, back off.
>
> JW: We earned this! Rosa Parks did that for this! Harriet Tubman did it so we could do this ignorant shit up here![71]

To be sure, I understand the absurdist impulse in this joke and its intent to refashion reparations in a language palatable to Williams and Robinson's target audience—an outlandish way of indicating their racial and sexual politics in the twenty-first century. Yet, can there be anything less oriented toward the common good of racial justice than a couple of white ladies coming to the houses of Black people, rocking out to Fleetwood Mac while folding up their underwear, or having exclusive sexual access to a white male actor? Racial justice manifests here as the domain of each private individual who is free to choose what justice means and looks like. Political consciousness in 2DQ has a neoliberal echo, often resembling that of the *Fearless Girl* statue on Wall Street, which as Yasmin Nair puts it "is a cynical testament to elite striving and the desire to be recognized symbolically without resisting materially."[72] This recognition, I fear, has the unfortunate potential to usher in a narrow ideal of Black women comics into mainstream culture at the possible expense of marginalizing those Black women comics who are deemed traditional and less "innovative" and whose comedy is less palatable to mainstream audiences. This is the updated version of the "sassy Black woman," repackaged, universalized, and disempowered.

Although the hosts come from Black middle-class backgrounds and the 2DQ podcast appeals to middle- and upper-middle-class audiences,[73] Williams and Robinson, like so-called urban Black comedy acts, often make use of traditional tropes of Black humor, especially when it comes to discussing experiences of anti-Black racism. For example, in an early-nineties routine on HBO's *Def Comedy Jam*, Adele Givens joked about the frustration of shopping while Black—or, being followed around in stores and assumed a thief. "I love to shop," Givens tells her audience, "'cause ladies like to shop, don't we girls? But don't you hate the bitches following you around in the store asking you stupid shit? Trying to keep you from stealing and shit . . ." After taking several items into the fitting room and having the clerk knock and suspiciously ask, "How do those fit?," Givens offers an enactment of sass that both exposes and turns the situation on its head. "Gee, they fit perfect, but my purse won't zip up now, bitch. Do you have a bigger bag I could use?"[74] Givens brazenly exposes not the individual racist actions of the clerk but the anti-Black logic that renders all Black people shopping thieves: "Don't you hate the bitches following you around in the store asking you stupid shit?" Givens's sass in this stand-up bit goes to the extreme for a symbolic, ephemeral win.

On a 2DQ episode titled "Get Outta My Window Seat," Jessica Williams recounts a story about buying a first-class Amtrak ticket and having a white ticket-taker question whether or not she was in the correct place.

> PR: Like, "Are you sure? This is for you?"
>
> JW: And I was like, "Yes bitch, this is Amtrak!"
> Fucking, the only difference here is I'm gonna get
> like, two bags of peanuts instead of one![75]

Although Givens may be considered an urban act and 2DQ is more in line with the alt scene, both routines have the same premise, which is that no matter the economic class, Black access is always restricted, questioned, and heavily policed. However, Givens's joke has a subversive, satirical edge. On 2DQ, there is a tone of "all we wanted to do was get on the train, leave us alone," whereas Givens simply abandons the system wholesale and makes a mockery of it.

Givens and the hosts of 2DQ are essentially interested in lodging the same critique of power, and the "bitch" in both jokes is anti-Blackness that polices and surveilles each of them at every turn. Indeed, the Black comics share experiences of racism across generations and genre, each needing to respond to it to assert their humanity. Yet, the expressions of sass, which I believe is articulated in both jokes, shifts aesthetically as it moves across genres. In Givens's stand-up routine, sass is embedded in the tone. In the podcast, sass is discernible in the narrative. The "bitch" in each joke is the target of sass, and in each case the comics express the anxiety of being subject to it, which illuminates their oppositional stances toward that "bitch." We can see how Black women comics, working across generic media, are demonstrating what happens "in the psychic-physical space of self-regard and that of social context," and what happens many times is a multiplicity of expressions of sass.[76]

Rather than buying into (figuratively and literally) trendy labels that do little more than imbue Black cultural products and their potential consumers with neoliberal illusions of "choice" and "diversity," we would do better to critically discuss how ideas about "creativity" and "innovation" can reify and perpetuate notions of good (intelligent, cultured, transgressive) Black comics versus bad (ignorant, one-dimensional, vulgar) Black comics. Perhaps we should expand the boundaries of the Black comic tradition instead of fragmenting it (and its subjects) into marketable, neatly circumscribed categories.

The 2 *Dope Queens* podcast has been praised as a necessary intervention in the pop cultural landscape, helping to break down the representations that have so often pigeonholed and marginalized Black women. Phoebe Robinson and Jessica Williams are rightfully lauded for their complex portrayal of Black women and Black life and for opening the door for other entertainers to follow suit. Indeed, 2DQ has been labeled a feminist podcast,[77] and both Williams and Robinson have embraced the feminist tag, especially the ways in which the podcast medium enables a particular kind of feminist ethic to flourish. "I'm just really jazzed about the future," Robinson said in 2016 interview for the website The Ringer. "I really am just, like, focusing on it just being equal. I'm not necessarily thinking about, like, 'Oh, we got to get rid of the guys.' It's more like, 'Oh, we got to bring more women to the forefront and more people of color to the forefront.'"[78] Robinson's statement lays bare an important paradox of the proliferation of Black women's alt-comedy in that it (un)wittingly embraces a neoliberal (feminist) orientation that, as Catherine Rottenberg argues, "is predominantly concerned with instating a feminist subject who epitomizes 'self-responsibility,' and who no longer demands anything from the state or the government, or even from men as a group; there is no longer any attempt to confront the tension between liberal individualism, equality, and those social pressures that potentially obstruct the realization of 'true' equality."[79] If podcasts like 2DQ signify a broader set of representations of diverse and distinct narratives of Black womanhood and are meant to give audiences more "freedom" and "choice" in their consumption of images of Black life and culture, why does it seem like Black womanhood is narrowly confined to a version of the fly, quirky, confident middle-class Black woman? The answer is likely that the "awkward Black girl" on Issa Rae's original web series was a springboard for successfully ascending to the mainstream throne of 2 *Dope Queens*.

The logic of the entertainment industry has enabled Black women's comedy to come to the mainstream in new ways. Black women's sass in neoliberal times is complex. The 2DQ podcast is a site where we can grasp how Black women's humor is reaching new audiences, yet the podcast and its hosts at times (re)produce neoliberal rhetorics that construct "a feminist subject who is not only individualized but entrepreneurial in the sense that she is oriented towards optimizing her resources through incessant calculation, personal initiative and innovation,"[80] which is problematic. Their audience is fluent in the constellation of signifiers that construct a deeply classed notion of being politically conscious while at the same time "living your best life."

The cultural, aesthetic, and stylistic terrain of contemporary Black women's comedy highlights anxiety, vulnerability, and a propensity for speaking in multiple voices. The women of this chapter share their desire to reveal their interiority through comedy, and their techniques range from intimate public disclosures to repudiating the "sassy Black woman" stereotype. The comics bring us on an affective journey from behind the "realimentary" camera through the soundscape of the podcast to the stage, foregrounding feelings of ambivalence, pleasure, relief, anxiety, and freedom. Imagination, vulnerability, and Black interiority factor into their performances, and many contemporary Black women comics are cultural articulators who use their craft to skillfully navigate between multiple worlds.

CHAPTER 5

IRREVERENCE RULES

SASS AND DIASPORA CULTURE

> Black is the manifestation of Africanist aesthetics....
> This Black is action, action engaged to enlarge capacity,
> confirm presence, to dare.
>
> —THOMAS DEFRANTZ

"I'm a proper Zulu girl," Celeste Ntuli explains, surveying her audience at the iconic Laugh Factory comedy club in Los Angeles in 2017. Ntuli wears her hair in a close-cropped blonde style similar to that of American comic Luenell, affecting a likewise gruff yet jovial attitude toward her audience. In the video of the performance she is wearing a dress that has a bright pattern on the top and is formfitting black at the bottom, with gold tie-up sandals that set off her golden hair. "Maybe you can tell by my accent," she continues, speaking quickly. "I don't do that '*What's up*,'" slightly bending her knees and flexing in a gesture mimicking American hip-hop. "No, I'm influenced by you guys, but I don't understand some of the shit that you do." Ntuli has the audience with her, judging by their robust laughter. "I'm Zulu and I must be African and Western every time. Whatever I'm doing. Even sexually. You must be *African* sexy and *Western* sexy. You know how fucking difficult that shit is? It's like, play *50 Shades* and slaughter a cow. You can't do both!"[1] The audience laughs at Ntuli's evocation of her ambivalence as a Black South African woman on the American stand-up stage. This performance represents the jagged pieces of the puzzle of what can be called the "Black experience" from the African perspective, an attempt to reconcile the experiences of a diverse cartography mapped onto a single Black body.

The tension between Ntuli's African and Western selves demonstrates the uneasiness with which Blackness acquires meaning within different locations, shaped by historical, temporal, and spatial contexts. Ntuli's joke is the mediating process by which Blackness, or what Amanda Kemp names the "slippery coast of Blackness that is and at the same time ain't,"[2] is produced. Ntuli's performance at the Laugh Factory suggests we read contemporary Black women's humor as an ongoing, historically situated genre of transformation in which the Black body cannot be finally constituted, ever in a state of becoming. It calls up questions about how Black women's stand-up comedy generates new approaches to diasporic flows of Black cultural material and about the ways Black women's humor is a component of diaspora culture that enables critique, empowerment, and the assertion of humanity. The comedic techniques and practices of Black women stand-ups in and from South Africa take up the concrete ways that Black people all over the world use performances, within theatrical or everyday practices, to critique, shape, and transform their worlds.

Stand-up comedy is an expression of diaspora culture, and global Black humor manifests transnational intimacies and affective affinities via the circulation of Black women's comic culture. I am concerned in this chapter with how Black stand-up comics outside of the United States make use of Black American women's cultural material (the language and practice of "twerking" and the unabashed use of vulgarity, for example) and enact the discourse of sass but remix those materials, cultural touchstones, and discourses to operate within their specific performative contexts. Pnina Werbner and Mattia Fumanti argue that "the transnational appropriation of aesthetic literary and embodied performative traditions, objects, sartorial styles or foods in the Diaspora points to the transformational power of mimesis: what appears on the surface to be derivative and imitative, taken from elsewhere, engenders authentically felt cultural competences and a sense of ontological presence."[3] I take up Werbner and Fumanti's articulation of aesthetics as "'sensuous participation'—the making of beauty, distinction and sensual pleasure as participatory performance, embedded and re-embedded in social worlds of literary art or celebration forged in Diaspora."[4] Black women's stand-up comedy enables us to orient our understanding of the inextricable link between aesthetic choices and diaspora as the locus of the production of Blackness and as a sensibility rooted in the struggles against colonialism, patriarchy, and anti-Black racism. Aided by close readings of live and recorded performances, I demonstrate how Black South African women stand-ups' styles and approaches manifest a global Black women's comic culture for audiences on the continent and in the diaspora.

Translation and Diaspora Culture

The language barrier in humor is a tough one to get over. I was in my twenties when I began studying the isiZulu language and traveled to live in South Africa. I will never be able to fully grasp the humor of any group of South Africans, Black or otherwise, regardless of my language proficiency or historical affinity as a Black person born in the crucible of anti-Black, capitalist, patriarchal oppression—features of contemporary Black life all over the world. Indeed, after attending live stand-up comedy performances in South Africa, one aptly named "99% Zulu Comedy," I understood that I could not have done this ethnographic fieldwork without the generous services of two native isiZulu speakers who translated and transcribed the recorded live comedy. Still, some components of the jokes, even translated into English, were difficult to understand contextually. For example, some Zulu words are translated and transcribed in ways that seem like obscenities in the context of US culture and custom but may not be taken in the register of curse words to native Zulu speakers. Many idiomatic phrases were incomprehensible to me before translation, and their register and resonance in terms of humor is difficult for a nonnative speaker to apprehend.

Keeping the limitations of translation in mind, I draw on scholars of diaspora who see Black culture as "profound process[es] of cultural formation, inflows, and outflows."[5] E. Patrick Johnson further defines Black culture as the mutual processes of constructing/deconstructing, avowing/disavowing, and expanding/delimiting in the production of Blackness.[6] Africa and the African diaspora are central to these processes of Black cultural production; as Catherine M. Cole notes, "Africa looms large."[7] Investigating Black South African women's comedic aesthetics enables us to see how Black women cultural producers are central to the idea of diaspora as "Black folk-geist," as "Harry J. Elam Jr. and Kennell A. Jackson put it. Each time the comics "cite this Black essence, the audience gets excited. It is like talking about a very public secret."[8] The travel of Black cultural material in the process of diaspora foregrounds movement, revision, and rearticulation within diaspora culture. To be sure, the appeal of Black American performance culture was entrenched in the making of urban South African culture during the twentieth century not only because of the "similarities in song structure," as David Coplan points out, but also because of the "comparable experience of the two peoples under white domination."[9] When analyzing humor cross-culturally, however, there is a lot lost in translation, yet there is much to be understood about the making of diaspora humor—one must first have even a vague understanding of the languages, the cultural touchstones, the salient political and social realities of gender and race relations, and, importantly, the way humorous affect is conveyed by way of performance.

From the 1960s through the formal end of apartheid in 1994, the expression of humor in the public sphere in South Africa existed on a very limited plane and, like all other aspects of sociocultural and political life, was heavily regulated by the state apparatus. According to Jennalee Donian, comedy existed in the apartheid state as a strategic tool to indoctrinate and challenge normative values that upheld the ideology of the state, whether the comedy was performed on film, on television, in the theater, or in the nascent forms of stand-up comedy that existed in that era. Comedy functioned in this period with three overlapping yet distinctive purposes: as a disciplinary tool, as a means to register grievance against state ideology, and as an instrument of radical politics.[10] The expression of humor in any genre was risky under the repressive regime, as Donian argues, and "the Publications and Entertainments Act of 1963, and later the Publications Act of 1974, resulted in the censoring and banning of films, television shows, plays, records, books, live performances and art work considered to be obscene, blasphemous, harmful to social relations, or derogatory towards Afrikaners or the State," and "humour primarily served as a propaganda machine—for both indoctrination and escapist pacification."[11] Political theater, though vastly underfunded compared with the theater of other racial groups, seemed to offer Black South Africans the widest avenue for social protest during the 1980s, and satirical humor functioned publicly as a means to challenge the racial exploitation and violence of the apartheid state.[12] Stand-up comedy is an American performance genre, and only a handful of white men enjoyed success in South Africa because of the limited framework for that type of public engagement with the kinds of subversion that usually accompany the practice. Before the twenty-first century, there were no professional Black women stand-ups in South Africa, though it is safe to say that many manifestations of Black women's humor were expressed in private settings.

The study of stand-up comedy in South Africa after 1994, when the policies of apartheid came to an end (constitutionally, if not materially), sheds light on the shifts in attitudes and consciousness, on new pathways to political expression, and on how cultural and social issues affect Black South African people. Robin K. Crigler argues that "humour as social commentary has deep roots in precolonial indigenous cultures as well as in apartheid-era township music and theatre."[13] Furthermore, "the landscape of humour in South Africa is rich and multifaceted, and as a young democracy still struggling in many ways with the dark legacy of apartheid, humour and politics are closely linked."[14] Yet, there is a distinct lack of critical attention to the history of South African humor, a gap Crigler intended to fill by looking at how white South African men's voices in stand-up have been historically amplified, given the fact that "for most of the country's history, white men have been at the forefront of crafting 'official culture' in South Africa, determining and policing the thresholds of what is funny and what is not, what can be subverted and what must remain stable."[15] The task of amassing a comprehensive history of South African humor is difficult, not least because of the eleven official languages recognized by the state and the nexus of indigenous comic sensibilities overlaid and deeply entwined with the brutal history of apartheid that shapes what is and is not funny to the diverse array of South African peoples.

In 2017 Celeste Ntuli, billed as the "Queen of Zulu Comedy," performed a set at an event to celebrate Black women's empowerment and International Women's Day, "Birthing Our Feminine Divine," where she discussed issues that get at the heart of being a Black woman in South Africa. In the recorded video of the performance, Ntuli's audience appears to be mostly Black women, many dressed in traditional indigenous attire. She tells a joke about the irony and unfairness associated with *lobola*, the dowry practice of traditional Zulu marriages where the male relatives on the bride's side of the family along with the groom negotiate a bride price:

> The *lobola* situation, me, I have a problem with that one. *Hhayibo* [no], you have a bunch of men deciding on your mileage. [*Laughter.*] You are not there to defend your situation. I think it's an unfair situation, 'cause we are judged. As women we are unfairly judged. You have a baby, no one is celebrating . . . so now you feel like *eish*, that means

your *lobola* goes down. Because you have a baby, you are like a car that was bought last year. You depreciate in value. [*Laughter.*] Which I feel it's very insane. 'Cause I think everyone knows, when you have a job, and you are looking for a job, experience counts! [*Laughter, cheering, hand waving.*][16]

Having lived in South Africa for several short periods and studied the isiZulu language in culture both in US and South African universities, I have the specific cultural knowledge to find this joke funny. It also helps that Ntuli performed most of this bit in English. Ntuli continued, "When you are a Black woman you are the bottom of the bottom. And when you are a Black, dark woman, *Jesus*! Can they just *kill* you already?! [*Laughter.*]" Ntuli locates herself as what Lawrence Mintz has called the negative exemplar, she who enacts certain traits to be "ridiculed, laughed at, repudiated and punished."[17] This marginal position, the Black woman at the bottom, is shared with Black women across the African diaspora, in terms of the overall social, political, and economic rung on which they are located on the global scale. Ntuli's joke unleashed the work of diaspora, where her humor that speaks back to the discursive and material practices that force Black women to "the bottom of the bottom" enables me to feel a sense of solidarity without repressing difference, an appreciation of a fragmented sense of particularity bound together by "alliances of anger."[18] While scholars agree that "there is no monolithic African feminism . . . African women's lives throughout Africa and the Diaspora have been linked through their commonalities of struggle, resistance and social transformation in relation to multiple oppressions—whether called 'feminist' or not."[19] The point here about translation is that Ntuli's humor of marginality as a Black woman in South Africa, articulated in English, is easy for me to translate to my own sense of humor and experience as a Black American woman.

The way Ntuli conveys her position as a Black woman at "the bottom of the bottom" enabled an intersubjective mood as I watched the stand-up set— the "we" of the community of laughter is at the heart of how humor works. Ntuli locates racist patriarchal power in this bit and the ways Black women, especially dark Black women, become subject to it. As she performs before a large group of Black women, speaking back to those structures of power that marginalize and (de)value, she subtly enacts her humanity with the sardonic punch line, "Can they just *kill* you already?!" Ntuli's bit is an enactment of the discourse of sass, where we see it move from her own claim on her humanity as the speaker, to the audience of Black women who laugh and cheer, perhaps recognizing their similar position and lodging their own critique in agreement, marked by their affirmative laughter. In other words, the medium of stand-up comedy opened this pathway of public critique and subversive agency, and it is important to remember the centrality of affective connection and cultural mobility that make up the engine of diaspora culture.

Black performance has always provided a space for resistance in Black communities, E. Patrick Johnson argues, and "Black performance has the potential of simultaneously forestalling and enabling social change."[20] The idea of Blackness as performance can help us think critically about how humor and comedy function in societies with deep histories of anti-Black racial oppression—wittingly or unwittingly, through gestures, movements, and play—in ways that stage "the collision of cultures and histories that constitute [Black women's] very conditions of existence."[21] Paul Gilroy explores Black performance practices as sites in which diasporic peoples learned tactics for survival and liberation, offering a metatheory of the function of Black expressive culture. The expressive arts during chattel slavery can be seen as cultural performances that had a threefold character for the enslaved: reconciling people to their conditions, offering them a way to partially compensate for it, and providing them refuge from the worst of its effects. "Apart from enacting their servitude and inferiority while guarding their autonomy," Gilroy explained, "people found significant everyday triumphs by mimicking and mastering their rulers, conquerors, masters, and mistresses."[22] Humor was one of those triumphs, and even though there is no direct comparison between Black people in the United States who experienced chattel slavery and its afterlives, and Black people in South Africa who endured centuries of anti-Black oppression enlivened by the ideology and policies of apartheid, there is something to say about the way humor has been fundamental to constructions of Blackness, especially in the late twentieth and early twenty-first centuries. Black comedic performance can be appreciated and understood in both contexts as a highly effective cultural production and mechanism for social and political critique.

Stand-Up in Context

Stand-up comedy has been a staple of the entertainment industry in South Africa in the decades since apartheid, flourishing in cities big and small, with comedy festivals cropping up at all times of the year, international exposure and success by many comics, and world-class comedy venues in Johannesburg and Cape Town. In 2018, a South African corporation teamed up with the

Just for Laughs brand, which hosts the largest comedy festival in the world each year in Montreal, Canada, to birth Just for Laughs Africa, the producers promising to "deliver a continent-wide mix of local comedy development, international comedy superstars and unprecedented opportunities for continental comedians to gain international exposure."[23] South Africans have put together their own comedy festivals, such as the Johannesburg International Comedy Festival and the Cape Town International Comedy Festival, to name only the most mainstream and largest.

Julia Katherine Seirlis discusses the connection between humor and democracy in postapartheid South Africa and the function of the sprawling stand-up comedy scene in the relatively new democracy. "The reasons for this recent boom are manifold," Seirlis explains. "Primary among them are the demise of the apartheid State, the end of its brutality, surveillance and censorship, and the emergence of a free and democratic South Africa."[24] Stand-up comedy functions in three interlocking ways to engender democratic freedom in the postapartheid state, Seirlis argues. First, stand-up is a cultural indicator, "providing a very fast compressed physical and symbolic topography . . . charting processes of exclusion and inclusion, of marginalization and indeed relegation."[25] Stand-up also functions to draw boundaries in terms of "who can enjoy the freedoms of the 'New' South Africa," especially when it comes to who has access to the stage and the seats in the audience, "point[ing] to the marking out of new social fractures, of new boundaries based, since 1994, more on class than race," Seirlis contends.[26] In the new democracy, stand-up comedy is an ordering mechanism by which various social, cultural, and economic identities cohere, express certain values, and reflect the ways various imagined communities define themselves within (and beyond) the postapartheid state. Lastly, stand-up is a licensed relationship, "a relationship based on 'permitted disrespect.'"[27] Taking Seirlis's classification of stand-up's function in postapartheid South Africa seriously, I want to push her analysis to think about how Black women have engendered new ways of interpreting and enacting freedom in the postapartheid state, especially about the insight their comedy gives into the cultural boundaries wrought by new arrangements since 1994, what is permissible to say, and what norms can be challenged on the public stage.

Alongside the mainstream acts, a rich culture of what South Africans call "vernac" comedy has emerged, which is performed in the indigenous languages of the country. Vernac comedy thrives on cultural intimacy between performer and audience. The documentary *In Stitches* has been in production for several years about the vernac comedy scene, and filmmakers Hannah

Rafkin and Meg Robbins show in the film how "vernac reclaims the pride of these mother-tongues through stories and jokes that audiences find relatable."²⁸ The majority of Black women comics in South Africa, most importantly Celeste Ntuli and Tumi Morake, have performed vernac comedy, even if they have crossed over into mainstream venues and audiences. Black stand-up comedy is a relatively new professional genre in South Africa, only going back to the early aughts. Given the history of racial segregation in the country, it is not surprising that Black South Africans developed their own styles and approaches to comedy, audiences to consume it, and venues in which it could be performed.

The biggest comedy brand in South Africa, Blacks Only Comedy was created by comic David Kau as a single night of comedy to showcase South Africa's most marginalized voices. Each year since 2004, Blacks Only has expanded, turning into one of the most anticipated comedy shows across the nation, with more than sixty shows happening at various stadium-sized venues. In 2004, the first poster for the event featured a stylized, generic Black man reading "Blacks Only," harking back to the era of apartheid when public and private spaces were segregated by race. Recognizing the sign in a news special on the tenth anniversary of the first Blacks Only show, Kau said the signs had been designed "to rip off all those apartheid rules and signs."²⁹ In fact, it was an advertisement on a telephone pole for a Blacks Only show in Durban in 2013 that I first learned of the iconic show and had the chance to attend for the first time at a large venue in the city's central business district. When a reporter asked two comics what they saw as the future of South African comedy in 2014, Thapelo "Shampoo" Seemise offered, "The future of comedy lies with us. We have the upper hand now that we can speak our home languages and English at the same time. So, we can, like, get the white people, Black people, and colored people to come and listen to us, where we can swap languages. We are the future."³⁰ Comedians who perform at Blacks Only receive massive exposure, filling arenas with thousands of seats and playing multiple-night engagements.

Each of the comics under study here have performed on the Blacks Only tour and are an integral part of the stand-up scene in South Africa. They stand on the shoulders of other Black South African women performers who have used the public sphere as a site where norms are transgressed, voices formerly silent can be heard, and political and social critiques can be lodged. In an introductory article of a special issue of *Agenda*, Pumla Dineo Gqola theorizes postcolonial feminism and the heterogeneous way African women articulate feminist politics, locating African women within a category called

"Blackwomen" who, across the continent and diaspora, have developed "an ability to carry mountains on [their] backs."[31] Gqola titled her essay "*Ufanele uqavile*," an isiXhosa phrase that, if directed at a woman, means "she speaks her mind, and is associated with socially transgressive behavior, perceived as good or bad depending on the audience."[32] Blackwomen, according to Gqola, have manifested a robust tradition of transgressive practices in creative media that are understood as outside the bounds of theory and politics typically associated with feminist agendas. Like being declared "sassy," to be hailed "Ufanele uqavile" may be perceived negatively or positively depending on the context, and similarly, one is regarded as such for carrying out a transgression of language and discourse that enables critique and is firstly about the assertion of one's humanity—the idea that one has regarded oneself as worthy of speaking back, even and especially in conditions of racialized gender disempowerment.

AboMshoza, for example, were Black women who participated in the *mapantsula*, a glamorous but gangster lifestyle in South African townships in the 1980s. AboMshoza were well known for their flashy dress, swagger, and particular style of dance.[33] "AboMshoza, the female mapantsula, were transgressive women," Gqola says, "dangerous women who questioned prescriptions on female behaviour in South African townships. They refused to be victims and were considered bad girls. They prioritised their own needs and pushed the boundaries of what it meant to be a Blackwoman in those days."[34] It is crucial to analyze the implications for this "something new" of Black women in comedy, which is heavily branded, marketed, and occupying a space in the global neoliberal economic climate, in the not-so-new environment of Black cultural traffic. It is also important to think through the ways contemporary Black women on the stand-up stage in South Africa have attempted to recover and redress the Black female body through various comedic strategies.

The Comics

Black women in comedy are relatively few in the booming South African scene, but they do exist and are thriving in the industry.[35] I have selected Khanyisa Bunu, Tumi Morake, Lihle Msimang, and Celeste Ntuli as exemplars of Black South African stand-up given their popularity, their professional success, and the fact that they all use some English in their material, which gives me a particular, if incomplete, ability to analyze their comedic techniques, aesthetics, and social efficacy. All are Black, and each is from one of the major geographical regions in the country: Khanyisa Bunu is from the Eastern Cape, Tumi Morake is from the Free State, Lihle Msimang hails from the township of Soweto, and Celeste Ntuli grew up in a township outside of Durban in KwaZulu-Natal. Each comic is professionally successful, and I would add that Morake, Ntuli, and Bunu can be said to be "celebrities," given their wide exposure on popular cable television shows and soapies. To be sure, each comic has moved through the ranks of the stand-up industry, from open mics to what is considered the top of the stand-up hierarchy in South Africa—headlining a one-person show tour.

Bunu was the first woman to win the Savanna Comics Choice Award in 2015 and earned a starring role in the soap opera *Ses'Top La*. Tumi Morake, billed as South Africa's "First Lady of Comedy," has been a comic and actress since 2005 after studying theater and drama at Wits University and was the first South African woman with a Netflix comedy special. Morake has been credited with many television roles and radio spots, as has Celeste Ntuli, who has been performing stand-up and acting in television roles since the mid-aughts. Ntuli has been dubbed the "Queen of Zulu Comedy" and is the first South African woman to record a one-woman show, *Seriously Celeste*. Ntuli is widely known in South Africa not only because of her comedy but also due to her role on the popular soap opera *Isibaya*. In 2022, Ntuli was featured on an episode of the Netflix series *Only Jokes Allowed*, where she performs a fifteen-minute set. Lihle Msimang won the 2011 Nando's Comedy Showdown, and like Khanyisa Bunu, she performs a "clean" act, without the aid of much blue material or profanity.

I have seen Tumi Morake and Celeste Ntuli perform live in multiple venues, both in arena-style venues in Durban and Johannesburg and in a nightclub in the affluent Sandton neighborhood in Johannesburg. My personal audio records of these live performances, along with the video-recorded performances available online, have enabled me to access verbatim transcripts (and translations where possible), and popular primary sources allow me to contextualize those performances with interviews about their lives, on the stage and off. Each comic performs in her own distinctive voice. Khanyisa Bunu inhabits the role of social critic. Lihle Msimang is a joke-heavy comic who embodies a style of humor that I have previously theorized in terms of Black American women who straddle multiple social locations and embrace "Black girl awkwardness."[36] Tumi Morake affects the no-nonsense domestic figure who is unafraid to talk about the ups and downs of family life—or critique social and cultural norms. Celeste Ntuli is a brash, engaging storyteller with blue material streaked all through her comedy.

Each of the comics makes use of her marginality in a society beset by vast inequities. In terms of health outcomes, poverty, and general social status, Black women, Celeste Ntuli pointed out, occupy a position at "the bottom of the bottom." Most of the comics embrace this role and the way it enables them to speak and be heard. Khanyisa Bunu believes that being a woman in stand-up is a marginal position that enables her to stand out and be seen in the race for time onstage and exposure. "For me, it works, because there are so many comedians and it's so hard to stand out," Bunu remarked. "But if you are a woman you've got the first advantage because there's few of us. So, people can always remember, 'That female comedian—yeah, she was good.'"[37] Celeste Ntuli remarked in a radio interview, "I feel like it's our time. There's no debate. Women have to give their input in a man's world. I feel like for women who want to do comedy, it's such a freeing space because we have a lot to say. We have stories to tell. No one has had it as bad as us."[38] Having stories to tell from the bottom of the bottom and being in conditions of perpetual constraint are affective and material strands that link Black women on the continent and in the diaspora, "connecting a range of texts that do not share national or cultural affiliations but do share motifs and strategies,"[39] namely the discourse of sass. Tumi Morake holds a different view of herself as a woman in stand-up comedy, commenting, "My biggest aspiration in comedy was to be seen as a comic, a kick-ass one, without the prefix of 'female.'"[40] Even still, in her stand-up she recognizes her unique position of being a Black woman in South Africa and how it contributes to conversations about conditions of post-coloniality and womanhood in ways that capitalize on her status.

As marginal comics within a sprawling global industry, Bunu, Msimang, Morake, and Ntuli use stand-up to call out certain cultural values that consign Black people, and more specifically Black women, to the margins by mocking and ridiculing those values. Social and cultural critique are performed in a stance where irreverence rules; as Khanyisa Bunu described her style, "Few, if any, subjects [are] taboo."[41] When irreverence rules, humor enables the four women to share their experiences with audiences in ways that subvert dominant discourses of Black womanhood. It becomes a site of celebration, in all its various incarnations. Moreover, Black women's stand-up in South Africa is in "sensuous proximity" to and in tension with Black American women's comic culture, enabling performers to express critique and assert humanity in new and exciting ways.

Taking Up Space

A general overview of the comedic material of the four comics reveals two interrelated themes central to Black women's comedy: presence and embodiment. Drawing on their experiences, each comic draws intersubjective connection between herself and audience members through codes of cultural familiarity and the celebration of Black female embodiment. "It took us years to get a proper platform," Ntuli explained on a segment of the show *Trippin' with Skhumba*, profiling her in her hometown of Empangeni. "We listen to people who do not live the culture, who do not understand the culture, who are not the culture, to dictate how we should share the culture. And now, it's a beautiful thing that most vernac comedians are given a platform."[42] Ntuli also remarked on the rise of comedy performed in indigenous South African languages, the genre of stand-up for which she is most well-known.

I first saw Ntuli perform live in Durban, South Africa, in July 2014 at the 99% Zulu Comedy show, where she shared the stage with several vernac comics, including Tumi Morake. True to its name, comics performed almost exclusively in isiZulu. The crowd was in stitches the entire night, and I barely grasped the content of a few jokes based on my seemingly elementary understanding of the language. The use of indigenous languages in stand-up is a powerful tool for comics, producing an intimate community of laughter based on a shared understanding of the cultural and linguistic particularity communicated in and through it. As Khanyisa Bunu put it, "There are some things that are funny only if you say them in Xhosa; no matter how you try to say them in English they won't be as funny as to say them in Xhosa because they have that Xhosa background."[43]

The nightclub Taboo is in the upscale Sandton neighborhood of Johannesburg. The VIP section was cordoned off with the classic velvet rope and contained about six tables; patrons could order bottle service (which came in buckets with a sparkler, delivered by a barmaid). The venue was a typical South African nightclub but with very expensive drinks. The room was dimly lit, the walls either painted black or made of a cork-like material; about fifteen disco balls hung in the main performance space. I attended the event with another person who happened to be the only white person in the place, and we took our seats in the next to last row on the end. The people came in—mostly young, between twenty and thirty-five, and dressed to impress—and began filling in the roughly 200 seats. By the time the show started, the place was packed, except for the first two rows. The host of the show, Sifiso Nene, welcomed the crowd, warming us up with several jokes, including about the "white girl" he had seen sitting in the crowd, a recurring theme throughout the show.

Celeste Ntuli headlined the show. She danced her way onstage, gripping the microphone and greeting the audience, "Hello!" She wore a camouflage-patterned dress with tights underneath and Chuck Taylor sneakers. Here hair was characteristically cropped close and dyed blonde, and she wore bright red lipstick. She had the crowd bent over laughing from the second she stepped on the stage, big belly laughter. People fell out of their seats laughing. People jumped up at certain points, encouraging Ntuli to keep bringing it. Her voice was gruff and confident. She spoke mostly in isiZulu, but she had a lot of English interspersed, which made it easier to follow along.

In one bit, Ntuli talked about a trip she made to Mozambique with her sister and the anxiety and fear of being stopped by the police. Ntuli led the crowd through the story of avoiding a ticket, and her use of vernacular was a crucial device to convey the message that this story was indeed based on her own experiences. The officer came up to the window to address Ntuli and a friend with her, who had been drinking. Ntuli relayed how the scene played out. "'Cause this nigga didn't see," she began, making use of the Black American vernacular term "nigga" to convey a relaxed, Black attitude. "*Akang'zwanga, aka khulumisanga nam* [he didn't even see me, didn't even speak to me], didn't speak a word. He was just looking at my legs, my friend's legs I'm like *hhaa. Waqala wakhulum' izinto ezi nasty 'yazi mangase lemilenze yakho angazi ngingay'faka imayonnaise' uyawaz' amadoda athembisa into angazazi.* [He then started talking about nasty things like 'You know if I could spread mayonnaise all over those legs of yours . . . ,' you know men when they start talking crazy making ridiculous promises.] [*Audience laughter.*]"

People were not just laughing during this joke but *dying* laughing and cheering her on to continue. More than simply being entertaining, it seemed like Ntuli's use of the isiZulu language interspersed with English conveyed a sense of authenticity and presence, and people hung on her every word with the stories she created onstage. Ntuli said that what she loves most about stand-up comedy is her ability to share her voice, that she "can be heard as a person within comedy."[44] Speaking in one's mother tongue onstage, even if interspersed with English or other colonial languages, is a way for performers to offer a corrective to the racial and cultural order that for so long denied the validity, beauty, and oftentimes even the use of indigenous languages in the public sphere. Ntuli's stage persona is thoroughly Zulu, and her language and the cultural references put a fine point on her Zuluness. However, she is also thoroughly outside of the norms of traditional Zulu culture, a culture that says a woman is diminutive, voiceless publicly, and fundamentally under the control, in one way or another, of a man. Ntuli's use of the isiZulu language and cultural touchstones is an act of speaking back to the dominating forces of white supremacy in South Africa. Her use of language is part of how Black people stake their claim as subjects empowered, conveying a defiant will to be present as Zulu and proud in a public sphere that for so long enforced language policy that consigned indigenous languages to the margins.

The four comics featured in this chapter use humor to draw distinctions between Black and white people to highlight and celebrate their in-group status: Blackness. At Ntuli's 2015 performance at Taboo, the white woman who went with me to the show, as mentioned above, became the butt of many jokes. At one point, Ntuli joked, "*Hheyi* [no], there is nothing like white people asking while you are in the middle of the groove. And they like, [*awkwardly*] 'So so which leg comes first?' *Hhayibo* [oh come on] move! You must ask for these instructions *before* we dance, not *during*. [*Laughs to self.*] Yes it happened to you [*pointing to my friend*], *hhe*? She feels very personal about this story; she's like 'Yesss!'" Under apartheid rules, a Black woman would never be able to openly ridicule white people, even less to subversively challenge their superiority the way Ntuli did in this joke. The audience embraced this small rebellion, which we can read as an enactment of sass given the way it illuminated the postapartheid fantasy of Black liberation and simultaneously disrupted the structures of white supremacy. Lihle Msimang performed at the venue The Box in Johannesburg and did a bit on Black versus white language: "I love studying the way people speak. When you are angry, English is the worst language to use. 'Cause you need a lot of words. [*Affecting a prim English accent*] 'Stop it. Right now. Stop it, I'm warning you! *Stop it!*' Whereas if you're Black, you don't need many words. In fact, you don't even need words. You need to look at a person and go [*raises eyebrows to a central point, gestures forward aggressively*] 'Hey!' [*Cut-eye.*] Nxe [*click with a curse word register*]!"[45]

As Seirlis points out, stand-up in postapartheid South Africa is a site where old ideologies and social orders can be challenged and subverted, especially whiteness and white supremacy. "In the new dispensation, whiteness has in many ways been neutralized and neutered," Seirlis argues. "If whiteness in its Afrikaner incarnation is set up as risible and outmoded, generic whiteness is rendered the ultimate unmarked category: dull and perhaps irrelevant."[46] This dullness and irrelevance are clear in the way white people are staged as dancers without rhythm, comically dry and verbose. Ntuli and Msimang use racial differentiation to disarm whiteness. The way they parody whiteness as awkward renders it wooden, dead—and Blackness as dynamic and enlivened. Blackness is celebrated as white people are cast as outsiders at best, useless relics at worst. These enactments of sass look different because the critique of power is in the context of diaspora culture. However, embodied gestures associated with sass—the cut-eye and click—are intimately proximate.

Self-deprecation is "an embodiment of the power of powerlessness," Joanne Gilbert argues, and is one of the primary techniques of marginal humor.[47] However, self-deprecatory humor can lead to the subversion of power; as Gilbert explains, "Capitalizing on their marginalized status is integral to the potentially subversive discourse these comics generate."[48] Tumi Morake opened her Netflix special saying, "I'm nervous. I'm an African fresh off the boat from Africa. On display in front of white people. And I've seen money exchanging hands. I'm a little nervous. It feels like déjà vu. Just putting it out there, it's a little awkward."[49] Morake is speaking to a largely white audience, judging from the camera's wide pans of the audience. Her joke calls up the Middle Passage, the journey Africans took from the continent to the Americas in the transatlantic slave trade, using the "rhetoric of victimage" to signify her relationship of marginality vis-à-vis her audience.[50]

As such, Morake, even as a South African not directly affected by the legacy of this instantiation of white racial terror, nonetheless brings that terror to the surface. The joke subverts the idea that Black South Africans are different from Black North Americans who were subject to chattel slavery, and even if it is a Black South African woman standing before them, her joke conveys to the Canadian audience that they are also implicated in the legacy of white racial terror. Essentially, Morake marks herself as discursively Black (and not generically African), and her audience is whitened, with all the meanings and implications that whiteness holds. She offers a subtle subversion—Black people are clearly marked as *formerly* victims of white terror. White people are still racist.

Celeste Ntuli had the crowd cracking up at Taboo with her impressions of white people. "White girls, you know they want everything," she started, the crowd already laughing. "[*Nasally voice*] 'Oh hug me Jonathan. Come to my workplace. Tell me bedtime stories.' [*Laughter.*] Uh-uh. *Thina* [us], we are not as needy. Just give us 40,000 and disappear for three weeks; we'll be fine!

[*Applause.*] We've been poor too long. We don't mess around." Ntuli's parody creates an intersubjective community of insiders (and outsiders), and that is crucially important, even if ephemeral, in a South Africa where in 2015, 64 percent of Black people still lived in poverty.[51] Stand-up can provide a sense of cathartic relief in laughter, but it can also generate solidarity among the most marginalized members of society around issues like entrenched poverty, capitalistic exploitation, and gender politics. Parody is an embodied expression of sass in the South African context of vernac comedy—it is a means by which the state is rendered ridiculous, ineffectual, and abject with the white targets as the stand-ins for the oppressive state and the institutions that undergird it.

Sass, Marginality, and the Carnivalesque

Ntuli and Morake use obscenity in their acts in ways that contribute to a mood of social transgression. An undated video on YouTube shows Celeste Ntuli in her younger days performing before a large arena-style audience, wearing a functional and not glamorous dress. It is clear from the video that she is at the beginning of her career. The person who translated and transcribed the bit for my analysis marked several instances of isiZulu and Afrikaans words and phrases that registered as obscenities. One joke featured an angry man exclaiming, "Eske nxa hhaga!" (Piss off) and "Tsek!" (Fuck off), expressions I would not have known without the aid of a native speaker.[52]

Susan Seizer has theorized obscenity in stand-up as a technique to communicate a relaxed mood, which "plays a large part in orienting audiences to the kind of playful communicative relationship that constitutes live stand-up comedy."[53] Ntuli showered her Taboo performances with obscenities in English, isiZulu, and some interesting (and funny) hybrids. In a bit about why Black folks do not engage in *50 Shades of Grey* kinds of sexuality, Ntuli joked, "Don't you dare give Dumisani a *sjambok*"—a leather whip with a thick, knobby handle—"these *motherfuckers* are angry!" Talking about women's dating behavior, Ntuli pronounced, "*Senza yonke ifucked* up" (We do all these fucked up things). Getting much applause and laughter at the Comic's Choice Awards, Tumi Morake started her routine, "It just pisses me off when Black women are in denial. 'I'm fit, no, I'm fit! This is an African gut.' No, you are fat. If you had an African body, you'd be a size zero 'cause Africa is starving, *bitch!*"[54] Seizer points out the function of obscenity as a comedic technique that alerts the audience that the performer is authentically "one of them," and they can feel like they are part of a conversation. Seizer simultaneously indexes the use of swear words as an expression of the carnivalesque, which relies on transgression of hegemonic norms, subversion of powerful ideas and positions, and the open celebration of excess. Seizer argues, "Obscenity in these performances serves to heighten and intensify the expression of the speaker's perspective, affect, and experience.... Such use puts the audience at ease and makes this dialogic performance event feel like colloquial, quotidian talk.... Their use of swear words signals to the audience that any formality associated with public speech acts need not hold here, that just as strictures on the audience's behavior are relaxed in the club setting, the comic too is hereby letting him or herself loose."[55]

If Joanne Gilbert is correct and "marginal traditions of humor are inevitably linked to power dynamics,"[56] then the carnivalesque is a useful frame to think about the way Black women comics in South Africa use humor to call into question those power dynamics and subvert or reorient dominant norms associated with Black womanhood, especially when it comes to discourses of the body. The carnivalesque evokes an atmosphere of freedom, Bakhtin theorizes, outside the strictures and rules of officialdom where an inversion of the bottom and top occurs in comic rites and rituals. It is no surprise that stand-up comedy is a site ripe for this kind of inversion and that Black women avail themselves of the techniques to partake in such inversion.

The carnivalesque relies on transgression or subversion of norms and an open celebration of that which, for Black women, has been framed as excessive or grotesque. "The transgressive behaviour and ideologies which characterise this space mean that we are always challenging the meanings attached to being Blackwomen," Gqola argues.[57] Black women employ carnivalesque aesthetics to question and move beyond ideals, especially when it comes to those pertaining to beauty and the body, a paradoxical site of repulsion and desire. Kathleen Rowe theorizes representations of the unruly woman, "an ambivalent figure of female outrageousness and transgression with roots in the narrative forms of comedy and the social practices of carnival."[58] The unruly woman in this case signifies the comedic power of subversion in which the excessive and grotesque function to (often visibly) challenge gendered social norms. Onstage, this looks like Black women exceeding the frame of legible Black womanhood; they are doing the most. As Janell Hobson has maintained, "Black women artists ... who wish to gesture toward an aesthetic of the black female body find themselves in need of an oppositional stance," and this aesthetic "must challenge dominant culture's discourse of the black body grotesque and articulate a black liberation discourse on the black body beautiful."[59] When they deploy carnivalesque aesthetics onstage, Black women stand-ups openly celebrate their experiences, their bodies, and their capacity to speak and be heard in contexts where they have often been silenced at best.

Celeste Ntuli is particularly adept at transgressing norms in carnivalesque form, especially those of sexual propriety. At Taboo, Ntuli entered the stage dancing and proclaimed, "Yah . . . hello *sengiya-twerka phela* [Yeah . . . hello I twerk these days]. *Sizama ukuyothola ama bhonasi, baholile abafana nathi siyo twerka int'engapheli* [We are going to try to spend their bonuses, the guys got paid and we are going to be twerking non-stop]." Again, Ntuli makes use of a Black American colloquialism, "twerking," to fit her needs in the moment. Ntuli establishes for her audience that she is comfortable and confident in her voluptuous embodiment, that she can and will publicly move in sexually suggestive ways, despite norms of femininity that bind sex and sexuality to the private realm. Ntuli instrumentalizes men and men's sexuality in this joke, setting them up as a foil to the notion that women are simply objects of the male gaze.

The joke earlier about the police officer who could not stop gawking at her body is also a joke that transgresses norms of feminine propriety, Ntuli's way of using sexually themed humor to embody the unruly Black woman. Her transgressions reflect that she is in fact already out of place; she stages a space where Black women are in control of their bodies, sexualities, and desires and make productive use of them, too. Her comedic transgressions of racialized gender norms reflect a broader lens through which we can see the ways Black women's sass travels—how Black women regard themselves as sexual subjects and their bodies as autonomous and claim their right to speak and be heard, regardless of social consequences.

Khanyisa Bunu's political transgressiveness is also interesting given how difficult it is for most Black women in South Africa to have an audience for their political speech. In an article about Bunu's career and style of comedy, a reporter referred to a joke Bunu performed in a city that strongly supported South Africa's ruling party, the African National Congress (ANC), where she offered the audience a scathing satire of the party's secretary-general at the time, Gwede Mantashe. "You know Gwede would walk in here and say, 'Ladies and gentlemen! I'm going to kill all of you—not directly, but through hunger, unemployment and corruption!' Yay! Gwede! Yay!"[60] Here, Bunu refuses to let off the hook neither the corrup members of the ANC government nor the people who perennially vote them into office, even knowing about the corruption, nepotism, and greed that has kept the masses of South Africans in poverty and landless.

Bunu contravenes norms of that which is sayable to the state because of the mood of the carnivalesque her comedic transgression inspires. As Seirlis maintains, "Comedy in South Africa is a compelling demonstration of the shift from the anger of political protest under the severe strictures of apartheid to the possibility of enjoyment in the freedoms promised by democracy,"[61] and Bunu's political satire is a relatively new freedom to be enjoyed publicly, an act of transgression that signifies Bunu's statement that when it comes to her comedy, "irreverence rules." Ntuli's and Bunu's security in their transgressive speech indexes that they are unconcerned about approval when it comes to their material and destabilizes the idea that Black women are to be seen, not heard. As Jacqueline Bobo has put it, "Black women's challenge to cultural domination is part of an activist movement that works to improve the conditions of their lives."[62]

"Before I go I want to share my problem with you," Bunu began her set on *The Bantu Hour* show. "I'm sure you have noticed. I'm battling with weight. I've tried so many things. . . . There is one ad that caught my attention. An ad for Herbix. I wanted to try Herbix, but I could not. There was this guy who . . . was two times bigger than I am. And he walked in front of the TV and filled the whole screen. . . . I lost 100 kilograms . . . so after six months, I disappear!"[63] Bunu's seeming unhappiness with her body is symptomatic of the way Black women's bodies have been represented and discursively produced in popular culture across the continent and in the diaspora as unruly and in need of being disciplined and controlled.

Louise Vincent surveyed and coded several years of discourse around obesity in English-language periodicals in South Africa and found that "in this coverage the fat body is overwhelmingly framed as diseased—to be fat is to be ill and therefore the legitimate subject of the intense gaze of a range of medical 'experts.'"[64] Bunu's joke counters the logic of the dominant discourse around fat Black bodies, and the supplement Herbix becomes the force threatening to do Bunu in, not her weight. "Reminiscent of the parading of Sara Baartman's flesh in European 'human zoos,'" Vincent contends, "the fat Black body reemerges in post-colonial South Africa as the legitimate object of the (westernized) medical gaze, to be prodded, measured, callipered and trained to better meet the requirements of 'civilization.'"[65] However, Bunu locates the medical gaze and instruments of training the fat body as a potential site where she, like Baartman, might be violated and disappeared.

Tumi Morake, like Celeste Ntuli, has publicly discussed her process of weight loss and uses this aspect of her life as part of her act. In her Netflix special Morake joked, "I've lost a little bit of weight. . . . I'm *thick* now. I used to be *fat*."[66] Morake's joke on the surface seems to be "subsumed within the logic of the dominant, overarching frame"[67] of fat as a negative attribute, but her use of the word "thick"—which is a colloquial term in Black American speech with a positive signification ascribed to Black women with large frames in ways that connote sexiness and health—is a subversive if incomplete means by which to convey to her audience that she has agency in the cultivation and training of her body, and even if that body is still outside of hegemonic standards of health and beauty, it is nevertheless a site of celebration. Morake uses self-deprecation to locate the big Black female body as a site of adoration, encouraging her audience to find ways to get positive affirmation as well. She implored Black women on a late-night talk show, "I want to just send this message to the big girls out there. Big girls: please, love yourself. If you don't feel good about yourself, find the nearest taxi rank and you will feel like the sexiest woman on earth."[68]

Celeste Ntuli has some of the most subversive and celebratory discourse about the Black female body. Her body and norms around Black women's bodies in general is a well-trod topic for Ntuli, who jokes often about her weight and skin tone. At the 2017 Johannesburg International Comedy Festival, Ntuli aggressively joked, "I know South Africans don't want me 'cause I'm dark. Apparently. That's how you know apartheid went down; men are fucked. He could be navy. 'I want a yellowbone.' 'But what about your *mother*?!'" This joke exudes sass and the carnivalesque. Ntuli has skewered the anti-Black racial politics of apartheid—not only the political arrangement itself but its legacy of self-hatred among Black people as well. "Navy" is a euphemism for a Black person's skin that is the darkest tone; in Black American culture there is a saying that some people are so Black they look blue. I believe Ntuli is using the same metaphor here.

This joke cuts like a knife at the heart of anti-Black racism, even and especially among Black people. "I want a yellowbone," the Black man says, another term borrowed from Black American culture that signifies an extremely light-skinned person. Ntuli symbolically punishes the man, putting him in his place—with his (dark) Black mother, the ancestral body he disavows in his desire for a light-skinned woman. In a sense, we can say that in this scene of inversion—in the proverbial Black "your mama!" moment—Ntuli subverts the man's position (and any self-hating Black man who refuses to date dark-skinned Black women), effectively becoming his mother. "Yellowbone" is the materialization of white supremacy—or colorism, the proximity to whiteness—across the diaspora. Comedically calling out colorism and disarming it—"But what about your *mother*?!"—are part of diaspora culture and the circulation of the discourse of Black women's sass across time and space.

In her Taboo set, Ntuli had an ongoing dialogue, interspersed between jokes of different topics, unabashedly celebrating her corpulent body, from the moment she came onstage twerking, confidently reveling in her own voluptuousness. "I'm no longer *fra now ngendaba yok'saba abafana hayi hayi* [frustrated now or scared about issues with guys]. If I catch myself on the mirror having sex *eer* . . . ," laughing to herself, "I'm no longer shy *hhe e'* [not at all]. *Ngize ngiy'bambe kahle ngithi "awu wadla sdudla"* [I even catch myself saying "Good going fat one/fatso"]." Ntuli refers to herself as *sdudla*, a Zulu word used to signify a big woman that has more of a positive than a negative register. Zulu culture celebrates *sdudla*, who is considered healthy and well-fed, and Ntuli's reference to herself as such in the joke suggests that she regards herself positively. She has brought the carnivalesque aesthetic to its apex as an enactment of sass: she has literally completed the process of "unmirroring," to borrow from Hobson, who is riffing on Lorraine O'Grady.[69] She sees herself first, once the object of an othering gaze, now gazing at herself—contemplating the beauty and sensuousness of her body, evaluating its worth based on that self-reflexive gaze, the hallmark of the discourse of sass and its expression as humor. The audience not only laughs but also cheers loudly at Ntuli's subversion of the suffocating cloak of self-consciousness that can define the affective state of individuals who feel like their bodies send the message that they are fat and undeserving of love and pleasure. Here, "the body represents the people: growing and renewed . . . grandiose, exaggerated."[70] In Ntuli's narrative, *sdudla*, "the fat one," reigns supreme. This rebellious joke is the ultimate embodiment of the carnivalesque, lowering that which is high in celebration of the excessive body.

"I Also Talk Like This and People Laugh"

The comedians in this chapter demonstrate the efficacy of stand-up comedy, how Black women make use of aesthetic practices and rhetorical choices that force us to generate new theories about diasporic flows of Black cultural material. The mood of irreverence is a crucial feature of Black women's comic culture in South Africa, and we can see that in the topics addressed, comedic styles and techniques, and aesthetic choices that demonstrate the complexity and artistry of their performances.

I have tried to tease out content that highlights Black American cultural material as part and parcel of Black South African stand-up, especially given that at least three of the comics explicitly stated that they were inspired to become professional comics after watching Black American stand-up. Ntuli revealed in an interview, "It was 2005 and I had just watched Richard Pryor and the Kings of Comedy with Steve Harvey and Bernie Mac and I fell in love and wanted to do what they do."[71] Tumi Morake was asked which international comedian was her all-time favorite, and she answered, "Richard Pryor. His gift of laughing at his own pain still inspires me."[72] Bunu is also influenced by American comedy, looking to comic Erin Jackson as a source of inspiration. "I also saw her in a competition called 'Last Comic Standing.' So I just saw this lady who was so powerful. . . . We're in contact now and we share ideas. I've told her I'd love to perform in America and she must come and perform in South Africa."[73]

I have also tried not to make too easy a connection between Black women's comedy in the United States and South Africa. Jacqueline Bobo reminds us that while "it would be a mistake to assume that Black women will always communicate across lines of sexuality, class, economic status, geographic location, and so on, there is still a need to examine the ways in which they do."[74] "Mimesis [is the] basis for newness," as Werbner and Fumanti argue, and furthermore, "through performance, diasporic groups enact narratives of Diaspora subjectivity."[75] This diaspora subjectivity is exemplified in Tumi Morake's "fresh off the boat" gag, yet there are also slippages that demonstrate some of the ways diasporic comics work to differentiate themselves from Black Americans, as Ntuli did in her joke performed in Los Angeles at the beginning of the chapter. Morake told a similar joke that gets at the seams of diaspora culture on her Netflix special.

"I feel like we've been abused a little bit by America, to be honest," Morake jokes. "Ah, America, they don't send us Jay-Z and Beyoncé, no!" Morake's joke takes an interesting turn. "They send us weird-looking mumbling guys 'rapping.' . . . These guys come and . . . they look weird; they scare me. They've got tattoos; they look like my high school desk. [*Laughter.*] What is wrong with you?!? He looks like he was doodled on by Sheniqua and Shaquanna [*laughter*], and this was detention [*pointing down the side of body*]."[76] The way Morake makes fun of Black women whom she produces as "ghetto" and the genre of American mumble rap reveals the uneasiness and incompleteness with which diaspora subjectivity coheres around (representations of) Blackness, and this joke locates Morake outside of Black American culture. It also manifests a disdain for lower-class Black linguistic and cultural practices, similar to the way Marina Franklin had done when she sent up a version of working-class Black womanhood with her castigation of the "sassy Black comic." In each case, there is a stylistic and ideological move in the service of differentiating Blackness, even in what might purportedly be a collective diaspora culture.

The comics of this study remind us that cultural practices in conditions of marginality provoke alliances and affinities between Black people all over the globe. Black South African women's comedy invites us to think about the mobility of and intimacy between diasporic cultural materials, like the discourse of sass, and about diasporic cultures as generative, dynamic, and multidirectional, beyond the sometimes-limited scope of concepts like hybridity and creolization.[77] These diaspora aesthetics adhere to what we might call irreverence rules, a politics of transgression in which diasporic women publicly and willfully express fears, anxieties, and desires in ways that subvert, and at times paradoxically uphold, norms of restrictive, traditional notions of Black womanhood—all in the service of articulating humanity in new and productive ways.

CODA

YOU DON'T QUIT, BITCH,
UNLESS YOU WANNA QUIT

When I tell people I research and write about Black women's humor and comedy, the question often follows: Who is your favorite comedian? Rarely do I offer a straight answer, instead opting to amplify the *many* wonderful comedians I have come to know over the course of my career and in my life. Truthfully, I have long had an answer. I want to end this book by honoring her, because it was she who first brought me into the world of comedy, not just because of her jokes but because of what those jokes can *do*. So I want to linger awhile on my favorite comedian, Adele Givens, because like the women whom I have discussed throughout *Sass*, when I first saw her perform, she had the disposition of a woman self-possessed. She had swag and a broad, toothy smile that never disappeared.

It was midnight on a Saturday in the mid-1990s and I was around ten years old. The volume on the old RCA console TV was turned down so low I strained to hear, and peals of laughter threatened to explode as Adele Givens delivered jokes that titillated my young, immature mind. When she graced the stage to perform on HBO's *Def Comedy Jam,* I felt like she was talking directly to me, as if we were the only ones in the room. Her humor drew me in as if we were kinfolk—she may as well have been one of my aunts or older cousins regaling me with the secrets of womanhood, what it is like to be older and wiser, to have the power to make people listen and laugh at the same time. "I know what you're thinking," Givens mused after a particularly raunchy bit, and I repeated it along with her (and still do rewatching her routines): "She's such a fucking lady!"

How could a person be so unimpeachably funny? How did she manage to speak directly to *me* from that stage? I did not understand it at ten years old, of course, but I now know as a scholar of Black humor that the intersubjective connection between the performer and audience I was experiencing that marks high-quality stand-up derives from a behind-the-scenes crafting of words and ideas and their performance, leaving you always wanting more. The laughter she evoked when I was ten and that continues to draw me in as a scholar and comedy lover comes from Givens's Black cultural material—most specifically the way she uses sass—as well as from her comedic dexterity and impeccable timing, with jokes so well-crafted their preparation is imperceptible. What I most love about Adele Givens is the sense of being brought into a uniquely Black woman's space, suffused with familiarity and a hint of illicitness—like going on a ride with your aunt to pick up milk, eggs . . . and a pack of cigarettes. Her language and the paralinguistic features of Givens's performance manifested a general aura that pulled me into the cozy quilt of Black women's humor. Johnnie M. Stover argues that during slavery, Black women's sass developed as a "tool of flagrant resistance," expressed via "mother tongue."[1] It is this palpable familiarity—this mother tongue—that drew me to Givens's comedy when I was a child, then only a nascent vibration, which I now appreciate as an epistemological frame of my Black womanhood, my sense of humor, and the way I have theorized sass as the most salient element of Black women's humor.

Reflecting on the humor of one of the most charismatic Black feminists of the twentieth century, Sherie Randolph notes that Black feminist activist and lawyer Florynce Kennedy's sharp wit and cutting satire was a powerful "weapon and shield." Indeed, as Randolph puts it, "Part of what annoyed [Kennedy's] adversaries and attracted some feminist followers was Kennedy's privileging of satirical amusement and unleashed pleasure as part of her political actions." Kennedy's performance of self-possession coupled with her penchant for political audacity frames how we might understand the contours of Black feminist humor, how it looks and sounds. Kennedy would organize protests and hold homemade posters while "loudly singing 'Stop the fuckers from fucking over you.'" As Randolph points out, Kennedy "argued that if U.S. leaders could use profane language, so could she."[2] The power of self-definition as political praxis deeply informed Kennedy's humor, she said: "Fashion, style, language, are the stuff of which societal reins on the oppressed are made. Grow a beard, wear a dashiki, say 'shit' or 'fuck' at the wrong time or place and you can get on the open-season-for-niggerizing list."[3] Adele Givens's self-possessed comedy is chock-full of political audacity, an expression of Black feminist humor invoked in her oxymoronic tagline, "She's such a fuckin' lady." This is also especially clear in a bit Givens performed in the 2000 *Queens of Comedy* special. It is worth quoting at length because it embodies the spirit of Black women's sass and underscores Black womanhood as a socially and culturally meaningful identity category, and we should expect that whatever has made it socially and culturally meaningful will be manifested in the humor of particular groups of people, however heterogeneous. After chiding an audience member who asked to hear one of her classic jokes, Givens tells the audience, no, she wants to talk about her grandmother:

> I love my grandma. In fact, she is the reason why I'm still standing here doing comedy . . . because you know I had got discouraged. I said I wasn't gon' do it because I had did a show and I gave it my all. I don't know if y'all know, but I use y'all for a therapist. I talk to y'all 'cause I know y'all can relate to the shit I'm talking about, you know? So, I talk to y'all and I put my heart into it. I gave a great show one night and a lady came up to me after the show and said, "Adele, we LOVED you, you were funny as shit." She said, "BUT . . . you have a filthy mouth." And I was all fucked up 'cause I wasn't thinking at the time that that's a control issue when somebody tell you how you should talk, that's a motherfucker that wanna control you. . . . I was discouraged that one of my fans thought I had a filthy mouth, and I said, "Fuck it, I'm through. I'm quitting, shit." My grandma talked to me and said, "Look, you don't quit bitch unless *you* wanna quit. You don't let nobody make you quit." She said, "Come here baby, lemme tell you something." She said, "The next time somebody tell you 'You got a filthy mouth,' you tell them: 'It ain't what come outcha mouth that make it filthy, it's what you put in there.'" She said, "Then you tell 'em you wash all the dicks you suck, hear?"[4]

Givens makes a point similar to the one Florynce Kennedy made decades before, reinforcing the idea that humor enables Black women to publicly problematize traditional scripts of womanhood and decorum from which we have been excluded and to produce alternatives at the same time. Black women's sass, like that which Givens enacts in this bit, is a combination of responding to how women are perceived in society at large and their reaction to it. But first and foremost, as Givens's conversation with her grandmother bears out, Black women's sass is about how they see themselves, how they regard themselves. The Black women in this study who make use of sass fundamentally regard themselves as human beings who have something to say, and even in conditions where speaking might be dangerous, sass is a genre that has enabled Black women to courageously unsilence themselves, asserting the humanity that many have tried to squelch.

This joke is playful and raunchy, yet deadly serious. It demonstrates one of the ways the category of Black womanhood is historically battered by commonsense notions about who can speak and what she can speak about and by the consequences of saying the unsayable. Givens foregrounds her emotional response to the experience of having someone try to discipline her behavior, and we see sass at work, the way she uses language, style, and *intent* to subvert the disciplinary forces that dare try to regulate her femininity and comedic artistry. Wresting control through the discourse of sass may seem inconsequential and fleeting. As I have demonstrated throughout this book, it kept many a Black woman alive and thriving. To flip the script within the context of disempowerment—across time and space—shows the brittleness of structures of domination and control, and flipping that script as an act of self-possession comes to be the primary means through which Black women take care of our spirits and make people laugh.

As Cynthia Willett and Julie Willett argue, "Laughter that comes from deep down can threaten the normal rules of social control with verve but also with aim and social purpose. . . . Belly laughs catalyze anger and transform negative affects and emotions toward liberation. . . . A contagious guffaw from the bottom up exerts undeniable biosocial force."[5] Givens emphasizes the affective power of Black women's sass—comedy routines become acts of self-care where vulnerability and the expression of one's interiority enables connection and reflection and inaugurates the possibility of life unfettered, for everyone. This is the spirit of a radical Black feminist ethos. The political force of Black women's sass is its power to expose the artificiality of hierarchies, but it also provides the agent and audiences attuned to its effects a bit of release in the defiant laughter it evokes.

NOTES

INTRODUCTION

1. Jada Pinkett Smith, "Crown Act," TikTok, March 22, 2022, www.tiktok.com/@jadapinkettsmith/video/7078010569235762475?is_copy_url=1&is_from_webapp=v1&item_id=7078010569235762475&refer=embed&referer_url=https%3A%2F%2Fpeople.com%2F&referer_video_id=7078010569235762475.
2. Bailey and Richardson, "'Will the Real Men Stand Up?,'" 111.
3. A rich body of scholarship on African American Women's Language (AAWL) has emerged since the mid-1970s, examining the communication strategies and styles Black women have developed in the ongoing context of chattel slavery, patriarchy, and anti-Black sexism. In particular, scholars have paid close attention to the ways Black women have used language as a way to negotiate their social, cultural, and political conditions and produce meaning and transformation within them. Adrienne Ronee Washington's article "'Reclaiming My Time'" offers an exemplary overview of the literature on the subversive qualities of Black women's language and discursive practices. These works, Washington summarizes, "explore the symbolic, creative and performative use of AAWL communicative practices among Black women to discursively unsettle and restructure institutionalised power relationships and hegemonic norms and to negotiate alternative realities, subjectivities, interpersonal relationships and identities" (364). For more sociolinguistic work on Black women's language, see Abrahams, "Negotiating Respect"; Bucholtz, "Black Feminist Theory"; Halliday, "Twerk Sumn!"; Lanehart, *Sista, Speak!*; Mitchell-Kernan, "Signifying and Marking"; M. Morgan, "Indirectness and Interpretation"; M. Morgan, "'I'm Every Woman'"; Richardson, "Gender Ideologies in Hip Hop Feminism"; Smitherman, *Black Talk*; Troutman, "'They Say It's a Man's World'"; and Washington, "'Reclaiming My Time.'"
4. Harris-Perry, *Sister Citizen*, 4.
5. Wood, *Cracking Up*, 4.
6. Bakhtin, *Rabelais and His World*, 10.
7. Hartman, *Scenes of Subjection*, 19.
8. Wood, *Cracking Up*, 9.
9. Willett and Willett, *Uproarious*, 103.
10. Baldwin, "Here Be Dragons," 689.
11. Baldwin, "Here Be Dragons," 690.
12. Nash, *Black Body in Ecstasy*, 2.
13. Miller-Young, "Hip-Hop Honeys," 280.
14. Miller-Young, *Taste for Brown Sugar*, 10.
15. Willett and Willett, *Uproarious*, 110.

16. Hartman, *Wayward Lives*, 283.
17. Hartman, *Wayward Lives*, 279–83.
18. Cooper, *Eloquent Rage*, 168 (emphasis in original).
19. Collins, *Black Sexual Politics*, 147.
20. Collins, *Black Sexual Politics*, 123.
21. Harris-Perry, *Sister Citizen*, 93.
22. Ekperigin interview.
23. Fulton, "Comic Views and Metaphysical Dilemmas," 92.
24. Ahmed, *Cultural Politics of Emotion*, 195.
25. Dobbins interview.
26. Dobbins interview.
27. Dobbins interview.
28. Cooper, *Eloquent Rage*, 2.
29. Cooper, *Eloquent Rage*, 1 (emphasis mine).
30. Warner, "They Gon' Think You Loud Regardless," 137.
31. Dunn, *"Baad Bitches" and Sassy Supermamas*, 3.
32. Cooper, *Eloquent Rage*, 7.
33. Cooper, *Eloquent Rage*, 151.
34. Cooper, *Eloquent Rage*, 150.
35. Cooper, *Eloquent Rage*, 5.
36. Cooper, *Eloquent Rage*, 2.
37. DeFrantz and Gonzalez, "Introduction," 3.
38. Hartman, *Scenes of Subjection*, 58.
39. Hartman, *Scenes of Subjection*, 77.
40. Frow, "Discourse Genres," 78.
41. Frow, "Discourse Genres," 74.
42. Dance, *Honey Hush!*; Stevens, *Smart and Sassy*.
43. Hanks, "Discourse Genres in a Theory of Practice," 670.
44. Hanks, "Discourse Genres in a Theory of Practice," 670.
45. Hanks, "Discourse Genres in Theory and Practice," 668 (emphasis mine).
46. Rickford and Rickford, "Cut-Eye and Suck-Teeth," 295 and 298.
47. Rickford and Rickford, "Cut-Eye and Suck-Teeth," 296.
48. Rickford and Rickford, "Cut-Eye and Suck-Teeth," 303.
49. Rickford and Rickford, "Cut-Eye and Suck-Teeth," 302.
50. Jamieson and Campbell, "Rhetorical Hybrids," 146, quoted in Frow, "'Reproducibles, Rubrics, and Everything You Need," 1630.
51. Max Read, "Watch Michelle Obama Throw World-Historical Shade at John Boehner," Gawker, January 1, 2013, https://gawker.com/5977763/watch-michelle-obama-throw-world-historical-shade-at-john-boehner.
52. Rickford and Rickford, "Cut-Eye and Suck-Teeth," 297.
53. Frow, "Discourse Genres," 77.
54. M. Morgan, "More Than a Mood or an Attitude."
55. Conquergood, "Performance Studies," 146.
56. Phelan, *Unmarked*, 7.
57. Morrison, "Unspeakable Things Unspoken," 8 (emphasis in original).

58. Hartman, *Scenes of Subjection*, 50.

59. Guy-Sheftall, *Words of Fire*, 21.

60. Wood, *Cracking Up*, 4.

61. Johnson, "Black Performance Studies," 452.

62. Stevens, *Smart and Sassy*, 18.

63. Krefting, *All Joking Aside*, 5.

64. D. Morgan, *Laughing to Keep from Dying*, 4.

65. Lorde, *Black Unicorn*, 31.

66. Website for San Francisco Comedy College, accessed October 20, 2020, www.sfcomedycollege.com.

67. Madison, *Critical Ethnography*, 195–96.

68. Ellison, *Shadow and Act*, 131.

69. Johnson, *Appropriating Blackness*, 2.

70. Johnson, *Appropriating Blackness*, 8.

71. J. Brown, *Babylon Girls*, 60.

72. Morrison, "Unspeakable Things Unspoken," 9.

73. Baderoon, "Surplus, Excess, Dirt," 260.

74. Gqola, "*Ufanele uqavile*," 20.

75. Kuumba, "African Feminisms in Exile," 5.

76. "Gina Yashere on New Comedy Tour: 'I'm Basically Telling Stories from My Life' | Prime," YouTube, June 23, 2023, www.youtube.com, www.youtube.com/watch?v=XmbKOTtoV-o&t=41s.

77. Hartman, *Wayward Lives*, 349.

78. Darren Taylor, "'Irreverence Rules' for S. African Comedy Queen," VOA News, April 5, 2013, www.voanews.com/a/irreverence-rules-for-south-african-comic-queen/1635552.html.

CHAPTER 1

1. Fannie Lou Hamer, "Testimony before the Credentials Committee, Democratic National Convention, Atlantic City, New Jersey—August 22, 1964," Say It Plain: A Century of Great African American Speeches, American Public Media, accessed April 20, 2021, https://americanradioworks.publicradio.org/features/sayitplain/flhamer.html. Later quotes from Hamer's testimony are also from this source.

2. Hartman, *Wayward Lives*, 28.

3. Cohen, "Deviance as Resistance," 38.

4. Morrison, *Paradise*, 62, cited in Stevens, *Smart and Sassy*, x.

5. "Annell Ponder," Digital SNCC Gateway, accessed April 20, 2021, https://snccdigital.org/people/annell-ponder.

6. Walcott, "Performing the (Black) Postmodern," 106.

7. Goffman, *Asylums*, cited in M. Morgan, "Shout-Outs to the Ancestors," 45.

8. Hartman, *Wayward Lives*, 29.

9. Hartman, *Wayward Lives*, 59.

10. *Heritage of Slavery*.

11. Richardson, "'To Protect and Serve,'" 680.

12. Clark, "Developing Diaspora Literacy and Marasa Consciousness," 42.
13. Majors, "'I Wasn't Scared of Them,'" 169.
14. Majors, "'I Wasn't Scared of Them,'" 170.
15. Richardson, "'To Protect and Serve,'" 680.
16. Cooper, "A'n't I a Lady?," 40.
17. Braxton, *Black Women Writing Autobiography*, 16.
18. Jacobs, *Incidents in the Life of a Slave Girl*, 17.
19. Jacobs, *Incidents in the Life of a Slave Girl*, 39.
20. Braxton, *Black Women Writing Autobiography*, 30–31.
21. Ugwu, *Let's Get It On*.
22. Braxton, *Black Women Writing Autobiography*, 1–3 (emphasis mine).
23. Stover, "Nineteenth-Century African American Women's Autobiography," 140.
24. Teague, "From A to Z," 1110.
25. Hurston, *Dust Tracks on a Road*, 2 (emphasis mine).
26. DeFrantz and Gonzalez, "Introduction," 8.
27. Hartman, *Scenes of Subjection*, 63.
28. Hartman, *Scenes of Subjection*, 77.
29. J. Brown, *Babylon Girls*, 5.
30. J. Brown, *Babylon Girls*, 7.
31. J. Brown, *Babylon Girls*, 63–64.
32. J. Brown, *Babylon Girls*, 57.
33. Stowe, *Uncle Tom's Cabin*, 37–41.
34. J. Brown, *Babylon Girls*, 82.
35. J. Brown, *Babylon Girls*, 83–84.
36. J. Brown, *Babylon Girls*, 77.
37. Levine, *Black Culture, Black Consciousness*, 300–303.
38. J. Brown, *Babylon Girls*, 5.
39. J. Brown, *Babylon Girls*, 84.
40. Dunn, *"Baad Bitches" and Sassy Supermamas*, 4.
41. J. Brown, *Babylon Girls*, 57–58.
42. Willett and Willett, *Uproarious*, 11.
43. Davis, *Blues Legacies and Black Feminism*, 24.
44. Elsie Williams wrote a well-researched study on the life and humor of Moms Mabley, *The Humor of Jackie Moms Mabley: An African American Comedic Tradition*. Further, Mel Watkins argues that Mabley was a pioneer of contemporary stand-up comedy; she "foreshadowed the shift to direct social commentary and stand-up techniques that would define humor by the late 1950s." Watkins, *On the Real Side*, 392.
45. Quoted in Watkins, *On the Real Side*, 392.
46. See Wood, *Cracking Up*; and Williams, *Humor of Jackie Moms Mabley*.
47. Wood, *Cracking Up*, 30.
48. Wood, *Cracking Up*, 28.
49. Wood, *Cracking Up*, 32.
50. Wood, *Cracking Up*, 36.
51. Wood, *Cracking Up*, 36.
52. Quoted in Wood, *Cracking Up*, 36.

53. Mintz, "Standup Comedy as Social and Cultural Mediation," 74.
54. Watkins, *On the Real Side*, 392.
55. Mintz, "Standup Comedy as Social and Cultural Mediation," 75.
56. Wood, *Cracking Up*, 50.
57. *Ask a Slave: The Web Series*, season 1, episode 1.
58. *Ask a Slave: The Web Series*, season 1, episode 1.
59. *Ask a Slave: The Web Series*, season 1, episode 2.
60. Hassan, "Question of Postmodernism," 30.
61. *Ask A Slave: The Web Series*, season 1, episode 1.
62. Carpio, *Laughing Fit to Kill*, 48.
63. Wood, *Cracking Up*, 27.
64. Mooney, *Black Is the New White*, 16.
65. Hartman, "Venus in Two Acts," 13.
66. Schechner, "Speculations on Radicalism, Sexuality, and Performance," 105–6.
67. Quoted in Giddings, *When and Where I Enter*, 24.
68. Wells-Barnett, *Southern Horrors*.
69. Giddings, *When and Where I Enter*, 28.
70. Nikole Hannah-Jones, public lecture at Middlebury College, Middlebury, VT, February 25, 2020.
71. Wells-Barnett, *Reason Why the Colored American*, 1.
72. "Executive Order on Establishing the President's Advisory 1776 Commission," November 2, 2020, Trump White House Archives, https://trumpwhitehouse.archives.gov/presidential-actions/executive-order-establishing-presidents-advisory-1776-commission/.
73. "Journalist Nikole Hannah-Jones on Ida B. Wells' Impact and Legacy," CBS News, July 17, 2021, www.cbsnews.com/news/nikole-hannah-jones-ida-b-wells/.

CHAPTER 2

1. "Luenell on Being a Prostitute, Katt Williams, VLADTV, The Comedy Game, & More," YouTube, November 11, 2022, www.youtube.com/watch?v=nWIVVr1lpwU.
2. "Luenell on Being a Prostitute."
3. "Liquor Does Crazy Sh*t—Luenell: Katthouse Comedy," YouTube, January 14, 2009, www.youtube.com/watch?v=L4hZfX_wapY.
4. Haggins, *Laughing Mad*.
5. "Luenell—Gift-Giving—Nasty Show Promo Clip," Vimeo, accessed March 4, 2021, https://vimeo.com/148384415.
6. Ahmed, *Cultural Politics of Emotion*, 85.
7. Ahmed, *Cultural Politics of Emotion*, 89.
8. Nash, *Black Body in Ecstasy*, 11 (emphasis in original).
9. Story, "(Re)Presenting Shug Avery and Afrekete," 25.
10. Stallings, *Funk the Erotic*, xi–xii.
11. Stallings, *Funk the Erotic*, xii.
12. Miller-Young, *Taste for Brown Sugar*, 10.
13. Zack, "Black Female Crossover Comedy," 38–39.

14. Zack, "Black Female Crossover Comedy," 48.
15. Stallings, *Mutha' Is Half a Word*, 3.
16. Felman, *Scandal of the Speaking Body*, 80.
17. Felman, *Scandal of the Speaking Body* 86 (emphasis in original).
18. Lindsey and Johnson, "Searching for Climax," 175.
19. Mintz, "Standup Comedy as Social and Cultural Mediation," 78 (emphasis mine).
20. Seizer, "On the Uses of Obscenity in Live Stand-Up Comedy," 211.
21. Kunze, "Tears of a Clown," 8 (emphasis mine).
22. On *Sane Advice*, the announcer calls her to the stage and describes her comedy as "indubitably soulful."
23. Stallings, *Mutha' Is Half a Word*, 116.
24. Page, *Pipe Layin' Dan*.
25. Stallings, *Funk the Erotic*, 11.
26. My concept of "corporeal orature" is not to be confused with Thomas DeFrantz's term by the same name, which he uses to theorize hip-hop dance. He defines corporeal orature as "a system of communication [that] aligns movement with speech to describe the ability of Black social dance to incite action. . . . Social dance may contain performative gestures which cite contexts beyond the dance." DeFrantz, "Bone-Breaking," 67.
27. Thiong'o, "Notes towards a Performance Theory of Orature," 7.
28. Page, *Watch It Sucker!*
29. Seizer, "On the Uses of Obscenity in Live Stand-Up Comedy," 214.
30. Page, *Watch It Sucker!*
31. Bakhtin, *Rabelais and His World*, 19.
32. Page, *Watch It Sucker!*
33. One of Page's catchphrases was "I'm gon' tell it like it T-I-is."
34. Williams interview.
35. For a fuller conversation about how the market influenced hip-hop to cater to broad audiences, see Neal, "Critical Noire"; and Neal, *What the Music Said*. Imani Perry discusses the link between Black consumerist impulses and hip-hop culture in *Prophets of the Hood*, especially chap. 7.
36. Williams interview.
37. On November 15, 2011, an article appeared in the *New York Times*, "Female Comedians, Breaking the Taste-Taboo Ceiling," which was entirely focused on white women comics making jokes about rape as their biggest transgression of taboos. See www.nytimes.com/2011/11/16/arts/television/female-comedians-are-confidently-breaking-taste-taboos.html.
38. Williams interview.
39. Flood interview.
40. Adele Givens, "Adele Givens on Def Comedy Jam," YouTube, July 29, 2012, www.youtube.com/watch?v=6gMUbECjSK4.
41. Givens, "Adele Givens on Def Comedy Jam."
42. Blake, "Framing the Video Vixen," 175.
43. The following comedians were surveyed: Hope Flood, Luenell, Chocolate, Adele Givens, Miss Laura Hayes, Mo'Nique, Sheryl Underwood, Cocoa Brown, Coco, Sommore, Edwonda White, Thea Vidale, Yvette Wilson, Ellen Cleghorn, Wanda Smith,

Dominique Whitten, Small Fry, Sonia D, Barbara Carlisle, Leighann Lord, and Melanie Camarcho.

44. "Simply Marvelous," YouTube, accessed April 2, 2022, www.youtube.com/watch?v=F2H1lHMljZA.

45. Sheryl Underwood, "Def Comedy Jam All Stars 5 Martin Lawrence and Sheryl Underwood PT 6," YouTube, May 27, 2019, www.youtube.com/watch?v=IAr-cxk2X30.

46. Blake, "Framing the Video Vixen," 173.

47. Higginbotham, *Righteous Discontent*, 14.

48. Hine, "Rape and the Inner Lives of Black Women," 912.

49. Carby, *Reconstructing Womanhood*, 39.

50. The Black women's club movement during the early twentieth century was an institutional site of policing lower-class Black women's sexualities and encouraging the performance of social propriety. Hazel V. Carby discusses the discourse of Black women's sexuality in the midst of the Great Migration in "Policing the Black Woman's Body." These performances of Black femininity were shot through with the rhetorical strategies of the "cult of true womanhood," adhering to the four virtues: "piety, purity, submissiveness, and domesticity," Patricia Hill Collins argues in *Black Sexual Politics*, 71. Katrina Bell McDonald addresses Black women's use of performances of femininity as a mode of resistance, specifically paying attention to the Black women's club movement during the early twentieth century and their programs aimed at inculcating lower-class Black women with notions of Black respectability. See McDonald, *Embracing Sisterhood*, 52–53.

51. Mercer, "Black Art and the Burden of Representation," 63.

52. On February 27, 2008, the popular tabloid website mediatakeout.com ran the story "RUMOR: Comedian Mo'Nique May Be Getting Her Stomach Stapled." The report reads, "Word is that she's been laying low and recovering from the surgery. And that, if all goes according to plans, she'll have her new physique in time for summer. Say it ain't so Mo'. You were always saying how proud you were to be a big girl." See www.mediatakeout.com/21939/rumor_comedian_monique_may_be_getting_her_stomach_stapled.html (accessed April 1, 2013, site discontinued).

53. Seth Abramovitch, "Mo'Nique: I Was 'Blackballed' after Winning My Oscar," Hollywood Reporter, February 19, 2015, www.hollywoodreporter.com/news/general-news/monique-i-was-blackballed-winning-774616/.

54. Stallings, *Mutha' Is Half a Word*, 115.

55. Therealmoworldwide, Instagram post, May 19, 2021, www.instagram.com/tv/CPdqpiSh-TZ/?hl=en.

56. Zack, "Black Female Crossover Comedy," 43.

57. Felman, *Scandal of the Speaking Body*, 87.

58. Lorde, *Sister Outsider*, 54.

CHAPTER 3

1. Rubin, "Of Catamites and Kings," 473.

2. Limon, *Stand-Up Comedy in Theory*, 4–6.

3. Willett and Willett, *Uproarious*, 138.

4. Late in Gadsby's more than hour-long set in *Nanette*, she comes back to an unfinished joke she told about a man who threatened to beat her up, mistaking her for a man. "It was a very funny story," she tells her audience; "I made a lot of people laugh . . . and the reason I could do that is because I'm very good at this job. . . . I'm pretty good at controlling the tension. . . . In order to balance the tension in the room with that story, I couldn't tell that story as it *actually* happened, because I couldn't tell the part of the story where that man, he realized his mistake. And he came back. And he said, 'Oh, now I get it. You're a lady faggot. I'm allowed to beat the shit out of you.'" Not even a beat goes on, "and he did it," she scowls, eyes wide and unflinching. Her voice breaks, as does the fourth wall. "He beat the shit out of me, and nobody stopped him!" Gadsby continues her anguished narration about how shame kept her from reporting the beating to the police or even seeking medical care. The violence she experienced was not just because of homophobia, Gadsby continues; it was because of her masculine self-presentation. "If I had been feminine, that would not have happened. I am incorrectly female. *I am incorrect.* And that is a punishable offense. And this tension, it's yours," she admonishes the audience. "You need to learn what this feels like, because this, this tension is what 'not-normals' carry inside of them *all* of the time, because it is dangerous to be different." This bit in *Nanette* is crucial for helping us think through the mutual imbrication of experience and aesthetics of failure in the comedic works of butch women comics. See *Hannah Gadsby: Nanette*.

5. Moore, "Lipstick or Timberlands?," 119.
6. Bridgforth, *Bull-Jean Stories*, 10.
7. Bridgforth, *Bull-Jean Stories*, 18–19.
8. Jaimee A. Smith, "The Triumph of Black Lesbian Feminist Resistance: Honoring Radical Poet and Activist Cheryl Clarke," Black Women Radicals, accessed September 25, 2023, www.blackwomenradicals.com/blog-feed/the-triumph-of-black-lesbian-feminist-resistance-honoring-radical-poet-and-activist-dr-cheryl-clarke.
9. Clarke, *Living as a Lesbian*, 12 and 26.
10. *Butch Mystique*.
11. Bing and Heller, "How Many Lesbians Does It Take to Screw in a Light Bulb?," 158.
12. Bing and Heller, "How Many Lesbians Does It Take to Screw in a Light Bulb?," 157.
13. Avilez, *Black Queer Freedom*, 5.
14. Avilez, *Black Queer Freedom*, 5.
15. "Combahee River Collective Statement," 272.
16. Bailey and Richardson, "Will the Real Men Stand Up?,'" 109.
17. Bey, *Them Goon Rules*, 68.
18. See Avilez, *Black Queer Freedom*.
19. Cohen, "Deviance as Resistance," 30.
20. Avilez, *Black Queer Freedom*, 152 (emphasis mine).
21. Hartman, *Scenes of Subjection*, 77.
22. See Davis, *Blues Legacies and Black Feminism*.
23. Stevens, *Smart and Sassy*, x.
24. See Wilson, *Bulldaggers, Pansies, and Chocolate Babies*.
25. Wilson, *Bulldaggers, Pansies, and Chocolate Babies*, 173.

26. Chauncey, *Gay New York*, 252.
27. Garber, "Gladys Bentley," 58
28. Hartman, *Wayward Lives*, 199 (emphasis mine).
29. Redmond, "Gospel Drag," 141.
30. Avilez, *Black Queer Freedom*, 152.
31. *I Be Done Been Was Is*.
32. "Marsha Warfield from 'Night Court' LIVE in San Francisco (1987)," YouTube, accessed July 25, 2023, www.youtube.com/watch?v=PvDJvuCmDpE&list=RDBht PjiNPPYg&start_radio=1.
33. *I Be Done Been Was Is*.
34. The original Facebook post was either deleted or is no longer publicly viewable. The Root published an article by Angela Helm, "Comedian Marsha Warfield Says That Her Mother Didn't Want Her to Come Out until She Was Dead, Defends Patti LaBelle," on December 17, 2017, containing the original text. See www.theroot.com/comedian-marsha-warfield-says-that-her-mother-didn-t-wa-1821159357.
35. Stallings, *Mutha' Is Half a Word*, 134.
36. *I Be Done Been Was Is*.
37. Quoted in Mizejewski, *Pretty/Funny*, 159.
38. Quoted in Mizejewski, *Pretty/Funny*, 159.
39. *Maury*, formerly known as *The Maury Povich Show*, was a syndicated daytime tabloid talk show that ran for thirty-one seasons, from 1991 to 2022, mostly on NBC. The show brought on guests dealing with various relationship issues, incorrigible teenagers who needed to be disciplined, transgender revelations, and most popularly, paternity tests. In the early years of the 2000s, *Maury* became known for paternity revelations with theatrical staging, dialogue, and explosive interview segments. Male guests would repeatedly storm offstage after finding out they had been deceived or that they had indeed fathered the child(ren) in question. Many times, the mothers of the children would dramatically berate the father-in-question, using some version of "That IS your baby!" or "You need to take care of your baby!" The host, Maury Povich, read the results from a small card, the audience in a state of high anticipation: either "You ARE the father!" or "You are . . . NOT the father!" These catchphrases are part of the pop cultural lexicon for castigating, punishing, and rendering humorous working-class (Black) people who publicly air their sexual dirty laundry.
40. Avilez, *Black Queer Freedom*, 5.
41. See D. Morgan, *Laughing to Keep from Dying*.
42. *Sam Jay: 3 in the Morning*.
43. Keeling, *Witch's Flight*, 125.
44. Shep Kelly, "Cosmic Comedy: A Celebration of Life," YouTube, accessed November 12, 2021, www.youtube.com/watch?v=vbWwEn_5K6Q.
45. Avilez, *Black Queer Freedom*, 8.
46. Takemoto, "Queer Art/Queer Failure," 86.
47. Avilez, *Black Queer Freedom*, 1.
48. Avilez, *Black Queer Freedom*, 156.
49. Halberstam, *Queer Art of Failure*, 95–96.

50. Bailey and Richardson, "'Will the Real Men Stand Up?,'" 111.
51. *Sam Jay: 3 in the Morning*.
52. Keeling, *Witch's Flight*, 130.
53. Avilez, *Black Queer Freedom*, 14.
54. Avilez, *Black Queer Freedom*, 3.
55. Avilez, *Black Queer Freedom*, 14.
56. Harper, "Evidence of Felt Intuition," 652.
57. Harper, "Evidence of Felt Intuition," 644.
58. Moore, "Lipstick or Timberlands?," 132–33 (emphasis in original).
59. Avilez, *Black Queer Freedom*, 2.

CHAPTER 4

1. "Meet Me in the Ladies Room, Cuz We Gotta Talk," Females in Comedy Association Convention, J Spot Comedy Club, Los Angeles, April 25, 2012.
2. *The Tonight Show Starring Sherwin*, season 2, episode 1, "Miss Laura Hayes," YouTube, accessed August 10, 2023, www.youtube.com/watch?v=1HiXnFPOEic.
3. Alexander, *Black Interior*, ix.
4. *Queens of Comedy*.
5. Rowe, "Nothing Else Mattered after That Wig Came Off," 22.
6. Rowe, "Nothing Else Mattered after That Wig Came Off," 23.
7. *2 Bees from Oakland*, accessed March 6, 2015, www.2beesfromoakland.com.
8. *2 Bees from Oakland*.
9. Phelan, *Unmarked*, 146.
10. Heddon, *Autobiography and Performance*, 31.
11. Heddon, *Autobiography and Performance*, 9.
12. Willett and Willett, *Uproarious*, 110.
13. Willett and Willett, *Uproarious*, 3.
14. "Luenell Talks w/ Pierre about Her Struggles & Becoming One of the Most Sought After Comedians—Full," aired on *Pierre's Panic Room*, video posted by Comic Pierre on January 26, 2023, YouTube, www.youtube.com/watch?v=iRsxxxxdkn0.
15. "Luenell on Being a Prostitute, Katt Williams, VLADTV, The Comedy Game, & More," YouTube, November 11, 2022, www.youtube.com/watch?v=nWIVVr1lpwU.
16. Stevens, *Smart and Sassy*, 33.
17. Fauset, "Gift of Laughter," 164.
18. *VH1 Presents: All Jokes Aside*.
19. *I Be Done Been Was Is*.
20. Fordham, "'Those Loud Black Girls,'" 10.
21. Fordham, "'Those Loud Black Girls,'" 10.
22. "Live @ The Apt" is a stand-up comedy web series recorded in an East Village apartment in New York City, and, according to the *New York Times*, it is "an unexpectedly ideal place for an indie comedy show." Elise Czajkowski, "When Getting Laughs Annoys the Neighbors," *New York Times*, June 19, 2014,

www.nytimes.com/2014/06/20/arts/live-the-apt-comedy-shows-really-happen-in-apartments.html. See www.liveapt.tv/about.

23. "About UnCabaret," UnCabaret, accessed November 17, 2023, http://uncabaret.com/our-story.

24. Hertz, "Alternative Comedy," 21.

25. E. Alex Jung, "The Sharp, Sensitive, and Surreal New Wave of Black Male Comedians," Vulture, April 1, 2015, www.vulture.com/2015/04/black-comedians-the-new-wave.html (emphasis mine).

26. Gillota, "Black Nerds," 21.

27. Gillota, "Black Nerds," 22.

28. Du Bois, *Souls of Black Folk*, 3.

29. Gillota, "Black Nerds," 17.

30. Blau and Brown. "Du Bois and Diasporic Identity," 221.

31. Thompson, *Beyond the Black Lady*, 2.

32. Ekperigin interview.

33. Ekperigin interview.

34. *Awkward Comedy Show*, liner notes.

35. Wanzo, "Precarious-Girl Comedy," 46.

36. Wanzo, "Precarious Girl-Comedy," 30.

37. *Awkward Comedy Show*.

38. Marina Franklin, live performance, Vermont Comedy Club, Burlington, March 5, 2016.

39. Bradley, "Awkwardly Hysterical," 149 (emphasis in original).

40. Du Bois, *Souls of Black Folk*, 3.

41. Eckert, "Vowel Shifts in Northern California and the Detroit Suburbs."

42. Lo, "'We Can't Even Play Ourselves,'" 177.

43. Tom Lamont, "Maya Rudolph: 'I'm Not a Woman in Comedy. I'm a Comedian,'" *The Guardian*, December 5, 2015, www.theguardian.com/film/2015/dec/05/maya-rudolph-im-not-a-woman-in-comedy-im-a-comedian-saturday-nigh-live-bridesmaids-sisters.

44. Lo, "'We Can't Even Play Ourselves,'" 161.

45. Brooklyn Comedy Festival, accessed March 12, 2017, https://bkcomedyfestival.com (site discontinued).

46. Sasheer Zamata, live performance, Vermont Comedy Club, Burlington, June 3, 2016.

47. Fauset, "Gift of Laughter," 164.

48. UCB Comedy, "Be Blacker: A SKETCH from UCB Comedy," online video clip, YouTube, posted February 14, 2013, www.youtube.com/watch?v=PefZk3q0U_U.

49. Becker, "Playing with Politics," 426.

50. Hariman, "Political Parody and Public Culture," 252.

51. Sarah Cooper, live performance, Largo at the Coronet, Los Angeles, September 20, 2021.

52. Wanzo, "Precarious Girl-Comedy," 45.

53. Wanzo, "Precarious Girl-Comedy," 46.

54. *Standups*. Ekperigin says "white woman" in the beginning of this bit with an affected, breathy, upper-class emphasis as part of the sendup of that classed whiteness that is the target of her joke. I have styled this pronunciation "WHite WHoman" to capture this part of her humor on the page.

55. Alexander, *Black Interior*, 5.

56. Emily Mahaney, "The *2 Dope Queens* Podcast Hosts on the One Joke They Never Want to Hear a Dude Make Again," *Glamour*, August 10, 2016, www.glamour.com/story/the-two-dope-queens-podcast-hosts-on-the-one-joke-they-never-want-to-hear-a-dude-make-again.

57. Allison P. Davis, "Yes, Queens," The Ringer, August 10, 2016, https://theringer.com/2-dope-queens-podcasting-phoebe-robinson-91bfe785ed4d.

58. E. Alex Jung, "The Sharp, Sensitive, and Surreal New Wave of Black Male Comedians," Vulture, April 1, 2015, www.vulture.com/2015/04/black-comedians-the-new-wave.html.

59. Meserko, "Standing Upright," 28.

60. Phoebe Robinson, "Two Dope Queens on Feminism," *Note to Self* podcast, WNYC, April 13, 2016, www.wnycstudios.org/podcasts/notetoself/episodes/feminist-podcasts-phoebe-robinson.

61. A "Khaleesi" is a queen in the fictional Dothraki language on HBO's *Game of Thrones*.

62. "Who Is Jeff Tweedy?," *2 Dope Queens* podcast, WNYC, June 13, 2017, www.wnyc.org/story/2-dope-queens-podcast-episode-36-who-jeff-tweedy/.

63. New York Public Radio Media Kit, Q2 2014, accessed November 29, 2023, www.nypublicradio.org/media/resources/2014/Jun/24/NY_Public_Radio_Media_Kit.pdf.

64. George Scialabba, "Welcome to Our Neoliberal World," comment on Radio Open Source, March 17, 2017, https://radioopensource.org/welcome-neoliberal-world/.

65. Thompson, *Beyond the Black Lady*, 6.

66. "Who Is Jeff Tweedy?"

67. W. Brown, "Neo-liberalism and the End of Liberal Democracy," 44 (emphasis mine).

68. Davis, "Yes, Queens."

69. Rottenberg, "Rise of Neoliberal Feminism," 428.

70. "Thank You, Harriet Tubman," *2 Dope Queens* podcast, WNYC, April 25, 2016, www.wnyc.org/story/2-dope-queens-podcast-episode-5-thank-you-harriet-tubman/.

71. "Mom Jokes with Kevin Bacon," *2 Dope Queens* podcast, WNYC, June 6, 2017, www.wnycstudios.org/podcasts/dopequeens/episodes/2-dope-queens-podcast-episode-35-mom-jokes-kevin-bacon.

72. Yasmin Nair, "Welcome to Our Neoliberal World," *Open Source* podcast, March 17, 2017, https://radioopensource.org/welcome-neoliberal-world/.

73. The New York Public Radio Media Kit elaborates on what the station means by "affluent" in describing trends of its core audience: its listeners are more than twice as likely to have incomes in excess of $250K and investments of more than $1 million.

74. "Adele Givens—*Def Comedy Jam*," video clip, YouTube, posted August 3, 2014, www.youtube.com/watch?v=TGi-ihN4EDA.

75. "Get Outta My Window Seat," *2 Dope Queens* podcast, WNYC, November 29, 2016, www.wnycstudios.org/podcasts/dopequeens/episodes/2-dope-queens-podcast-episode-24-get-outta-my-window-seat.

76. Stevens, *Smart and Sassy*, 33.

77. Isabelle Khoo, "Feminist Podcasts That Will Leave You Feeling Empowered," Huffpost, March 13, 2017, www.huffingtonpost.ca/2017/03/13/feminist-podcasts_n_15336944.html.

78. Davis, "Yes Queens."

79. Rottenberg, "Rise of Neoliberal Feminism," 411.

80. Rottenberg, "Rise of Neoliberal Feminism," 422.

CHAPTER 5

1. Celeste Ntuli, "ZULU GIRL IN LA," Instagram video, October 9, 2017, www.instagram.com/p/BaBVoy9gEuM/?igshid=13j6wdr84v8b5.

2. Kemp, "This Black Body," 123.

3. Werbner and Fumanti, "Aesthetics of Diaspora," 151.

4. Werbner and Fumanti, "Aesthetics of Diaspora," 149.

5. Elam and Jackson, *Black Cultural Traffic*, 19.

6. Johnson, *Appropriating Blackness*, 2.

7. Cole, "When Is African Theater 'Black'?," 43.

8. Elam and Jackson, *Black Cultural Traffic*, 5.

9. Coplan, *In Township Tonight*, 5.

10. Donian, "Comedy-Scape in Apartheid South Africa," 1.

11. Donian, "Comedy-Scape in Apartheid South Africa," 2.

12. Donian, "Comedy-Scape in Apartheid South Africa," 8.

13. Crigler, "No Laughing Matter?," 168.

14. Crigler, "No Laughing Matter?," 155.

15. Crigler, "No Laughing Matter?," 168.

16. "Birthing Our Feminine Divine Conference: Celeste Ntuli," YouTube, posted October 9, 2017, www.youtube.com/watch?v=Hp8-E2Oii2U.

17. Mintz, "Standup Comedy as Social and Cultural Mediation," 75.

18. Nixon, *Homelands, Harlem, and Hollywood*, 3.

19. See Collins and Kuumba cited in Kuumba, "African Feminisms in Exile," 7–9.

20. Johnson, "Black Performance Studies," 447.

21. Mercer, "Black Art and the Burden of Representation," 63.

22. Gilroy, ". . . To Be Real," 14.

23. "New Just for Laughs Festival Heading to Africa in 2018," Suburban, August 1, 2017, www.thesuburban.com/arts_and_entertainment/entertainment/new-just-for-laughs-festival-heading-to-africa-in-2018/article_8410d5a0-770d-11e7-ac9d-3f0907c9b5a1.html.

24. Seirlis, "Laughing All the Way to Freedom?," 513.

25. Seirlis, "Laughing All the Way to Freedom?," 515.

26. Seirlis, "Laughing All the Way to Freedom?," 519.

27. Seirlis, "Laughing All the Way to Freedom?," 526.

28. Penelope Mack, "In Stitches' Highlights Rise of Vernac Comedy in South Africa," Bowdoin Orient, November 30, 2018, https://bowdoinorient.com/2018/11/30/in-stitches-highlights-rise-of-vernac-comedy-in-south-africa/.

29. "Blacks Only Comedy Show," YouTube, July 31, 2014. www.youtube.com/watch?v=0BIQnDL_6xA.

30. "Blacks Only Comedy Show."

31. Gqola, "Ufanele uqavile," 13.

32. Gqola, "Ufanele uqavile," 22.

33. See the documentary film *Lady Was a Mshoza*, directed by Nokuthula Mazibuko, for a fuller explication of Black women's experiences in the *mapantsula* lifestyle.

34. Gqola, "Ufanele uqavile," 19.

35. Black and colored women in South Africa perform distinctive styles to diverse audiences. I am including colored comics here because many of them were influenced by and identify with Black American comics, as well as with many of the styles and aesthetics of diasporic comics, both in the United States and in South Africa. These comics include Tumi Morake, Celeste Ntuli, Anele Mdoda, Khanyisa Bunu, Lihle Msimang, Noko Moswete, Judy Jakes, Nonkululeko Mthethwa, Lindy Johnson, Mel Jones, Shimmy Isaacs, Samkelo Ndlovu, and Brenda Ngxoli.

36. See Finley, "From Awkward to Dope."

37. Darren Taylor, "'Irreverence Rules' for S. African Comedy Queen," accessed July 15, 2019, www.voanews.com/africa/irreverence-rules-s-african-comedy-queen.

38. Cheryl Kahla, "Trippin' with Skhumba: In Conversation with Celeste Ntuli," The South African, September 4, 2019, www.thesouthafrican.com/lifestyle/trippin-with-skhumba-celeste-ntuli-interview/.

39. Avilez, *Black Queer Freedom*, 12.

40. "Funny Girls," News24, July 13, 2012, www.news24.com/Archives/City-Press/Funny-girls-20150430.

41. Taylor, "'Irreverence Rules' for S. African Comedy Queen."

42. Kahla, "Trippin' with Skhumba."

43. Taylor, "'Irreverence Rules' for S. African Comedy Queen."

44. Amanda Ndlangisa, "5 Min with the Hilarious Celeste Ntuli," Bona, accessed November 17, 2023, www.bona.co.za/celebrity/5-min-with-the-hilarious-celeste-ntuli/.

45. "Best Stand Up Comedians: Best Stand Up Comedians Comedy Video Just for Fun by Lihle Lindzy!!," YouTube, accessed September 28, 2018, www.youtube.com/watch?v=jFuyaaxreuQ (video discontinued).

46. Seirlis, "Laughing All the Way to Freedom?," 517.

47. Gilbert, *Performing Marginality*, 159.
48. Gilbert, *Performing Marginality*, 17.
49. *Comedians of the World.*
50. Gilbert, *Performing Marginality*, 137.
51. Pumza Fihlani and Dominic Bailey, "South Africa Elections: Charting Divides 25 Years after Apartheid," BBC News, May 1, 2019, www.bbc.com/news/world-africa-48050197.
52. "Afrotaking Celeste Ntuli 99% Zulu Comedy 6," YouTube, posted November 4, 2013, www.youtube.com/watch?v=iRXVQ9Q1GHQ.
53. Seizer, "On the Uses of Obscenity in Live Stand-Up Comedy," 211.
54. "The Brilliant Tumi Morake at the Comic's Choice Awards," YouTube, July 6, 2011, www.youtube.com/watch?v=zgS9QapMXJE.
55. Seizer, "On the Uses of Obscenity in Live Stand-Up Comedy," 230.
56. Gilbert, *Performing Marginality*, 19.
57. Gqola, "*Ufanele uqavile*," 20.
58. Rowe, *Unruly Woman*, 20.
59. Hobson, "'Batty' Politic," 89.
60. Taylor, "'Irreverence Rules' for S. African Comedy Queen."
61. Seirlis, "Laughing All the Way to Freedom?," 528.
62. Bobo, *Black Women as Cultural Readers*, 22.
63. "Khanyisa Bunu," YouTube, August 17, 2017, www.youtube.com/watch?v=W0tS2D7wfWo.
64. Vincent, "Fat in a Time of Slim," 915.
65. Vincent, "Fat in a Time of Slim," 923.
66. *Comedians of the World.*
67. Vincent, "Fat in a Time of Slim," 915.
68. "Tumi Morake Stand Up Comedy on Late Night with Kgomotso2.mp4," YouTube, February 25, 2011, www.youtube.com/watch?v=5ygf_4084Mo.
69. Hobson, "'Batty' Politic," 89.
70. Bakhtin, *Rabelais and His World*, 19.
71. Ndlangisa, "5 Min with the Hilarious Celeste Ntuli."
72. "Tumi Morake—Comedy and Feminism," KASIBIZ/MAHALA, July 8, 2015, https://kasibiz.co.za/?p=8681.
73. Taylor, "'Irreverence Rules' for S. African Comedy Queen."
74. Bobo, *Black Women as Cultural Readers*, 60.
75. Werbner and Fumanti, "Aesthetics of Diaspora," 151–56.
76. *Comedians of the World.*
77. Hybridity is limiting as a way of theorizing racial and cultural formation because it assumes that two autonomous and exclusive races or cultures come into contact and fuse into an entirely new (hybrid) race or culture. Using hybridity to theorize Black culture and identity neglects the fact that there are many divergent elements of Blackness in that constitution alone. Creolization refers to the intermixture of various elements of different races and cultures that results in a multicultural/multiracial identity or culture.

CODA

1. Stover, "Nineteenth-Century African American Women's Autobiography," 141.
2. Randolph, *Florynce "Flo" Kennedy*, 156.
3. Randolph, *Florynce "Flo" Kennedy*, 156.
4. *Queens of Comedy*.
5. Willett and Willett, *Uproarious*, 102.

BIBLIOGRAPHY

INTERVIEWS BY THE AUTHOR

Campbell, Luenell. August 18, 2011.
Dobbins, Karinda, July 9, 2011.
Ekperigin, Naomi. August 10, 2011.
Flood, Hope. April 28, 2012.
Hayes, Laura. April 26, 2012.
Williams, Michael. October 26, 2012.
Yashere, Gina. July 17, 2015.

NEWSPAPERS AND WEBSITES

American Radio Works
CBS News
Gawker.com
Instagram
Mediatakeout.com
Netflix
New York Times
The Root
SNCC Digital
TikTok
Vimeo
VOA News (South Africa)
Vulture
YouTube

FILMS, TELEVISION SHOWS, AND RECORDINGS

Ask a Slave: The Web Series. 2013. Seasons 1 and 2. Created by and starring Azie Mira Dungey, directed by Jordan Black. www.askaslave.com/home.html.
The Awkward Comedy Show. 2010. Directed by Victor Varnado. Supreme Robot Pictures.
Butch Mystique. 2003. Directed by Debra A. Wilson, written by Donna Rowell and Debra A. Wilson. Moyo Entertainment.
Comedians of the World. 2019. Season 5, episode 2, featuring Tumi Morake. Netflix.
Comedy after Dark with Host Heather Hunter. 2003. Image Media.
Hannah Gadsby: Nanette. 2018. Written by and featuring Hannah Gadsby, directed by Madeleine Parry and Jon Olb. Netflix.
The Heritage of Slavery. 1968. Directed by Peter Davis and George Foster. CBS News: Film Associates.
I Be Done Been Was Is. 1984. Directed by Debra Robinson. Women Make Films.
I'ma Be Me. 2009. Directed by Beth McCarthy-Miller. HBO.
In Treatment. 2021. Season 4, episode 3. Aired May 24 on HBO.
Lady Was a Mshoza. 2000. Written and directed by Nokuthula Mazibuko. Cape Town: Midi.
Page, LaWanda. 1973. *Pipe Layin' Dan*. Laff Records, A-150.

———. 1977. *Watch It Sucker!* Laff Records, A-195.
———. 1979. *Sane Advice*. Laff Records, A-205.
The Queens of Comedy. 2001. Directed by Steve Purcell. Paramount Home Entertainment.
Sam Jay: 3 in the Morning. 2020. Written by and featuring Sam Jay, directed by Kristian Mercado. Netflix.
The Standups. 2021. Season 3, episode 2, featuring Naomi Ekperigin. Netflix.
VH1 Presents: All Jokes Aside: Black Women in Comedy. 2017. Directed by Eric Parker. VH1 Productions.

JOURNAL ARTICLES, ESSAYS, AND DISSERTATIONS

Abrahams, Roger D. 1975. "Negotiating Respect: Patterns of Presentation among Black Women." *Journal of American Folklore* 88 (347): 58. https://doi.org/10.2307/539186.

Baderoon, Gabeba. 2018. "Surplus, Excess, Dirt: Slavery and the Production of Disposability in South Africa." *Social Dynamics* 44 (2): 257–72. https://doi.org/10.1080/02533952.2018.1494243.

Bailey, Marlon M., and Matt Richardson. 2019. "'Will the Real Men Stand Up?' Regulating Gender and Policing Sexuality through Black Common Sense." In *Black Sexual Economies: Race and Sex in a Culture of Capital*, edited by Adrienne D. Davis, 108–23. Urbana: University of Illinois Press.

Baldwin, James. 1985. "Here Be Dragons." In *The Price of the Ticket: Collected Nonfiction, 1948–1985*, 685–98. Boston: Beacon Press.

Becker, Amy B. 2014. "Playing with Politics: Online Political Parody, Affinity for Political Humor, Anxiety Reduction, and Implications for Political Efficacy." *Mass Communication and Society* 17 (3): 424–45. https://doi.org/10.1080/15205436.2014.891134.

Bing, Janet, and Dana Heller. 2003. "How Many Lesbians Does It Take to Screw in a Light Bulb?" *Humor—International Journal of Humor Research* 16 (2): 157–82. https://doi.org/10.1515/humr.2003.009.

Blake, Felice. 2019. "Framing the Video Vixen: Intraracial Readings of Unruly Desire." In *Black Sexual Economies: Race and Sex in a Culture of Capital*, edited by Adrienne D. Davis, 166–84. Urbana: University of Illinois Press.

Blau, Judith R., and Eric S. Brown. 2001. "Du Bois and Diasporic Identity: The Veil and the Unveiling Project." *Sociological Theory* 19 (2): 219–33. https://doi.org/10.1111/0735-2751.00137.

Bradley, Regina N. 2015. "Awkwardly Hysterical: Theorizing Black Girl Awkwardness and Humor in Social Media." *Comedy Studies* 6 (2): 148–53. https://doi.org/10.1080/2040610x.2015.1084176.

Brown, Wendy. 2003. "Neo-Liberalism and the End of Liberal Democracy." *Theory and Event* 7 (1). https://doi.org/10.1353/tae.2003.0020.

Bucholtz, Mary. 2013. "Black Feminist Theory and African American Women's Linguistic Practice." In *Rethinking Language and Gender Research: Theory and Practice*, edited by Victoria L. Bergvall, Janet Mueller Bing, and Alice F. Freed, 267–90. London: Routledge, Taylor and Francis.

Carby, Hazel V. 1992. "Policing the Black Woman's Body in an Urban Context." *Critical Inquiry* 18 (4) (Summer): 738–55.

Clark, VéVé. 1991. "Developing Diaspora Literacy and *Marasa* Consciousness." In *Comparative American Identities*, edited by Hortense Spillers, 40–61. New York: Routledge.

Cohen, Cathy J. 2004. "Deviance as Resistance: A New Research Agenda for the Study of Black Politics." *Du Bois Review: Social Science Research on Race* 1 (1): 27–45. https://doi.org/10.1017/s1742058x04040044.

Cole, Catherine M. 2005. "When Is African Theater 'Black'?" In *Black Cultural Traffic: Crossroads in Global Performance and Popular Culture*, edited by Harry J. Elam Jr. and Kennell Jackson, 43–58. Ann Arbor: University of Michigan Press.

"The Combahee River Collective Statement." 1983. *Home Girls: A Black Feminist Anthology* 1:264–74.

Conquergood, Dwight. 2002. "Performance Studies: Interventions and Radical Research." *TDR/The Drama Review* 46 (2): 145–56.

Cooper, Brittney. 2010. "A'n't I a Lady? Race Women, Michelle Obama, and the Ever-Expanding Democratic Imagination." *MELUS* 35 (4): 39–57.

Crigler, Robin K. 2018. "No Laughing Matter? Humour and the Performance of South Africa." *South African Theatre Journal* 31 (2–3): 155–71. https://doi.org/10.1080/10137548.2018.1451360.

DeFrantz, Thomas F. 2016. "Bone-Breaking, Black Social Dance, and Queer Corporeal Orature." *Black Scholar* 46 (1): 66–74. https://doi.org/10.1080/00064246.2015.1119624.

DeFrantz, Thomas F., and Anita Gonzalez. 2014. "Introduction: From 'Negro Expression' to 'Black Performance.'" In *Black Performance Theory*, edited by Thomas F. DeFrantz and Anita Gonzalez, 1–16. Durham, NC: Duke University Press.

Donian, Jennalee. 2021. "The Comedy-Scape in Apartheid South Africa: A Historical Overview." *Phronimon* 22:1–15.

Eckert, Penelope. 2008. "Vowel Shifts in Northern California and the Detroit Suburbs." Unpublished essay. www.stanford.edu/~eckert/vowels.html.

Fauset, Jessie Redmon. (1925) 1997. "The Gift of Laughter." In *The New Negro*, edited by Alain Locke, 161–67. New York: Simon and Schuster.

Finley, Jessyka. 2018. "From Awkward to Dope: Black Women Comics in the Alternative Comedy Scene." In *The Joke Is on Us: Political Comedy in (Late) Neoliberal Times*, edited by Julie Webber-Collins, 221–45. Lanham, MD: Lexington Books.

Fordham, Signithia. 1993. "'Those Loud Black Girls': (Black) Women, Silence, and Gender 'Passing' in the Academy." *Anthropology and Education Quarterly* 24 (1): 3–32. https://doi.org/10.1525/aeq.1993.24.1.05x1736t.

Frow, John. 1980. "Discourse Genres." *Journal of Literary Semantics* 9 (2): 73–78.

———. 2007. "'Reproducibles, Rubrics, and Everything You Need': Genre Theory Today." *PMLA* 122 (5): 1626–34. https://doi.org/10.1632/pmla.2007.122.5.1626.

Fulton, DoVeanna S. 2004. "Comic Views and Metaphysical Dilemmas: Shattering Cultural Images through Self-Definition and Representation by Black Comediennes."

Journal of American Folklore 117 (463): 81–96. https://doi.org/10.1353/jaf.2004.0010.

Garber, Eric. 1998. "Gladys Bentley: The Bulldagger Who Sang the Blues." *OUTLook: National Lesbian and Gay Quarterly* 1 (Spring): 52–61.

Gillota, David. 2013. "Black Nerds: New Directions in African American Humor." *Studies in American Humor* 28 (January): 17–30. https://doi.org/10.2307/23823874.

Gilroy, Paul. 1995. ". . . To Be Real: The Dissident Forms of Black Expressive Culture." In *Let's Get It On: The Politics of Black Performance*, edited by Catherine Ugwu, 12–33. Seattle: Bay Press.

Gqola, Pumla Dineo. 2012. "*Ufanele uqavile*: Blackwomen, Feminisms, and Postcoloniality in Africa." *Agenda* 16 (50): 11–22. https://doi.org/10.1080/10130950.2001.9675990.

Halliday, Aria S. 2020. "Twerk Sumn! Theorizing Black Girl Epistemology in the Body." *Cultural Studies* 34 (6): 874–91. https://doi.org/10.1080/09502386.2020.1714688.

Hanks, William F. 1987. "Discourse Genres in a Theory of Practice." *American Ethnologist* 14 (4): 668–92. https://doi.org/10.1525/ae.1987.14.4.02a00050.

Hariman, Robert. 2008. "Political Parody and Public Culture." *Quarterly Journal of Speech* 94 (3): 247–72. https://doi.org/10.1080/00335630802210369.

Harper, Phillip Brian. 2000. "The Evidence of Felt Intuition: Minority Experience, Everyday Life, and Critical Speculative Knowledge." *GLQ: A Journal of Lesbian and Gay Studies* 6 (4): 641–57. https://doi.org/10.1215/10642684-6-4-641.

Hartman, Saidiya V. 2008. "Venus in Two Acts." *Small Axe: A Caribbean Journal of Criticism* 12 (2): 1–14.

Hassan, Ihab. 1981. "The Question of Postmodernism." *Performing Arts Journal* 6 (1): 30–37. https://doi.org/10.2307/3245219.

Hertz, Emily. 2010. "Alternative Comedy: Women in Stand-Up." PhD diss., Central European University.

Hine, Darlene Clark. 1989. "Rape and the Inner Lives of Black Women in the Middle West." *Signs: Journal of Women in Culture and Society* 14 (4): 912–20. https://doi.org/10.1086/494552.

Hobson, Janell. 2003. "The 'Batty' Politic: Toward an Aesthetic of the Black Female Body." *Hypatia* 18 (4): 87–105. https://doi.org/10.1111/j.1527-2001.2003.tb01414.x.

Jamieson, Kathleen Hall, and Karlyn Kohrs Campbell. 1982. "Rhetorical Hybrids: Fusions of Generic Elements." *Quarterly Journal of Speech* 68 (2): 146–57. https://doi.org/10.1080/00335638209383600.

Johnson, E. Patrick. 2006. "Black Performance Studies: Genealogies, Politics, Futures." In *The Sage Handbook of Performance Studies*, edited by D. Soyini Madison and Judith Hamera, 446–63. Thousand Oaks, CA: Sage Publications.

Kemp, Amanda Denise. 1998. "This Black Body in Question." In *The Ends of Performance*, edited by Peggy Phelan and Jill Lane, 116–29. New York: New York University Press.

Kunze, Peter Christopher. 2012. "Tears of a Clown: Masculinity and Comedy in Contemporary American Narratives." PhD diss., Florida State University.

Kuumba, M. Bahati. 2003. "African Feminisms in Exile: Diasporan, Transnational, and Transgressive." *Agenda* 17 (58): 3–11.

Lindsey, Treva B., and Jessica Marie Johnson. 2014. "Searching for Climax: Black Erotic Lives in Slavery and Freedom." *Meridians* 12 (2): 169–95.

Lo, Valerie M. 2017. "'We Can't Even Play Ourselves': Mixed-Race Actresses in the Early Twenty-First Century." PhD diss., University of Hawai'i at Mānoa.

Majors, Yolanda J. 2004. "'I Wasn't Scared of Them, They Were Scared of Me': Constructions of Self/Other in a Midwestern Hair Salon." *Anthropology Education Quarterly* 35 (2): 167–88. https://doi.org/10.1525/aeq.2004.35.2.167.

Mercer, Kobena. 1990. "Black Art and the Burden of Representation." *Third Text* 4 (10): 61–78. https://doi.org/10.1080/09528829008576253.

Meserko, Vince. 2015. "Standing Upright: Podcasting, Performance, and Alternative Comedy." *Studies in American Humor* 1 (1): 20–40.

Miller-Young, Mireille. 2007. "Hip-Hop Honeys and Da Hustlaz: Black Sexualities in the New Hip-Hop Pornography." *Meridians* 8 (1): 261–92. https://doi.org/10.2979/mer.2007.8.1.261.

Mintz, Lawrence E. 1985. "Standup Comedy as Social and Cultural Mediation." *American Quarterly* 37 (1): 71–80. https://doi.org/10.2307/2712763.

Mitchell-Kernan, Claudia L. 1986. "Signifying and Marking: Two Afro-American Speech Acts." In *Directions in Sociolinguistics: The Ethnography of Communication*, edited by John J. Gumperz and Dell Hymes, 161–79. New York: Blackwell.

Moore, Mignon R. 2006. "Lipstick or Timberlands? Meanings of Gender Presentation in Black Lesbian Communities." *Signs: Journal of Women in Culture and Society* 32 (1): 113–39. https://doi.org/10.1086/505269.

Morgan, Marcyliena. 1991. "Indirectness and Interpretation in African American Women's Discourse." *Pragmatics* 1 (4): 421–51.

———. 1998. "More Than a Mood or an Attitude: Discourse and Verbal Genres in African-American Culture." In *African-American English: Structure, History and Use*, edited by Guy Bailey, John Baugh, Salikoko S. Mufwene, and John R. Rickford, 251–80. New York: Routledge.

———. 2000. "Shout-Outs to the Ancestors: 'Here Come the Drum.'" *Black Scholar* 30 (3–4): 44–50.

———. 2005. "'I'm Every Woman': Black Women's (Dis)placement in Women's Language Study." In *Language and Woman's Place: Text and Commentaries*, by Robin Tolmach Lakoff; edited by Mary Bucholtz, 252–59. New York: Oxford University Press.

Morrison, Toni. 1988. "Unspeakable Things Unspoken: The Afro-American Presence in American Literature." *Michigan Quarterly Review* 28 (11): 123–63.

Neal, Mark Anthony. 2000. "Critical Noire: *Like Water for Chocolate*: Common's Recipe for Progressive Hip Hop." *Pop Matters*, May 5, 2000.

Redmond, Shana L. 2019. "Gospel Drag: Intimate Labor and the Blues Stage." In *Black Sexual Economies: Race and Sex in a Culture of Capital*, edited by Adrienne D. Davis, 139–50. Urbana: University of Illinois Press.

Richardson, Elaine. 2002. "'To Protect and Serve': African American Female Literacies." *College Composition and Communication* 53 (4): 675–704. https://doi.org/10.2307/1512121.

———. 2009. "Gender Ideologies in Hip Hop Feminism and Performances of Black Womanhood." In *African American Women's Language: Discourse, Education and*

Identity, edited by Sonja L. Lanehart, 291–304. Newcastle upon Tyne: Cambridge Scholars.

Rickford, John Russell, and Angela Rickford. 1976. "Cut-Eye and Suck-Teeth: Masked Africanisms in New World Guise." *Journal of American Folklore* 89 (353): 294–309.

Rottenberg, Catherine. 2014. "The Rise of Neoliberal Feminism." *Cultural Studies* 28 (3): 418–37.

Rowe, Kristin Denise. 2019. "'Nothing Else Mattered after That Wig Came Off': Black Women, Unstyled Hair, and Scenes of Interiority." *Journal of American Culture* 42 (1): 21–36. https://doi.org/10.1111/jacc.12971.

Rubin, Gayle. 2006. "Of Catamites and Kings." *Transgender Studies Reader*, no. 1: 487–97.

Schechner, Richard. 1969. "Speculations on Radicalism, Sexuality, and Performance." *Drama Review: TDR* 13 (4): 89–110. https://doi.org/10.2307/1144485.

Seirlis, Julia Katherine. 2011. "Laughing All the Way to Freedom? Contemporary Stand-Up Comedy and Democracy in South Africa." *Humor—International Journal of Humor Research* 24 (4): 513–30. https://doi.org/10.1515/humr.2011.028.

Seizer, Susan. 2011. "On the Uses of Obscenity in Live Stand-Up Comedy." *Anthropological Quarterly* 84 (1): 209–34. https://doi.org/10.1353/anq.2011.0001.

Story, Kaila Adia. 2015. "(Re)Presenting Shug Avery and Afrekete: The Search for a Black, Queer, and Feminist Pleasure Praxis." *Black Scholar* 45 (4): 22–35.

Stover, Johnnie M. 2003. "Nineteenth-Century African American Women's Autobiography as Social Discourse: The Example of Harriet Ann Jacobs." *College English* 66 (2): 133–54.

Takemoto, Tina. 2016. "Queer Art/Queer Failure." *Art Journal* 75 (1): 85–88.

Teague, Charlotte. 2013. "From A to Z: Zora's Use of Sass in Framing Cultural Identity and Individuality." In We Build Our Bridges Together conference proceedings. Scarborough, ME: National Association of African American Studies and Affiliates, 1107–13.

Thiong'o, Ngũgĩ wa. 2007. "Notes towards a Performance Theory of Orature." *Performance Research* 12 (3): 4–7. https://doi.org/10.1080/13528160701771253.

Troutman, Denise. 2006. "'They Say It's a Man's World but You Can't Prove That by Me': African American Comediennes' Construction of Voice in Public Space." In *Speaking Out: The Female Voice in Public Contexts*, edited by Judith Baxter, 217–39. New York: Palgrave Macmillan.

Vincent, Louise. 2016. "Fat in a Time of Slim: The Reinscription of Race in the Framing of Fat Desirability in Post-Apartheid South Africa." *Sexualities* 19 (8): 914–25. https://doi.org/10.1177/1363460716640730.

Walcott, Rinaldo. 1999. "Performing the (Black) Postmodern: Rap as Incitement for Cultural Criticism." *Counterpoints*, no. 96: 97–117.

Wanzo, Rebecca. 2016. "Precarious-Girl Comedy: Issa Rae, Lena Dunham, and Abjection Aesthetics." *Camera Obscura: Feminism, Culture, and Media Studies* 31 (2): 27–59. https://doi.org/10.1215/02705346-3592565.

Warner, Kristen J. 2015. "They Gon' Think You Loud Regardless: Ratchetness, Reality Television, and Black Womanhood." *Camera Obscura: Feminism, Culture, and Media Studies* 30 (1): 129–53. https://doi.org/10.1215/02705346-2885475.

Washington, Adrienne Ronee. 2020. "'Reclaiming My Time': Signifying, Reclamation, and the Activist Strategies of Black Women's Language." *Gender and Language* 14 (4): 358–85.

Werbner, Pnina, and Mattia Fumanti. 2013. "The Aesthetics of Diaspora: Ownership and Appropriation." *Ethnos* 78 (2): 149–74. https://doi.org/10.1080/00141844.2012.669776.

Zack, Naomi. 2013. "Black Female Crossover Comedy: Freedom, Liberty, and Minstrelsy." In *Philosophical Feminism and Popular Culture*, edited by S. Crasnow and J. Waugh, 37–50. Lanham, MD: Lexington Books.

BOOKS

Ahmed, Sara. 2004. *The Cultural Politics of Emotion*. New York: Routledge Taylor Francis Group.

Alexander, Elizabeth. 2004. *The Black Interior: Essays*. Minneapolis: Graywolf Press.

Avilez, GerShun. 2020. *Black Queer Freedom: Spaces of Injury and Paths of Desire*. Urbana: University of Illinois Press.

Bakhtin, Mikhail. 1984. *Rabelais and His World*. Translated by Hélène Iswolsky. Bloomington: Indiana University Press.

Bey, Marquis. 2019. *Them Goon Rules: Fugitive Essays on Radical Black Feminism*. Tucson: University of Arizona Press.

Bobo, Jacqueline. 1995. *Black Women as Cultural Readers*. New York: Columbia University Press.

Braxton, Joanne M. 1989. *Black Women Writing Autobiography: A Tradition within a Tradition*. Philadelphia: Temple University Press.

Bridgforth, Sharon. 1998. *The Bull-Jean Stories*. Washington, DC: Redbone Press.

Brown, Jayna. 2008. *Babylon Girls: Black Women Performers and the Shaping of the Modern*. Durham, NC: Duke University Press.

Carby, Hazel V. 1995. *Reconstructing Womanhood: The Emergence of the Afro-American Woman Novelist*. New York: Oxford University Press.

Carpio, Glenda. 2008. *Laughing Fit to Kill: Black Humor in the Fictions of Slavery*. New York: Oxford University Press.

Chauncey, George. 2019. *Gay New York: Gender, Urban Culture, and the Making of the Gay Male World, 1890–1940*. New York: Basic Books.

Clarke, Cheryl. 2014. *Living as a Lesbian*. New York: A Midsummer Night's Press.

Collins, Patricia Hill. 2004. *Black Sexual Politics: African Americans, Gender, and the New Racism*. New York: Routledge.

Cooper, Brittney C. 2019. *Eloquent Rage: A Black Feminist Discovers Her Superpower*. New York: St. Martin's.

Coplan, David Bellin. 1985. *In Township Tonight! South Africa's Black City Music and Theatre*. New York: Addison-Wesley Longman.

Dance, Daryl C. 1998. *Honey Hush!: An Anthology of African American Women's Humor*. New York and London: W. W. Norton.

Davis, Angela Y. 1999. *Blues Legacies and Black Feminism: Gertrude "Ma" Rainey, Bessie Smith and Billie Holiday*. New York: Vintage.

Du Bois, W. E. B. (1903) 2005. *The Souls of Black Folk*. New York: Barnes and Noble Classics.

Dunn, Stephane. 2010. *"Baad Bitches" and Sassy Supermamas: Black Power Action Films*. Urbana: University of Illinois Press.

Elam, Harry J., Jr., and Kennell Jackson, eds. 2005. *Black Cultural Traffic: Crossroads in Global Performance and Popular Culture*. Ann Arbor: University of Michigan Press.

Ellison, Ralph. 1964. *Shadow and Act*. New York: Random House.

Felman, Shoshana. 2003. *The Scandal of the Speaking Body*. Redwood City, CA: Stanford University Press.

Giddings, Paula. 2007. *When and Where I Enter: The Impact of Black Women on Race and Sex in America*. New York: HarperCollins.

Gilbert, Joanne R. 2004. *Performing Marginality: Humor, Gender, and Cultural Critique*. Detroit: Wayne State University Press.

Goffman, Erving. 1973. *Asylums: Essays on the Social Situations of Mental Patients and Other Inmates*. Chicago: Aldine.

Guy-Sheftall, Beverly. 1996. *Words of Fire: An Anthology of African-American Feminist Thought*. New York: New Press.

Haggins, Bambi. 2007. *Laughing Mad: The Black Comic Persona in Post-Soul America*. New Brunswick, NJ: Rutgers University Press.

Halberstam, Jack. 2011. *The Queer Art of Failure*. Durham, NC: Duke University Press.

Harris-Perry, Melissa V. 2013. *Sister Citizen: Shame, Stereotypes, and Black Women in America*. New Haven, CT: Yale University Press.

Hartman, Saidiya V. 1997. *Scenes of Subjection: Terror, Slavery, and Self-Making in Nineteenth-Century America*. New York: Oxford University Press.

———. 2019. *Wayward Lives, Beautiful Experiments: Intimate Histories of Social Upheaval*. New York: W. W. Norton.

Heddon, Deirdre. 2008. *Autobiography and Performance*. Basingstoke, UK: Palgrave Macmillan.

Higginbotham, Evelyn Brooks. 1994. *Righteous Discontent: The Women's Movement and the Black Baptist Church, 1880–1920*. Cambridge, MA: Harvard University Press.

Hurston, Zora Neale. (1942) 1995. *Dust Tracks on a Road*. New York: Harper Perennial.

Jacobs, Harriet Ann. 2009. *Incidents in the Life of a Slave Girl: Written by Herself, with "A True Tale of Slavery" by John S. Jacobs*. Edited by Jean Fagan Yellin. Cambridge, MA: Harvard University Press.

Johnson, E. Patrick. 2003. *Appropriating Blackness: Performance and the Politics of Authenticity*. Durham, NC: Duke University Press.

Keeling, Kara. 2007. *The Witch's Flight*. Durham, NC: Duke University Press.

Krefting, Rebecca. 2014. *All Joking Aside: American Humor and Its Discontents*. Baltimore: Johns Hopkins University Press.

Lanehart, Sonja L. 2002. *Sista, Speak!* Austin: University of Texas Press.

Levine, Lawrence. 1977. *Black Culture, Black Consciousness: Afro-American Folk Thought from Slavery to Freedom*. New York: Oxford University Press.

Limon, John. 2000. *Stand-Up Comedy in Theory, or, Abjection in America*. Durham, NC: Duke University Press.

Lorde, Audre. 1978. *The Black Unicorn: Poems*. New York: W. W. Norton.

———. 1984. *Sister Outsider: Essays and Speeches*. Trumansburg, NY: Crossing Press.

Madison, D. Soyini. 2005. *Critical Ethnography: Method, Ethics, and Performance*. Thousand Oaks, CA: Sage.

McDonald, Katrina Bell. 2007. *Embracing Sisterhood: Class, Identity, and Contemporary Black Women*. Lanham, MD: Rowman and Littlefield.

Miller-Young, Mireille. 2014. *A Taste for Brown Sugar: Black Women in Pornography*. Durham, NC: Duke University Press.

Mizejewski, Linda. 2014. *Pretty/Funny: Women Comedians and Body Politics*. Austin: University of Texas Press.

Mooney, Paul. 2010. *Black Is the New White: A Memoir*. New York: Gallery Books.

Morgan, Danielle Fuentes. 2020. *Laughing to Keep from Dying: African American Satire in the Twenty-First Century*. Urbana: University of Illinois Press.

Morrison, Toni. 1998. *Paradise*. New York: Alfred A. Knopf.

Nash, Jennifer C. 2014. *The Black Body in Ecstasy: Reading Race, Reading Pornography*. Durham, NC: Duke University Press.

Neal, Mark Anthony. 1998. *What the Music Said: Black Popular Music and Black Public Culture*. New York: Routledge.

Nixon, Rob. (1994) 2022. *Homelands, Harlem, and Hollywood*. New York: Routledge.

Perry, Imani. 2004. *Prophets of the Hood: Politics and Poetics in Hip Hop*. Durham, NC: Duke University Press.

Phelan, Peggy. 1993. *Unmarked: The Politics of Performance*. New York: Routledge.

Randolph, Sherie M. 2015. *Florynce "Flo" Kennedy: The Life of a Black Feminist Radical*. Chapel Hill: University of North Carolina Press.

Rowe, Kathleen Karlyn. 2005. *The Unruly Woman: Gender and the Genres of Laughter*. Austin: University of Texas Press.

Smitherman, Geneva. 1994. *Black Talk: Words and Phrases from the Hood to the Amen Corner*. Boston: Houghton Mifflin.

Stallings, L. H. 2007. *Mutha' Is Half A Word: Intersections of Folklore, Vernacular, Myth, and Queerness in Black Female Culture*. Columbus: Ohio University Press.

———. 2015. *Funk the Erotic: Transaesthetics and Black Sexual Cultures*. Urbana: University of Illinois Press.

Stevens, Joyce West. 2002. *Smart and Sassy: The Strengths of Inner-City Black Girls*. New York: Oxford University Press.

Stowe, Harriet Beecher. 1852. *Uncle Tom's Cabin*. Leipzig, Ger.: Tauchnitz.

Thompson, Lisa B. 2009. *Beyond the Black Lady: Sexuality and the New African American Middle Class*. Urbana: University of Illinois Press.

Ugwu, Catherine, ed. 1995. *Let's Get It On: The Politics of Black Performance*. Seattle: Bay Press.

Watkins, Mel. 1994. *On the Real Side: Laughing, Lying, and Signifying- The Underground Tradition of African-American Humor That Transformed American Culture, From Slavery to Richard Pryor*. New York: Simon and Schuster.

Wells-Barnett, Ida B. 1892 (2005). *Southern Horrors: Lynch Law in All Its Phases*. Project Gutenberg EBook, www.gutenberg.org/files/14975/14975-h/14975-h.htm. Accessed November 16, 2023.

———. 1893. *The Reason Why the Colored American Is Not in the World's Columbian Exposition*. Edited by Mark Ockerbloom. https://digital.library.upenn.edu/women/wells/exposition/exposition.html. Accessed November 16, 2023.

Willett, Cynthia, and Julie Willett. 2019. *Uproarious: How Feminists and Other Subversive Comics Speak Truth*. Minneapolis: University of Minnesota Press.

Williams, Elsie A. 1995. *The Humor of Jackie Moms Mabley: An African American Comedic Tradition*. New York: Garland.

Wilson, James F. 2010. *Bulldaggers, Pansies, and Chocolate Babies: Performance, Race, and Sexuality in the Harlem Renaissance*. Ann Arbor: University of Michigan Press.

Wood, Katelyn Hale. 2021. *Cracking Up: Black Feminist Comedy in the Twentieth and Twenty-First Century United States*. Iowa City: University of Iowa Press.

INDEX

Academy Awards, 1–4
activism: and Black women, 176, 182; and Hope Flood, 79; and Fannie Lou Hamer, 37; and Nikole Hannah-Jones, 63, 64; maverick, 61; and Annell Ponder, 39; and Ida B. Wells-Barnett, 62
African Americans: and Civil War, 39; comedians, 27, 32, 133–35, 72, 157–58, 198n35; and creativity, 147; culture of, 47, 103, 160, 177–79; experiences of, 30–32; and girl groups, 105; Issa Rae, 145; marginalization of, 64; and minstrelsy, 48; Obama family, 22, 133; performance culture of, 160; and racial Blackness, 30; and sass, 31, 46; satirists, 27, 133; and sexuality, 175; and South Africans, 172; speech of, 44, 46, 176; stand-ups, 135; Ida B. Wells-Barnett, 62, 64; and women, 5
Ahmed, Sara, 13, 70
Alexander, Elizabeth, 127, 129, 147
America, 39, 62; and comedy, 133; and culture, 24, 48, 58, 78, 85, 140; history of, 65; and music, 100–101; and racism, 63, 153; and sass, 14; and slavery, 65
"Americanness," 24; slavery and, 63–65
American South, 52, 56–57, 67
anger: alliances of, 162; and Black women, 19, 21, 38, 119, 121, 184; and eros, 17, 19; and Jackie "Moms" Mabley, 54; and political protest, 176; politics of, 15; righteous, 16
apartheid: and cultural practices, 31, 161, 177; end of, 160, 163–64; and humor, 161; policies of, 163, 165, 171, 176–77;

and racial order, 35; and violence, 160–61
Ask A Slave (web series), 57, 59–60; Lizzie Mae, 57–60
audiences: and awkwardness, 134–36; and Black performers, 105, 107–9, 127–28, 131, 134–37, 166, 182; of Black women's comedy, 13, 43, 67–70, 72–77, 79–82, 86, 92–96, 102, 111–15, 119, 121–23, 126, 129, 142–51, 157–58, 160–62, 164, 166, 169–75, 177–78, 183, 192n4, 193n39; and comedy, 111; experiences of, 6, 27–28, 72, 77, 80, 95; global, 32; public, 96; reactions of, 2, 76–77, 79, 82, 84; and vulnerability, 96; white, 18, 139–40, 153
Avilez, GerShun: and aesthetic redress, 100; and bathrooms, 121–22; and comics, 104; and gender expression, 114; and otherwise-genders, 102, 124; and sass, 104; and space of injury, 99; and vulnerability, 107
awkwardness: and alternative comedy, 134–35, 146; "Black girl," 136–38, 145, 155, 167, 171–72; celebration of, 133; and function of, 140–41, 145–46; and sass, 133, 147; and self-deprecation, 172; and whiteness, 172

Baderoon, Gabeba, 31
Bailey, Marlon M., 2, 99, 116
Bentley, Gladys, 101–4, 107
"bitches": bad, 146–47; bitchiness, 51; "Black," 12; and Black women, 67, 69, 80, 84, 114, 126, 154, 173; and Blaxploitation films, 15; butch, 112–13;

"bitches" (*continued*)
    and comedy, 76, 79–80, 112, 117–18, 123–24, 154; and Sam Jay, 115; and raunchiness, 81–82, 123–24; regular, 118; and sass, 154; skinny, 84; trans, 118
Black culture: and Black comics, 99, 136, 169; and Black women, 98, 176, 185n3; and cultural formation, 98, 159, 166; and discourse, 99; and experiences, 130, 136; and hybridity, 199n77; and identities, 140, 144, 183; and institutions, 131–32, 138; and marketplace, 100; and material, 98, 100, 104, 143, 155, 158–60, 178, 180, 182; and pop culture, 108; and practices, 179; and rituals, 109; and roots, 136; signifiers of, 133, 136; and South Africa, 171
Black feminine propriety, 1
Black feminism, 14, 16, 18, 77; and activism, 127, 182; and comedy, 7–8, 52; and comics, 57, 60; and diaspora, 35; and discourse, 12; ethos, 94, 127, 184; and heroes, 86; and humor, 7–8, 60, 182–83; and performance, 8, 34; and politics, 3, 8, 27, 56, 82, 94, 101; radical, 71, 99; and rage, 11; and sass, 25–26; and stand-up comedy, 26; and stereotypes, 86
"Black girl awkwardness," 136–38, 167
Black Girl Giggles Comedy Festival, 112–13, 115, 120
Blackness: anti-, 154; and authenticity, 142, 145; celebration of, 172; constructions of, 163; and cultural identification, 144; definitions of, 30, 125; elements of, 199n7; expectations of, 129, 140, 158; experiences of, 144; "failed," 94; fantasies of, 151; and "femaleness," 117; and humor, 31, 95; idea of, 163; (mis)representations of, 48, 58; norms of, 137; performance of, 27, 125; post-slavery, 58; production of, 159; racial, 30; and racial hegemony, 145; reception of, 68, 140, 158; representations of, 131, 140, 179; and Maya Rudolph, 138; and sass, 20, 30; and status, 171; and stereotypes, 135

Black performance tradition, 19–20, 130–32, 142, 155

Black women: and authority, 15; and awkwardness, 137, 146; and behavior, 87; and blackface, 48; "butch bitches," 113; and carnivalesque, 173–74; and comic culture, 159–60, 162, 167–68, 170; as comics, 13–14, 25, 28, 30–32, 34–35, 51–52, 54, 72–73, 78–87, 89, 92, 97–98, 107–9, 111, 114, 129–34, 140–41, 149–50, 153–56, 158, 161–62, 165–66, 168, 173–76; dehumanization of, 2, 4, 12, 15, 18; demonization of, 12; and drag performances, 56; and enslavement, 2; and entertainment industry, 51–52, 105, 135–36, 159, 177–78; and essentialism, 128; experiences of, 26, 101–2, 126, 179; and explicitness, 11; and female masculinity, 101, 121; and feminism, 25, 34, 82; and freedom, 4, 40–41, 51, 164; and gender, 119; humor, 24, 32–33, 42–45, 47–48, 50, 54, 157–58; as humorists, 5–6, 24–28, 30–31, 60–61, 147–48; humor tradition of, 24–25; inner lives of, 4; and Harriet Jacobs, 46; language of, 43–44; and liberation, 5, 23, 25, 28, 45; and literacy, 43; and lynching, 62; masculine, 123–24; and master-slave dialectic, 54; as musicians, 9–10, 12, 50; as performers, 9; and podcasting, 152; and pornography, 71; and public performance, 128; racism toward, 151–52; rage of, 14, 17; and sass, 5–7, 14–23, 26–27, 31, 33, 41, 50–51, 54–55, 74, 104, 108, 184; and self-defense, 44; and sexual desire, 12; and sexual domination, 44; and sexual imagery, 75; and sexuality, 60, 83; singers, 105; and slavery, 31, 47, 59, 78, 185n3; and Will

212 INDEX

Smith, 3; and "unwoman" (term), 2; and vaudeville, 47; violence toward, 8, 12, 60; and "WAP," 7, 10; and womanhood, 183–84

bodies, 89; and autonomy, 102; Black, 121, 133, 173; and Black female comics, 52, 54, 69–70, 79, 82; Black female masculine, 105; and Black humanity, 49; butch body politics, 34, 52, 94–95, 98, 100, 111, 120; and erotic pleasure, 34, 75; fat, 176; female, 92, 94–96, 113–14, 117, 134, 137, 166, 174–79; function of, 151; and harm, 121; and humor, 6, 33, 158; and liberation, 174; and ownership, 50; and LaWanda Page, 76; pained, 47; and race, 30; and sass, 54; and white imaginary, 30; and womanhood, 140

Brown, Eric S., 133

Brown, Jayna, 30, 47–50

Bunu, Khanyisa, 35, 166–69, 175, 198n35

butchness: Black, 34, 52, 54, 91, 94–96, 98–100, 106, 111, 114–16, 118–20, 123, 192n4; and comfortability, 93; and comics, 105, 111; expressions of, 107; and femmeness, 111; and Sam Jay, 110; and legibility, 111, 116; and lesbians, 98; and masculinity, 91–92, 100; and physicality, 34; and poetry, 97; presentation of, 108, 118; and sass, 99, 102, 104, 107, 116–17, 119, 121–22, 124; signifiers of, 113, 116; theories of, 110; and womanhood, 94

Byer, Nicole, 34, 132, 141–43

Cardi B, 6–7, 9–10, 12

Caribbean, 43

Chicago, 29, 52, 80, 136

Cho, Margaret, 132, 143

comedy, 3, 74, 116, 127–28, 153; and abjection, 95, 145; alternative, 130–37, 149, 155, 182–83; and autoethnography, 29; Black, 29, 50, 78–79, 133, 135, 143, 148, 153, 165–66, 195; Black butch, 105, 111, 114, 123; and Black culture, 158; Black feminist, 7–8, 26, 52, 82, 129; and Black masculine women, 34; and Black women, 78, 145, 148, 159, 174, 181, 184; business of, 80; as career, 48; clubs, 14, 67, 73, 78, 92, 95, 157; and community of laughter, 13; and economy of humor, 34; and efficacy, 178; and erotic pleasure, 73; and femininity, 116; festivals, 17, 109, 112, 163–64; and freedom, 68; industry, 79, 109, 129, 149; and interiority, 128; and knowledge, 20; and live performances, 28, 32, 84, 173; and Luenell, 68; marketplace, 149–50; and monologue style, 51; and national tours, 84; and Celeste Ntuli, 170; LaWanda Page, 73–74; and performance, 128, 141, 148, 160; podcasts, 147; politics of, 35, 83; and power, 100; public, 96, 98; and raunch, 72, 79; and sass, 5, 89, 97, 128; and sex, 79, 88; and sexual politics, 25, 77; and shock, 68, 74; shows, 14, 17, 28–29, 11, 119, 135–36, 141, 148; skits, 6; and slavery, 48; in South Africa, 35, 159, 161, 163–64, 166–70, 175–79; specials, 17, 108–11, 117, 141, 146, 167, 172, 176, 179, 183; venues, 28, 100; vernac, 164–65, 173; and vulgarity, 75, 79; and vulnerability, 129, 156; Marsha Warfield, 105–6; women, 98, 125–26; working class, 81; writers, 57, 99, 109; Gina Yashere, 87; Sasheer Zamata, 139–40

comic culture, 28, 35, 78, 107, 158–59, 168, 178

comics: alternative, 134; Black, 158–59, 168–69; Black lesbian, 106, 119–21; Black women, 13–14, 25, 28, 57, 68–69, 72, 99, 109–12, 114, 117, 120, 129–32, 136, 138–41, 155, 158–59, 165–66, 169, 174, 178–79; and comic license, 56; and comic personae, 52, 54, 68, 74, 83–84,

comics (*continued*)
86, 106, 133; and comic style, 14, 74; experiences of, 29; and feminism, 57; and genre, 95–96; and Just for Laughs festival, 17; and monologues, 121; and "The Nasty Show," 88; observational, 107; subversive, 10

Cooper, Brittney, 11, 14–16, 19, 44, 87

Cooper, Sarah, 143–45

Cornelius, Don, 95

corporeal orature, 190n26; and Gladys Bentley, 101; and LaWanda Page, 75–77; and raunch, 34; and sass, 72; and sex, 75; and Sheryl Underwood, 82

cross-dressing, 101–2

cultural production: Black, 155, 159, 163; and Black women, 13, 43, 52, 128, 132, 150; and Nicole Byer, 141; and Megan Thee Stallion, 9; and power, 62; and race, 59–60, 64, 147; and sass, 46

culture: cultural formation, 26, 164; cultural identity, 32, 46, 140, 144; cultural imagination, 12, 24, 77, 79, 82, 85, 125, 134; cultural institutions, 131, 138, 170; cultural knowledge, 13, 15, 30, 42, 68, 128, 161–62; cultural marginalization, 28; cultural marketplace, 47, 50, 100; cultural norms, 20, 83, 96, 167–68; cultural performance, 26; cultural politics, 25, 35; cultural practice, 12, 31, 44, 179–80

Def Comedy Jam (television series), 32, 78, 80–81, 92, 130, 153, 182

defeminization, 2

DeFrantz, Thomas, 19, 46, 190n26

democracy, 12, 161, 164, 176

diaspora culture, 35, 158–60, 163, 172, 179–80

Diop, Jo-Issa Rae, 132, 136, 145, 155

discourse genre: and Black women, 4, 21, 47, 124; definition of, 21–22; and sass, 14–16, 20, 23, 41–42, 51, 120, 130, 146

disempowerment, 13, 18, 27, 43, 50, 153, 166, 184

domination: and Black women, 19, 23, 31–32, 45–46; critiques of, 50; cultural, 176; and freedom, 152; and oppression, 42; and patriarchy, 5, 32; racial, 151; sexual, 44, 61; and slavery, 47; structures of, 16, 60, 184; and violence, 5; white, 160

Dungey, Azie Mira, 57

Dunn, Stephane, 15, 50

Ekperigin, Naomi: and autoethnography, 28; and Black women's humor, 13; as comic, 28, 34, 132, 134–35, 146–47, 149; and sass, 13

empowerment: and Black women, 1, 28, 50, 74, 96, 98–99, 158, 161, 171; forms of, 71; and liberation, 40; and pleasure, 75; political, 7; and sass, 19; and violence, 13

enslaved people, 63, 163; and freedom, 25, 40; and inversion, 49; and performance, 25; practices of, 47; and women, 2, 41, 44–45, 57–59, 78

entertainment culture, 6

Females in Comedy Association Convention, 78–79, 92, 111, 125, 131

femininity: Black, 115, 191n50; comedic, 137, 184; failure of, 116; female, 91, 116, 119; heteronormative, 54; and masculinity, 117; norms of, 91, 112, 127, 175; presentation of, 3; and sass, 101; standards of, 2, 115, 118; tropes of, 92

feminism: Black, 18, 23–27, 44, 86, 99, 162; and collectivity, 127; and comics, 57; and diaspora culture, 35; discourse of, 12; and humor, 7–8, 10, 60, 123, 129, 182–83; and ideology, 16; and neoliberalism, 152; and performance practices, 34; and podcasts, 155; and politics,

3, 34, 56, 72–73, 82, 94–95, 101, 134, 149, 165–66; postcolonial, 165; radical Black, 71, 184; and rage, 11, 14; and sass, 51; second-wave, 77; and stand-up comedy, 52; and subjects, 155–56
Flood, Hope, 28, 79–80, 92–94, 125
Franklin, Marina, 34, 132, 135–38, 140, 150, 179
freedom: Black, 8, 62, 64; and Black women, 24–25, 33, 41, 51, 56, 81, 99–100, 114–15, 155–56, 174; democratic, 164, 176; dialectic of, 105; and failure, 114, 121; and fantasy, 102; feeling of, 11; forms of, 100; and gender, 99; ideals of, 101; meaning of, 3–4; and neoliberalism, 151–52; practice of, 109; and slavery, 39; and social justice, 27; state of, 112; struggle for, 37–40; and Ida B. Wells-Barnett, 61

Gadsby, Hannah, 95–96, 123, 192n4
gender, 122, 137, 142, 158; and Black gender common sense, 99, 110–11, 119–20; and Black gender-transgressive women, 123; and Black women, 41, 74, 81, 83, 97, 99–100, 102, 110, 112, 118; and diaspora culture, 35; disempowerment, 166; dynamics, 126; expression, 116–17; and humor, 6; and inequity, 6, 52; logics of, 19; and marginality, 10; minorities, 25; nonconformity, 110; normativity, 114; norms, 61, 98, 101, 104, 115, 174–75; oppression, 85; passing, 131; perceptions of, 57; performance, 2, 30, 34, 54, 99, 104, 124; performativity, 99; politics, 57, 105–6, 128, 148, 160, 173; presentation, 30, 34, 91, 96, 104, 121, 123; racialized, 98, 101, 110, 114, 175; and South Africa, 31; structures of, 59–60; subversion of, 11, 81; variance, 107, 115, 120, 124; and violence, 5, 58, 71

genre: and comedy, 130, 132–33, 135, 148, 165, 169; definition of, 21; and female masculinity, 102; and genre-bending, 95; and humor, 24, 160; and language, 21; and music, 100; performative, 5; and podcasting, 152; and racism, 154; and rap, 179; and sass, 31, 143, 184; and stand-up, 32, 35; theory, 16; transformative, 8, 158
"The Gift of Laughter" (essay), 130
Gillota, David V., 133
Goldberg, Whoopi, 25
Gonzalez, Anita, 19, 46
Gregory, Dick, 56, 106

Hamer, Fannie Lou, 37–41, 43
Hannah-Jones, Nikole, 62–66
Hartman, Saidiya, 11, 20, 25, 42, 47, 61, 102, 112
Hayes, Laura ("Miss Laura"), 28, 125–29, 132
heterogender, 2
Hilliard, Chloe, 132
hip-hop culture, 69, 81–82, 157, 190n26, 190n35
Hollywood, 1–2, 68, 85, 87
Hood Adjacent (television series), 17
humanity: assertion of, 28, 51, 79, 119, 158, 166, 168, 184; and authority, 7, 20, 32, 72; Black, 49; of Black women, 60–62, 66, 72, 79, 86–87, 95, 116, 124, 180; claiming of, 79, 86–87, 92, 97, 101, 104–5, 108, 113, 128, 130, 162; and domination, 31; and empowerment, 28; enactment of, 3, 107, 112, 114, 118, 146, 147, 154, 162; and enslaved people, 58; expression of, 13; and humor, 5, 24, 41, 50, 56; and interiority, 19; and politics, 34; and power, 72; and rights, 7; and sass, 3–4, 16–17, 23–24, 33–34, 39–41, 45–47, 56, 81
humorists, 5, 8, 23–27, 30–32, 60, 102, 130–31, 133, 148

interiority: Black, 127; and Black women, 5, 41, 46, 52, 68, 128, 137, 142, 144–45, 156; and butch bodies, 100; expression of, 19, 141, 144, 184; externalization of, 140; interpretation, 78; and performance, 130; radical, 135; and sass, 137; and self-possession, 46; and stand-up, 96

Jackson, Ketanji Brown, 2
Jacobs, Harriet, 44–46
Jefferson, Thomas, 58
Johnson, E. Patrick, 26, 30, 159, 163
Johnson, Jessica Marie, 73
Johnson, Lyndon Baines, 38
Johnson, Punkie, 120

Keeling, Kara, 110
Kennedy, Florynce, 25, 182–83

laughter: affirmative, 163; and Black satire, 28; and Black sexuality, 79, 118; and Black women, 18, 25, 93, 120, 127–28, 136–39, 147, 151; and catharsis, 173; community of, 18, 162, 169–70; and cussing, 85–86; and interiority, 41; intersubjective, 82–83; outcomes of, 13; production of, 17, 25, 50, 73–74, 120, 182, 184; and raunchiness, 69–72, 75–77; and sass, 19, 42, 47, 65; and slavery, 49, 72; and stand-up comedy, 123, 157; and Wanda Sykes, 108; and vulgarity, 33, 87–88, 106; and womanhood, 120
literacy, 43–44, 136, 142, 151
Los Angeles (CA), 87
Luenell: and acclaim, 28, 92; and Arkansas, 67; and comedy, 68, 125, 128, 132, 157; and "The Nasty Show," 71; and raunch, 69–70; and sex, 71; and *2 Bees from Oakland*, 129

Mabley, Jackie "Moms," 25, 51–55, 60, 69, 102, 127, 188n44

mainstream culture, 4, 105, 153
marginality, 10–11, 13, 27, 95–96, 162, 168, 172–73, 179
marginalization, 8, 11, 26, 28, 33, 35, 72, 75, 164
masculinity: Black, 71, 132–33; Black female, 91–92, 97–98, 101–2, 104, 107, 110–21; hyper-, 116; patriarchal, 3; phallic, 71; toxic, 114
Megan Thee Stallion (Megan Jovon Ruth Pete), 7, 9, 12
Misadventures of Awkward Black Girl (web series), 145
Mississippi Freedom Democratic Party, 37, 39–40
Mooney, Paul, 28, 61
Morake, Tumi, 35, 165–69, 172–73, 176–79, 198n35
Morrison, Toni, 25, 30–31, 40
Msimang, Lihle, 166–68, 171–72, 198n35

Nash, Jennifer C., 9, 71
"The Nasty Show," 68–69, 71, 87–88
Ntuli, Celeste: and acclaim, 158, 161; and comedy, 162, 167–68, 171–73, 175–79, 198n35; and Laugh Factory, 157; and participant observation, 35; and racism, 162; and South Africa, 165–70

Obama, Barack, 22, 133
Obama, Michelle, 3, 16, 22–23, 85, 87, 108–9, 138–39
obscenity, 73, 159, 173–74
Orji, Yvonne, 130, 132

performance: American, 160; Black, 19–20, 45–46, 49–50, 95–96, 160, 163; Black feminist, 8, 60; of Black women, 24–26, 30, 43, 52, 54, 89–90, 94, 99, 108, 111, 121, 128, 134, 142, 146–48, 150, 157, 161, 169, 171, 174, 179, 182; culture, 160; drag, 56; ethnography, 29; expressive, 19; gender, 2, 54, 104; and liberation, 23; masculine, 74;

and music, 8–9, 12, 48; participatory, 158; and politics, 26–27, 94; practice, 34; public, 98, 102; queer, 56; and raunchiness, 83; and sass, 26, 28, 30, 56; and satire, 27; theory, 16, 24; vernacular, 44, 47, 52

performance culture, 160

Perry, Tyler, 14–15

pleasure: and Black feminism, 18, 34; of Black women, 11, 13, 16, 20, 24, 43, 57, 78–82, 99–100, 104–5, 178, 182; and Black women's humor, 6–8; and Cardi B, 9; and Megan Thee Stallion, 9; and performance, 26, 156; and politics, 81, 182; and raunch, 81; and sass, 4, 33, 47; sensual, 158; sexual, 54, 69–77, 82, 89–90

political discourse: and Black women, 2, 15, 17, 96, 143; and comedy, 14, 163, 165; and deviance, 100; and digital media, 149; and gender, 160; and pleasure, 89; and sass, 17, 19, 108

political practice: and apartheid, 177; Black, 26; and Black women, 6, 41–42, 56, 72, 97, 119, 129, 143, 148; and Fannie Lou Hamer, 39; and humanity, 92; and humor, 52, 73; and literacy, 43; and race, 63–64; and rape, 129; and sass, 17, 30, 62, 121, 183–84; and self-definition, 183; and slavery, 62–64

politics: and actors, 24–26, 82, 87, 161–62, 182; butch body, 34, 94, 98, 100, 111, 120; and consciousness, 8, 24, 35, 50, 77–78, 105, 153; and conventions, 45, 73, 161, 185n3; cultural, 25, 35; and efficacy, 6, 25, 65, 90, 124; and empowerment, 7; and expression, 24–25, 177; gender, 57, 105–6, 128, 148, 160, 173; and identity, 31–32, 34; and performance, 94; racial, 5, 11, 19–20, 25, 60, 130, 153, 177; racialized sexual, 25; and sass, 19, 97; sexual, 25, 153; and speech, 60, 102, 175–76

Ponder, Annell, 39–41, 45

popular culture, 114, 120, 130, 140, 151, 156, 176; American, 48, 52, 68, 78; Black, 6, 36, 47, 77, 99, 133, 155, 169, 177; and Black women, 6, 12, 14–16, 23–24, 47–48, 50, 101–2, 107–8, 136–37, 176; clash of, 25; and defeminization, 2; discourse, 87; imaginary, 51; map, 92; and music, 100, 105–6; and neoliberalism, 150; and race, 148; and sexual desire, 74

power: and Black women, 8, 11, 13–16, 19, 28, 49–50, 135, 145–46, 184, 185n3; critiques of, 2, 4, 12, 40, 51–52, 108, 119, 147, 154, 172, 182; disciplinary, 5, 116; forms of, 130; and gender, 74; and hegemony, 115; inversion of, 45, 47, 123; and masculinity, 113; and mimesis, 158; patriarchal, 2, 4, 33, 162; political, 7, 25, 35, 183; relations, 41–42, 53, 59, 62, 65, 70–71, 100; sexual, 11; speaking back to, 21, 32, 41, 72, 81, 85, 87, 109, 118, 146–47; structures of, 8, 10, 17, 22, 26–27, 60, 147, 162; subversion of, 172, 174

public culture, 6, 43–44, 48, 82–83

The Queens of Comedy (film), 126–27, 183

racial ambivalence, 133, 138, 140, 144–45

racism: anti-Black, 30, 35, 63, 153–54, 159, 177; and Black satirists, 27, 148; and Black women, 8, 12, 16, 26, 148; and patriarchy, 42; scientific, 63; and slavery, 59; and South, 52, 56; and United States, 61

radical tradition, 13

rage, 11, 14–16

raunch: and Gladys Bentley, 102, 104; and Black women's humor, 33–34, 69–72, 74–76, 78–80, 86–90, 129, 182, 184; and Cardi B, 7, 9, 11; and Megan Thee Stallion, 9, 11; and LaWanda Page, 78–82; and pleasure, 75–76, 83; and politics, 81; and sass, 85

representation: "angry Black woman," 12; and Blackness, 48; of Black women, 108, 110, 128; burden of, 84; hegemonic, 94; "sassy Black woman," 137, 142; and stereotypes, 136; of white women, 94
respectability, 12, 50, 74, 78, 83, 86, 191n50
Richardson, Elaine, 43
Richardson, Matt, 2, 99, 115
Rickford, Angela, 21–23
Rickford, John, 21–23
Robinson, Phoebe, 132, 148–51, 153, 155
Rock, Chris, 1–5

sass: and aesthetics, 146; and agency, 16, 19; and Black artists, 9; and Black women, 13–14, 66, 129, 175, 177, 182–84; butch, 99, 102, 104, 105, 107, 111, 113–14, 116–22, 124; and Cardi B, 9, 11; and comics, 34; and Brittney Cooper, 15–16; and cultural practice, 12; and dehumanization, 43; deployment of, 22, 62, 86–87; as discourse genre, 19–21, 23–24, 26–27, 35, 50, 53, 65, 108, 130, 158, 162, 168, 180; and efficacy, 5–6; enactments of, 17, 40–41, 46, 51, 81–82, 109, 112, 114, 128, 140, 143, 147, 154, 171–72, 178; and explicitness, 71; expression of, 41–43, 46–49; and fantasy, 83; and femininity, 101; function of, 40–42, 51, 92, 173; and humanity, 32, 39, 46, 62, 101, 130; and humor, 7, 40, 84; and Zora Neale Hurston, 46; and individuality, 46; and interiority, 130; and language, 44; and liberation, 15, 18, 33, 45, 72; limitations of, 148; and Lizzie Mae, 60; and Luenell, 70; and Jackie "Moms" Mabley, 53–54, 56–57; and Megan Thee Stallion, 9, 11; and neoliberalism, 155; and Michelle Obama, 3, 23, 108; performance of, 28; and pleasure, 78; as political liberation, 15, 71; and politics, 19, 97, 86–87, 128; and power, 5; and queerness, 57; and raunch, 33, 89; and sassiness, 23, 46, 50, 166; and sassy Black women, 12–15, 17–19, 21, 41, 81, 107–9, 133, 135–37, 140–43, 147, 153, 156, 179; and satire, 57–60; as self-defense, 44; and self-definition, 85; and Jada Pinkett Smith, 2, 4–5; and social redress, 74; and subversion, 58, 141; as technique, 133; theory of, 25; and violence, 13, 40; and Ida B. Wells-Barnett, 61

satire: Black, 27–28, 58–60, 137, 140, 142, 182; political, 176; and race, 27–28; satirists, 27, 56, 61; social, 102; and South Africa, 160, 175–76; and subversion, 16, 57–58, 61, 154
Saturday Night Live (*SNL*), 12, 109, 120, 138
Schlesinger, Iliza, 17–19
segregation, 42, 63, 126, 165–66
Seizer, Susan, 73, 76, 173–74
self, the: and Black women, 24, 35, 45, 47, 57, 77, 127–28, 141; and bodies, 47; and collective, 20; and political consciousness, 50; presentation of, 52, 83, 86, 94, 102, 104, 110, 112, 115, 140; and race, 147; and subjectivity, 45
self-consciousness, 178
self-definition, 84–85, 99, 183
self-deprecation, 115–16, 172, 177
self-efficacy, 26–27
self-possession: and Black female comedy, 54, 97, 106, 182–84; and Black women, 4, 54, 56, 101, 181–84; and interiority, 46
self-presentation, 83, 94, 98, 115, 124, 192n4
Set It Off (film), 110
sexuality: arousal, 9, 11, 73–74; Black, 89; and Black comedy, 173, 175; Black

female, 7, 10, 15, 30, 33–34, 52, 54, 71, 74, 77–79, 83, 96–99, 106–7, 110, 134, 137, 148, 173, 175, 179, 191n50; and butch women, 34; and culture, 71; desire, 12, 42, 54, 72, 81; deviance, 70–71, 75, 79, 83; and discursive production, 6; domination, 44, 61; heterosexuality, 123; hypersexuality, 51, 72, 81, 85, 133; and normativity, 81; pleasure, 7, 11, 54, 75–77, 81, 150; practices, 2, 71, 73–75, 83, 88, 95; production of, 6; queer, 57, 60; racialized, 9, 72; and relationships, 101; sexual politics, 25, 153; sexual propriety, 175

sexual violence, 31, 44–45, 59, 118; racialized, 44, 58–59, 61

slavery: and African diaspora, 31; aftermath of, 60, 62; and colonialism, 71; conditions of, 27, 62; and cultural performance, 163; and dehumanization, 58; end of, 39; experiences of, 25, 163, 172, 185n3; institution of, 42, 47; legacy of, 14, 63; and patriarchy, 60, 185n3; proximity, 51; and racism, 59; role of, 33; and sexual deviance, 71; and sexual violence, 44

Sloan, Dulce, 132

Smith, Jada Pinkett, 1–5

Smith, Lydia, 57

Smith, William, 1–4

songs: and Blackness, 79; and Black women, 11, 33, 90, 105, 142; and butchness, 93; and lyrics, 9, 79; popular, 101; and sexual pleasure, 7; and South Africa, 160; structure of, 160; and "WAP," 8–9, 89

South Africa, 28–32, 35, 42, 158–69, 171–79, 198n35

Southern Horrors (pamphlet), 62–63

Stallings, L. H., 71, 73, 85, 106

stereotypes: and Black comedy, 131, 134–36, 140; of Black men, 133; of Black women, 12–13, 41, 77, 82, 101, 134, 141, 143, 147, 156; degrading, 48, 50; negative, 26, 81, 86; reinforcement, 89; and representations, 16, 24, 136; saturation of, 51

Stevens, Joyce West, 20, 26, 129

street culture, 79

subjectivity: and Black women, 73–74, 78, 90, 100, 104, 111, 117, 128, 131; diaspora, 179; erotic, 56; full, 46; intersubjectivity, 150; postmodern, 137; queer, 114; self, 45; sexual, 33, 71, 78

Sykes, Wanda, 107–9

Topsy (character), 47–50

Trump, Donald, 7–8, 10, 64–65, 143

Underwood, Sheryl, 81–82

"unwoman," 2

vernac comedy, 164–65, 169–70, 173

vernacular performance, 44, 47, 52, 164, 170

Vidale, Thea, 131

vulnerability: of Black queer people, 107; of Black women, 102, 117, 127–29, 135, 144–45, 150; and laughter, 184; and masculinity, 112, 116; perception of, 96

Warner, Kristen, 15

Washington, DC, 7

Washington, George, 57–59

Washington, Martha, 57–58

Wells-Barnett, Ida B., 61–66

whiteness, 147, 151, 171–72, 177, 196n54

white racial terror, 172

white supremacy: and anti-Black violence, 61; authority of, 40; and Black humiliation, 145; and Black women, 18, 41, 52, 61; definition of, 46; and feminist comedy, 52; forces of, 171; ideology of, 61; illegitimacy of, 62; materiality of, 6, 63, 177; and patriarchy, 2, 5, 41;

white supremacy (*continued*)
  rationality of, 49; and slavery, 46; structures of, 171; undermining of, 40; and violence, 39; and whiteness, 171
Williams, Jessica, 132, 148–55
Williams, Michael, 78–79, 92
Williams, Serena, 15

Yashere, Gina, 32, 83, 87–89

Zamata, Sasheer, 34, 132, 138–41
Zulu people: and comedy, 159, 161, 167; and culture, 178; and isiZulu (language), 159, 162, 169–71, 173; and marriages, 161; and native speakers, 159; Celeste Ntuli, 157, 167

www.ingramcontent.com/pod-product-compliance
Lightning Source LLC
Chambersburg PA
CBHW021855230426
43671CB00006B/394